PRIVATE EYE ANNUAL 2017

EDITED BY IAN HISLOP

GNUS   FAKE GNUS

Published in Great Britain by
Private Eye Productions Ltd
6 Carlisle Street, London W1D 3BN
www.private-eye.co.uk

© 2017 Pressdram Ltd
ISBN 978-1-901784-65-7
Designed by Bridget Tisdall
Printed and bound in Italy
by L.E.G.O. S.p.A

2 4 6 8 10 9 7 5 3 1

PRIVATE EYE ANNUAL 2017

EDITED BY IAN HISLOP

"He spends all day staring at his phone"

HOW AMERICAN POLITICS HAS CHANGED

THEN

NOW

Fake Sheikh Exposed!

by Our Crime Staff **Roy al-Twitt**

FOR years he dressed up in Arab costume in order to fool his victims, many of them innocent Saudi princes, into agreeing to dodgy deals which they would later regret. But now at last the man they call "the Fake Sheikh" can be revealed as none other than Chazza Mahmood, aka Charles Windsor.

His technique was always the same, to go to the Middle East in a stupid headdress, accompanied by an unhidden camera team, and suggest to his gullible prey that they buy billions of pounds' worth of arms, aircraft and missile systems.

The next thing they knew, they were splashed all over the papers and portrayed as important business partners for British industry.

Why did they keep falling for it? Everyone knew that Chazza was up to no good and would stop at nothing to get their signatures on the papers.

Said one innocent prince, Shufti Al-Baqhanda, "I had no idea I was actually buying enough equipment to invade Yemen. I went along with it because he seemed a nice bloke and offered me access to Windsor Castle. He seemed very well connected and claimed to be closely related to the Queen. How was I to know that his disguise masked a ruthless, cynical arms dealer and organic biscuit salesman, who worked for a discredited organisation known as Britain?'"

DAILY BREXPRESS

BREXIT WILL CREATE MILLIONS OF NEW JOBS – IT'S OFFICIAL

By Our Brexit Staff **Yuri Sceptik**

A LEAKED, top-secret government document has revealed that Britain's decision to leave the EU will immediately lead to the creation of three million jobs.

This stunning news is yet more proof that pulling out of the EU is the best thing that has ever happened to Britain.

The new jobs, according to the secret document, will all be needed under the government's plan to hire huge numbers of new civil servants to work out in practical terms how Britain can possibly extricate itself from Europe over the next 20 years.

The document reveals that, until recently, ministers had no idea how complicated it might be to negotiate an end to British membership of the EU.

As the explosive secret memorandum admits, "It has unfortunately been brought home to us since June 23, that when the British people voted to Leave, no one had actually given any though as to how this might be achieved.

"It has now been pointed out that we not only have to sort out this trade business, but we also have to negotiate new arrangements for agriculture, fisheries, justice and home affairs, foreign and defence policy, access to the Single European Sky, and God knows what else.

"Apparently, there are 35 different areas that we hadn't even thought about, and we no longer have anyone in government who understands any of it."

At this point, it is clear that the authors of the document underwent some sort of nervous breakdown, as the sentences became ever more disjointed and hysterical in tone.

The final paragraph concludes, "We're going to need hundreds of thousands of civil servants to sort out this bloody mess... No – make that millions."

Last night the prime minister, Theresa May, angrily denied that such a report existed.

"This is all nonsense," she told the Brexpress. "I can assure you that everything is under control. I have every confidence that our negotiations will run very smoothly and that we shall, in good time, be able to tell the British people what we plan to do, just as soon as these millions of new people have worked out what on earth it is."

GRAYLING ANNOUNCES HS2 TIMETABLE

Transport Secretary Chris Grayling this week announced plans for the high-speed train. The timetable for completion of the new line will be as follows:

2033 delay – leaves on the line

2043 delay – homes on the line

2053 delay – jobs on the line

2063 delay – trains on the line
(continued to 2094)

BREXIT LATEST

THEN

NOW

A statement by the Prime Minister the Rt. Hon. Theresa May on the Hinkley Point nuclear power station

O F ALL the decisions I knew I would have to make when I at last took office, I knew that none needed more careful thought than whether it would be right to go ahead with Mr Cameron and Mr Osborne's completely mad idea of getting the Chinese and the French to build a nuclear power station at Hinkley Point.

That is why, in a defining first act of my premiership, I called in the decision so that I could give very careful thought to all the arguments for and against proceeding with the project.

This is how I set out the pros and cons which enabled me to come to a firm, sensible and considered decision.

Arguments against Hinkley

● It will be the most expensive power station ever built in the history of the world.

● In order to persuade the Chinese and the French to build it, we have had to allow them to sell the electricity to us at twice the normal price.

● From all the evidence, this type of reactor can probably never be made to work.

● We could have bought four nuclear power stations from Korea for half the price and they have been proved to work.

● The Chinese are clearly only interested because it will allow them access to whatever nuclear secrets Britain may have left and will give them control of Britain's future energy policy, enabling them to switch off our lights whenever they choose.

Arguments for Hinkley

● In a very constructive telephone call with President Xi, he told me that if we cancelled the deal, his country would never do any business with Britain again.

After responsibly weighing up the arguments on both sides, I have decided that it would be in Britain's best interests to carry on with this excellent deal and that we are deeply grateful for the very generous help being offered to us by the People's Republic of China and its illustrious and far-seeing President Xi, of whom a large statue will be placed on the fourth plinth in Trafalgar Square as a mark of the undying respect in which this great world statesman will be held by the people of Britain for generations to come.

Signed
Mrs Theresa May

Anyway, to cut a long story short, I threw the ring into the fire

Moose

We don't want a second referendum, say hundreds of people who clearly do

by Our Policy Correspondent
Hugh Turn

A committee of prominent Remain supporters have made clear that they definitely don't want another referendum.

"Look, it's over," said one prominent Remainer. "The will of the British people has been made clear, and we are going to leave the EU." He then added, *sotto voce*, "Unless, of course, we have another referendum because Remain would win by a landslide."

Another said, "We're not trying to fight old battles. The key thing now is that we make this process as successful as we possibly can." After a long pause, she murmured, "Except, of course, that it's going to be a complete disaster."

A third added, "Look, it's important that we heal the wounds of the referendum campaign and move on. We have to pull together as a nation to show that more things unite us than divide us. And I think we can all agree the last thing anyone wants is a second referendum!"

A few seconds later, he added, almost inaudibly, "But we definitely want one and we think we're going to get it."

'No Major Effect' From Brexit So Far

THE Office for National Statistics (ONS) says its findings that Brexit has so far had little effect on the UK economy are most likely down to the fact that we haven't had Brexit yet.

"Amazingly, the economy is continuing as if we are still at present a member of the European Union and able to trade tariff-free across the 27 member states," said an ONS spokesman.

"This is because until Theresa May invokes Article 50, we are still at present a member of the European Union and able to trade tariff-free across the 27 member states.

"To put it in more technical terms, the shit hasn't hit the fan yet, as Theresa May tries to delay turning the fan on for as long as possible."

Those tell-tale signs you have asthma in full

Rasping/wheezing sounds When you're asked why you were granted exemption to take powerful steroids

Tightness in your chest When the IOC drug testers call

Gasping for breath When Russian hackers release your medical files

Winning the Tour de France

BRITISH NAVY RESPONDS TO RUSSIAN WARSHIP IN CHANNEL

FEAR OVER HACKED PIPPA PHOTOS

by Our Technology Staff **I. Cloud**

BUCKINGHAM Palace was bracing itself last night for the publication of stolen photographs of Pippa Middleton, the sister of the Duchess of Cambridge.

The photos are believed to be of a "revealing nature" and apparently show Ms Middleton "as she has never been seen before".

Among the 3,000 hacked photos, one in particular has horrified royal officials which purports to show Pippa "doing some work".

Said a spokesman for the palace, "We were expecting some pretty graphic images, but this one actually shows her sitting fully clothed at a desk staring at a computer screen.

"It could damage her reputation irrevocably and it is pretty low for someone to expose her in this compromising way, rather than just partying, drinking, giggling and ligging."

He concluded, "This shows Ms Middleton in a very different light and it may lead to her being ostracised by minor members of the royal family who do not approve of this type of behaviour."

Pippa Middleton is 26-24-38.

POETRY CORNER

**In Memoriam
Jimmy Perry, creator of
Dad's Army and other
legendary sitcoms**

So. Farewell
Then Jimmy Perry,
Not hi-de-hi, alas
But bye-de-bye.

Unlike your work,
You will never
Be seen again.

Let's hope you
Are not going
To where "It ain't
Half hot mum".

But if you are,
And you meet a
Man with horns
And a pitchfork,
Don't tell him
Your name,
Perry!

E.J. Thribbute
(17½ repeats per week)

NEW BOOK: NAZIS WERE ALL ON DRUGS

High Hitler

It's Kristallmethnacht

"I'm afraid I don't know how babies are made, sorry"

7

ANGELINA BLAMES BRAD PITT FOR SPLIT

You've acted atrociously

We both have – remember *Mr & Mrs Smith*?

Sarah Vain

It's not about you!

OMG! I couldn't believe it! When I heard the news, my first reaction was: the editor will be wanting 1,000 words by lunchtime.

It's the split of the century, as the world's most famous power couple go their separate ways. No, not me and Michael. It's not the end of what everyone in Westminster enviously calls "Goveyvaina".

We've had our ups and downs and lived our life in the glare of the media spotlight and yes, it's had its price, as the strains of living in the goldfish bowl have taken their toll.

Michael grew a straggly beard, then shaved it off. I was subjected to endless pieces of tabloid nonsense about myself,

written by myself. And even our children had to read about themselves in the pages of the *Daily Mail*, to their immense embarrassment.

But we've come through it and I consider myself to be older, stronger and still with a column, which is quite an achievement, given that my husband's no longer a Cabinet Minister.

But this isn't a story about me. It's about Brad and Angelina and the end of the iconic Hollywood relationship, Brangelina, that has defined this millennium.

So, what do I think about their relationship? Well, it's clearly exactly like mine, except that we're still together, her husband wasn't in the Cabinet and, whatever else she may have achieved, poor Angelina has never had a column in the *Daily Mail*.

Sad, sad, sad. I could go on, but I notice that I'm now just three letters away from hitting my word count. OMG!

I'm a bit of a foodie, how about you?

I'm a bit of a drinkie

Who will replace Brangelina? You decide who should be the next internationally famous couple with a portmanteau name

| Willgelina | Brandgelina | Bongelina | Trumpelina | Nigelina | Hiddlelina | Vazelina | Angelina |

LATE NEWS: Port and Manteau to split. "Irreconcilable differences." "We wanted to lead separate lives." "No other word is involved."

8

Theresa May's secret plan to slash immigration to zero

by Our Whitehall Staff
Christopher Hopeful

FOR months, the prime minister, Theresa May, has been working on a top-secret strategy to bring down Britain's immigration figures to not just "tens of thousands", but to none at all.

Mrs May's three-point plan, the Daily Telegraph has learned, is so radical that it has been kept strictly under wraps, and shared only with her husband, Phil.

The plan is simple but devastating and, for the first time, the Daily Telegraph can reveal its contents in full:

1. We ensure that Brexit is a total disaster by bringing a complete halt to our trade with the EU.

2. Britain's economy collapses.

3. Would-be immigrants see that there is no longer any point in coming to Britain and go to Germany instead.

This, Mrs May has calculated, is the only way that she can keep her pledge to reduce the numbers of Tory voters migrating to Ukip to zero. *(Is this right? Ed.)*

League table of businesses 'named and shamed' for employing foreign workers

Manchester City

Tottenham Hotspur

Arsenal

Liverpool

Everton

Manchester United

Chelsea

Crystal Palace

West Bromwich Albion

(continued down to League 94)

New Galaxy To Stop Production

THERE was shock and disbelief yesterday when God announced that he would be stopping work on the production of his latest galaxy, citing potentially harmful design flaws.

"I've just made this galaxy – the Milky Way – and I honestly thought it was the best thing I've ever done," said the ashen-faced omnipotent deity yesterday.

"It seemed flawless, state of the art, but then I found humans in its software, which meant it was liable to completely blow up at any moment.

"Until I work out how they got there and make them less dangerous, I have no choice but to remove this galaxy from the universe and halt production of any further galaxies."

God is three billion and sixteen.

Meeting breaks out at Ukip fight

UKIP has reacted angrily after allegations that a meeting broke out during a routine brawl at the European Parliament.

Mike Hookem said, "These reports of a meeting are seriously defamatory. Our party is a modern political machine and we are more than capable of solving our problems by taking off our coats and kicking the shit out of each other."

Stephen Woolfe, meanwhile, insisted that a scheduled punch-up had proceeded completely as planned, and that allegations that two of the MEPs present had discussed points of policy in-between blows were wholly untrue.

He's face down and unconscious in the morning...

...perfect Ukip leader!

 # TWITTER NEWS

Tragic Python Star Has Dementia

■ There was widespread sympathy today as the news was confirmed that Monty Python legend John Cleese has gone mad.

Cleese was diagnosed after being seen on Twitter calling the editor of the Spectator a "half-educated tenement Scot" and rambling about how Scottish people had come over here and taken over all the English media.

Said one comedy fan, "It's a tragic spectacle seeing his decline from silly walk to silly talk," and another fan said of the Fawlty Towers legend, "Don't mention the bore. I just have, but I think I've got away with it."

ZUCKERBERG ANNOUNCES REVOLUTIONARY NEW FOUNDATION TO ELIMINATE DISEASE

by Our Social Affairs Staff **Bill Outstanding**

THE genius founder of Facebook, Mark Zuckerberg, has announced an inspiring new foundation to which he and his wife will donate huge amounts of their fortune in a bid to defeat all disease over the next century.

"It's called the government," said Mr Zuckerberg. "For such a long time I've been pondering how I can make a real difference with the enormous fortune I've amassed by concocting clever tax structures that minimise any tax liability from my firm.

"Imagine my shock when it turned out that this 'government' is devoted to ending disease. Not

only that, it also has side projects dedicated to running schools, hospitals, a road system, parks, a national infrastructure, and lots of other worthy projects which make this planet a decent place to live.

"I'm proud to announce that I'll be giving lots of this money to the 'government', as I've decided to call it, and I fully expect to get a lot of really fantastic publicity out of it."

I HEAR YOU'VE GOT A GREEK BLOKE WORKING HERE

TORY WIN5   FOREIGN WORKER REGISTER?

ERDOGAN ARRESTS ENTIRE COUNTRY

by Our Turkish Staff **D. Tained** and **I.M. Prisoned**

TURKEY'S President Recep Erdogan yesterday arrested 80 million people on charges of having supported the recent attempt to overthrow him in a failed coup d'état.

In the morning, he ordered the arrest of all Turkey's 5,612 judges, 816 generals and the entire police force.

By the afternoon, he had added all the nation's teachers, lawyers, scientists, doctors and intellectuals, and closed down all of Turkey's newspapers.

By the evening, he had widened his net to include all men, women and children, on a blanket charge of having had the thought that he was perhaps not the most entirely responsible or suitable person to be running the country.

Mr Erdogan defended his actions and hit out at "the lies" of his opponents. "It is quite untrue to say that I have arrested everyone in Turkey," he claimed. "You can see for yourselves that I myself am still completely free and at perfect liberty to imprison anyone foolish enough to disagree with me."

Boris Johnson, the Foreign Secretary, on the current proposals for triggering Article 50 and leaving the European Union

Cripes! Now let's not have a big whingeroo about our old chum Johnny Turk wanting to string up everyone who doesn't agree with him. Look, let's give Matey Mustapha a break and stop wagging the finger at him every time he wants to line his opponents up against the wall!

Ok, so the kebab-munchers are a bunch of rotters and I should know, I'm one of them but... hang on, I appear to have got the wrong briefing here and Bungling Bozza has launched forth on the wrong topic of the day.

Whoops! I'm in for a spanking from Mrs T, so I'd better stuff the briefing notes down the back of the trousers and return to the subject in question. Namely... er... how do we get out of the jolly EU with the best deal possible for us and without upsetting all the prickly foreign chummies who need a bit of diplomatic finesse to smooth over all the jaw-jaw round the table.

So here's a list of Bozza's foolproof measures:

1. Tell the Eyeties that we won't be buying any more of their fizzy pop if they insist on cutting up rough.

2. Mention the fact that "*prole*-secco" isn't half as good as genuine champers anyway and they're lucky that everyone in Britain is so poor they can't afford proper Bolly.

3. Suggest to Signor Cornetto that he wave the white flag, surrender and retreat because historically that's what the Italians are good at.

4. Give interview to Czech newspaper using technical diplomatic term "bollocks" to describe EU position on Freedom of Jumping on Back of Lorry to Blighty, etc.

5. Tell rest of media that story about Bojo using unsuitable language is "bollocks".

6. Get bollocked by Mrs T on previous five diplomatic gafferoonies and get told to stop embarrassing us over Europe and return to safe subject of Friend Fez-weaver.

Quite right! And here's Bozza's last thought: Being strung up didn't do me any harm *(see pic)*!

Yours diplomatically,
The Boz Man

REPUBLICANS 'STUNNED AND HORRIFIED' BY TRUMP

by Our US Political Correspondent **John Soapopera**

SENIOR Republicans have sought to distance themselves from Donald Trump, after an extremely embarrassing tape emerged last week, featuring Trump saying appalling and disturbing things.

The tape, which was a recording of an obscure television programme called *The Second Presidential Debate,* shows Mr Trump talking to a married woman called Mrs Clinton, whom he threatens to "bang up" if he becomes president.

Mr Trump also declared that he wanted to "reach out" to women in America, but "not in the way that had got me into trouble on previous occasions".

Mr Trump claimed that Mr Clinton had set a precedent for sex maniacs in the White House, but Mrs Clinton said he would only be there at weekends.

Mr Trump has since apologised for his comments on the controversial video, saying that he had made them a long time ago – over three days before. He said, "I owe the American people an apology, as well as a great deal of tax."

He also denied accusations of misogyny, saying, "Misogyny? Is she a friend of Miss Universe?"

Republicans have since distanced themselves from Mr Trump. "If only there'd been some way of knowing earlier what a horror Trump was," said one senior Republican. "How were we supposed to know that a man who calls women 'pigs, slobs and dogs' had a disrespectful attitude to women? We're not mind readers."

---

g2

Is the Guardian dead?

by **Zoe Willthisdo**

As the world becomes more and more boring, the question being asked by many satirists is a tough one: Is it no longer possible to be duller than real life?

And does this mean it's all over for Britain's Guardian?

In its heyday, the Guardian was a byword for wonderfully boring articles, features and editorials, but has that now been outstripped by the sheer tedium of everyday existence?

Said one former Guardian writer, "I don't even try any more. I've given up being boring. In my opinion, boredom is finished as a genre. I hate to say it, but the Guardian is no longer dead boring – it's just dead.

"In the old days, readers could choose from any number of brilliantly boring borists, but now you have to go to the United States to find really dull newspapers and the top borists now are all in America."

However, defenders of the Guardian hit back, telling satirists, "It's really unfair. The Guardian still has the capacity to induce a yawn and there are still flashes of inspired dullness. For example, there was a piece by Zoe Williams in G2 last week, which was a model of *(cont. p94)*

"Dawn's no good for me... how about pistols at lunch?"

SYRIAN CHILD REFUGEES 'NOT ANGELIC OR DEAD ENOUGH'

by Our Immigration Staff
Charity Fatigue

THERE was widespread outrage in many newspapers today that the Syrian child refugees arriving in Britain weren't tiny, angelic or dead enough to engender any sympathy.

"How dare these youngsters who look like adults still expect sympathy?" said outraged newspaper editors.

"We have made it very clear that the only Syrian refugees we feel sorry for are toddlers who have the good grace to be either angelic or too dead to be a drain on Britain's heavily over-stretched public services."

They continued, "We feel quite sorry for the ones who are dragged out of bombed-out buildings in Aleppo, but only if they don't grow up and don't come over here to *(You're fired. Ed.)*

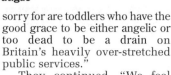

🌴 BIBLICAL TIMES 🌴

Children of Israel 'clearly adults'

BY OUR ROD AND STAFF WRITER
FERDINAND MOUNT-SINAI

There was anger last night at the arrival in the promised land of the first refugees from the Middle East (Egypt) who had walked all the way across the Red Sea.

Said one furious resident of Sinai, "These so-called children of Israel are nothing of the sort. Some of them have beards and the ring leader, Moses, looks at least 700."

He continued, "They are coming over here to take all our milk and honey and it's quite clear that they are trying to cheat the system and abuse our goodwill."

Many others suggested that there should be a commandment

against bearing false witness about your age and there were even calls for the "children" to be sent back across the now unparted Red Sea to resume a life of slavery, which they were unreasonably trying to escape.

But Moses was unrepentant, saying, "Throughout Biblical history, age assessment has been somewhat unreliable. My friend, Methuselah, claims to be 969, but I think he might be older and *(cont. p94)*

THE Sun SAYS

WHAT a disgrace ex-footballer and crisp salesman Gary Lineker has proved to be!

Fancy tweeting rubbish about the ages of Syrian child migrants being accepted into Britain!

Tweet after tweet showed Lineker had no clue about what was going on and was just happy to spout falsehoods about migrants.

If that's what he wants to do, why doesn't he come and work for the Sun? *(You're fired. Rupert)*

WHAT THE NEW POUND LOOKS LIKE

CUMBERBATCH: Tom, let me make it clear that I'm not going to ask any embarrassing questions about the role of spoons in your private life, even though that's the only thing people want to hear about.

HIDDLESTON: Thank you, Ben, I appreciate that.

CUMBERSOME: So let's talk instead about spoons in your cinematic oeuvre. You are known as something of an expert on spoons, a spoonéaste, one might say.

HIDDLEDIDDLE: That's for others to judge, Ben, but I *am* passionate about the craft of the spoonmaker and its effect on world cinema.

CUMBERJACK: Do spoons feature prominently in your role as the evil Loki in your new film Thor 94…

HIDDLECLASS: Loki is an immensely rich and complex character who exists in a mythical realm inspired by the Norse gods, but in terms of utensils, Thor's hammer is rather more important than any spoons Loki might have.

CUMBLEDORE: Amazing, Tom.

HIDDLYWINK: So are you, Ben. I first saw you in a performance of "Love's Ladle's Lost" at the Donmar which, spoon-wise, was a masterclass in cutlery-related performance.

CUMBERSANDWICH: Thanks, Tom. You were fantastic on TV as the Spoon Manager, which set new standards for location catering scenes. I'd love to see you as Bond… Maybe something like "The Spoon Who Loved Me".

HIDDLEBATCH: Thanks, Ben, and thanks for not mentioning Taylor Swift.

CUMBERSTON: Pleasure. One last question: Has anything interesting ever happened to you in connection with a spoon?

HIDDLE-ME-REE: Taylor Swift stuck one up my nose…

CUMBERLANDSAUSAGE: Hahahaha.

NEXT WEEK: *Darcey Bussell, "Me And My Bustle".*

Eye Film Review

The Jungle Book

The heartwarming tale of a young boy who is lost in the Jungle and hopes desperately to get out and go and live in the civilised world (well, Dover anyway). Unfortunately, he's photographed at a bad angle and deemed to look "far too old" by the British tabloids, so has to remain in the Jungle with his friends. Eventually, the Jungle is destroyed and he is taken to a Village somewhere in France, where he teams up with the other cartoon children who cannot get into Britain, including: Peter Pan, who may be any age up to 80 after living in Neverland for so long; Pinocchio, who is made of wood and cannot possibly be a real child and Bambi who, though disguised as a deer, isn't fooling anyone with his claim that his mother was killed.

EYE RATING: He Wants To Be Like You.

Revenge Pawn

1936	2016
Prince to marry American divorcee	**Prince to marry American divorcee**
Constitution in crisis	**Constitution, who cares?**
Think of England, Sire!	**Lie back and think of England!**
It's all over for the Monarchy	**It's leg-over for the Monarchy**
Oh no, it's Abdication!	**Oh yes, it's Fornication!**

Bananas complain at 'intrusion of privacy'

by Our Fruit Correspondent
Roy Al Gala

TWO of the world's most famous bananas have pleaded with the press to leave them alone following widespread publication of them together in a seemingly intimate embrace.

"My relationship with this banana is serious," said one of the bananas, in an unprecedented statement for a top piece of fruit, "and I don't want it jeopardised by an irresponsible American actress sneaking up and taking a photo of such a private moment, then posting it online for all to see."

The photographer, Meghan Markle, was unapologetic, saying, "These fruit are in the public eye, and therefore shouldn't be surprised if people want to see what they're up to.

"The bananas are clearly

meghanmarkle   + Follow

Sleep tight xx

25.1k likes   480 comments   Instagram

bananas about each other. They should just come forward and let the press take photos of them, preferably peeled."

But a spokesman for the bananas was adamant that further harassment could lead to the worst possible outcome – a banana split.

Government to crack down on prison strikes

by Our Justice Staff
Phil Gaols

THE justice minister, Liz Truss, last night unveiled her masterplan for ending the wave of unrest in Britain's overcrowded prisons.

Ms Truss threatened that, if prison officers continue to break the law by striking, then she would have no alternative but to send them all to gaol.

"Of course," she added, "our prisons are already so overfull that in order to make room for the 20,000 lawbreaking prison officers, we will have to release back into the community an equivalent number of convicted murderers, rapists and disabled families who've failed to pay the bedroom tax.

"This will present no problems to the community, as the ex-prisoners will be kept under strict supervision by our probation service, now outsourced to the highly capable G4S, working in conjunction with the Amazon drone fleet, who will monitor all ex-prisoner movements 24/7."

When asked who would be responsible for looking after the prisons containing all the former prison officers, Ms Truss looked momentarily nonplussed.

"Oh," she said, "I hadn't thought of that. Perhaps we could bring in the army. I must check whether we still have one of those."

Ms Truss is the Lord Chancellor of England (*surely shome mistake? Ed.*)

GOVERNMENT LAUNCHES NEW INQUIRY INTO OLD INQUIRY

by Our Inquiry Staff **E.N. Quiry**

THE Prime Minister Mrs Theresa May yesterday announced the setting up of a full-scale, top-level independent inquiry into every aspect of the failure of the previous full-scale, top-level independent inquiry into every aspect of child abuse that was set up two years ago by Mrs May herself.

"The historical abuse inquiry has become one of the most scandalous examples of mismanagement, incompetence and the wasting of public money in history," said one of the victims of this fiasco, a Mrs Theresa May.

"That is why it is necessary that we should commission a comprehensive inquiry into why such an administrative disaster was allowed to happen.

"As a nation, it is vital that we establish all the causes of this shambles," the prime minister went on, "even if it costs £200 million and takes 25 years to report."

Mrs May's initiative got off to a somewhat shaky start when the respected judge from Fiji, whom she had invited to chair the inquiry, resigned half an hour later, saying he hadn't realised it was such a long way from Fiji to England.

He was quickly replaced by a senior female judge from the Northern Circuit, who lasted ten minutes, after a colleague tweeted that she had once been heard observing, "If we're going for the poofy bishops, I suppose we've got to say something about all the Paki paedos up north."

In her resignation statement, issued on Facebook, she said, "I am regretfully having to step down because I had no idea how far it was to London from my agreeable home in the Yorkshire Dales."

At the time of writing, the latest head of Mrs May's inquiry is a retired social worker who lives within Zone One of the London Underground and is widely respected by all the people who will shortly be calling for her resignation.

LATE NEWS

● Prime Minister Theresa May last night announced a new inquiry into the apparent failure of the inquiry she launched yesterday into the failure of the previous inquiry. There was some surprise when she confirmed that the head of this inquiry would be another antipodean Dame, Dame Edna Everage, who said, "Hello possums! This sounds like a farce, which is right up my (cont. p94)

"I never realised old people were so obsessed with sex and violence"

WE WANT 'LACK OF CONTROL' SAYS PUBLIC

by Our Staff Hugh Extremely Angry Bastard

BRITAIN was yesterday in the grip of furious confrontation as both sides in the Brexit crisis called for "less reasoned debate" and more "rabid abuse".

Said one leading Brexiteer, "I hate everyone who disagrees with me and they should all be locked up for treason."

A senior Remainer, however, disagreed violently, shouting, "How dare you disagree with me? You should be locked up for incitement to hatred."

Meanwhile, the Prime Minister reassured the nation, as it descended into violent threats, murderous trolling and hysterical abuse.

"There is no danger of civil war, it is going to be very uncivil indeed."

Nursery Times

Friday, Once-upon-a-time

KISS-THE-GIRLS-AND-MAKE-THEM-CRY-GATE
New Revelations

By Our Political Correspondent Georgie Porgie Washington

THE boy at the centre of allegations of sexual harassment and inappropriate behaviour, Trumpy-Pumpy-Pudding-and-Pie, has refused to apologise for his conduct in the playground.

"These girls made the whole thing up. All nine of them. I never kissed anyone without their consent, so I don't have to apologise for anything."

However, a number of boys came out to play a secret recording, in which Trumpy-Pumpy boasted that he could kiss any girl he liked because he was a famous nursery rhyme character and they wouldn't dare cry.

Mr Trump then ran away, shouting, "That is just guy stuff. It's locker-room banter and if you want to talk about caveman behaviour, just look at what Bill Clintstone got up to whilst his wife, Hillma, turned a blind eye. That's what I call being in deep yabadabadoodoo!"

Nurseryland supporters of Trumpy-Pumpy were shocked by these revelations about his behaviour.

Said Little Boy Blue Collar and Robin Redneck, "The guy's

a wimp. Why did he just kiss them? Why didn't he grab them by the Puss-in-Boots *(cont. p94)*

On other pages

● Peter Pan cleared of Lost Boy charges – "The Nurseryland Broadcasting Company ruined my life," said Sir Peter. "I am now going to put it all behind me and go on a summer holiday. No more working for a week or two, fun and laughter on a summer holiday, no more worries for me and Yewtree **2**
● Big Bad Woolfe punched by Little Pig. Ukip in crisis **3**
● Fears for Moos probe after cow goes missing after lunar leap **94**

"Good luck at uni, son. Don't come back"

TIM BALES

THE CROWN

Ten Facts On The Hit Netflix Series Everyone Is Talking About

1 The series cost $100bn (£100bn) to make, which is greater than the wealth of the actual monarchy

2 The Queen's stunning coronation dress took a team of 38 Philippino seamstresses nine years of solid work, and was commissioned by Netflix seven years before anyone even thought of making the series

3 To prepare for his role as the Duke of Edinburgh, Matt Smith spent three weeks in an orange box

4 To prepare for the role of the Queen, Claire Foy ruled a small nation in East Africa for three years

5 To prepare for the role of Winston Churchill, John Lithgow met and beat up a professional Hitler lookalike

6 To get the atmosphere of the coronation scene right, Netflix rebuilt Westminster Abbey in Southern California and recruited 470 actual Dukes to advise on protocol. The filming of the scene took six months, which is actually exactly the same length as the 1953 coronation itself

7 The series' writers needed to capture the Queen's natural voice, so they constructed a 'Liz-Bot' to listen to all her speeches and reproduce lines of dialogue exactly as Her Majesty would do. The Liz-Bot was put into storage after killing two series' electricians for minor breaches of protocol

8 Er...

9 *(That's enough boring PR puff about The Crown. Ed.)*

THIS WEEK

ALAN BENNETT

Do you have a favourite spoon?

There is, I suppose, one spoon of which I am particularly fond, which Rupert and I found whilst browsing in Mr Midgely's antique shop at the end of Kirkby Road in Harrogate. We'd been to look around the little church of St Peter's in Dudley, where there's supposed to be some fine medieval stained glass, but there was a wedding going on and we had to eat our sandwiches in the graveyard. The vicar apologised, which was kind of him, but I was disappointed by how ordinary he seemed. He didn't even have a moustache. I am sure vicars used to be camper in the old days, but then along came Mrs Thatcher and put an end to all that. Anyway, we treated ourselves to a fruit scone in Giggleston, where Virginia Woolf once tried to seduce the Lady Mayoress by pretending to play the tuba in the colliery band (the subject of my 1972 play "Mucky Brass" at the National, with Thora Hird as the great Elsie Trumpington and Frances de la Tour doubling up as Mrs Woolf and W.H. Auden). We ended up, as we so often do, in Midgely's where Rupert spotted this teaspoon – nothing flashy mind – just a decent 19th-century stainless steel spoon from the Sheffield factory of Smutt & Wimsey, which would be of little interest to all the rich young bankers busy ruining perfectly good local houses with their fancy renovated kitchens filled with expensive silverware, but was the sort of honest spoon that could be used to add sugar to a cup of tea in a book-lined study in Primrose Hill on a wet afternoon in February. John Gielgud used it once and said to me, "It's like you, Alan... sweet, but a bit of a stirrer," which, in a way, was....

Has anything amusing ever NOT happened to you in connection with a spoon or anything else?

No, I don't think so.

NEXT WEEK: Wayne Bridge, *Me And My Bridge*.

DIARY

SIR ROY STRONG: MY ROYAL SECRETS

The Duke of Edinburgh is blessed with a wonderfully salty sense of humour. Needless to say, he loves to "josh" with yours truly! To be discreet, I refused to include the following anecdote in my published diaries, but one couldn't help relaying it to one's many admirers at the West of England Books and Chunky Marmalade Festival last week.

The occasion? Dear HRH Princess Alice's memorial service in 2004. The venue? St George's Chapel, Windsor, no less!

Myself: "I trust, sir, you have left your coach and horses outside!"

HRH Duke of Edinburgh: "Fuck off, you oily little creep!"

A classic jest from the doughty Duke! Like many of our greatest men, methinks he doth much to disguise his warmth with ribaldry – but to no avail!

One was brought up never to let the proverbial feline out of the cloth container (!). Never let it be said that the youngest-ever Director of the V&A was the type to break a confidence!

I would, par exemple, never breathe a word about the day I came across poor, dear Cecil Beaton lying in a pool of his own vomit (at least, one trusts it was his own!), clad only in a pair of singularly tatty "Y-Fronts" after "one too many" schooners of shop-bought sherry.

It would so hurt Cecil were hundreds of thousands of readers privy to this supremely embarrassing episode. So, for reasons of loyalty, I make it a firm rule to put discretion first, and one's lips remain buttoned, one's quill firmly sheathed!

Equally, one has long harboured protective feelings towards several of the more, shall we say, sophisticated members of our Royal Family. For all their many faults (some of them, as Prince Charles once privately acknowledged, simply too ghastly for repetition!), one utterly reveres the monarchy – its pomp, its colour, its magic, its profound links with histoire.

For this reason, I took pains to omit from my published diaries any damaging stories about my dear departed friend Her Majesty Queen Elizabeth the Queen Mother. Discretion is one's middle name. As befits a man widely praised as not only the youngest but the most successful Director of the V&A!

However, the mousey little audiences at literary festivals, in all their be-jeaned and anoraked glory, bless them, have a ghastly habit of pressing one for information about those well above their social standing.

Sadly, their only hope of meeting the Queen would be to undergo a "tragic railway accident" or something equally disagreeable, and have her visit them à l'hôpital. But alas, they would then be wrapped in plaster, with their milk-white limbs strapped to a variety of hideous "gurneys" – hardly a look with which to endear them to Her Majesty! Exquisitely well-brought-up, she would never allow her distaste to become visible, but she would allot them a couple of minutes, racing through her usual list of dreary questions. Never in a million years would she think of passing on anything remotely "juicy" concerning her nearest and dearest in such circumstances! So one feels something of an obligation to offer these pitiful "punters" a few shavings from the carpenter's block, as it were.

"*Entre nous*," I said to the 800-strong audience at the West of England Books and Chunky Marmalade Festival, "my very dear friend the Queen Mum was, one must sadly confess, the most tremendous tippler. I shall never forget the day she arrived at my home for elevenses bearing a 2-gallon flagon of Woodpecker's Cider and a packet of paper straws. As the conversation progressed, her language became increasingly fruity, her opinions more and more outspoken. "Send them back to where they came from – and throw away the key!" she said, after I told her how much I had enjoyed The Black and White Minstrel Show on the magic lantern the previous evening. And when the topic changed to the Prime Minister of the day, Edward Heath, she leaned over and whispered, "Have you seen the way he conducts? That awful way he has of revolving his unmentionables! Thrust! Thrust! Thrust! It's really too unspeakable, Roy! His sense of rhythm is the giveaway, you know. The fellow's as black as the Ace of Spades!"

Strictly between these *quatre murs*, did I ever tell you of the day the Duke of Edinburgh took me to one side and whispered in my ear, "Breathe not a word to a soul, Roy, but Diana appeared on the Panorama television programme a few nights ago, being most dreadfully rude about poor Charles!"

Not a soul knew about the offending broadcast, and I kept silent about it from that day to this. But in the interests of history, I believe the time has come to "tell all", regardless of consequences.

I count The Prince of Wales among the firmest of friends. The two of us are the most terrific gigglers! We tease each other mercilessly! The last time I bumped into him was at the funeral of his dearly beloved grandmamma.

"Where DID you get that simply GHASTLY tail-coat?" I hooted, as he sat there putting on his "look at me, I'm so upset" expression. "I've seen better on an East End navvy!"

How the poor man managed to stifle a fit of the giggles at my jest, I shall never know! Instead, he just stared straight ahead, battling to maintain a straight face!

As I told the audience at the West of England Books and Chunky Marmalade Festival, in the strictest confidence, I have it on the very highest authority that the Princess of Wales once spent an evening dancing with the handsome Hollywood film-star John Travolta. Meanwhile, the poor, weedy Prince looked on morosely with the most ghastly "hangdog" expression on his face!

Needless to say, there would be the reddest of faces around Buckingham Palace if ever this information were to "hit the news-stands". Our beloved Royal Family have surely earned their privacy – one must defend them from malicious tittle-tattle, however fresh and juicy.i

As told to

CRAIG BROWN

"It goes on for ever"

"Brexit...? How about never...? Is never good for you...?"

With Acknowledgements & Apols

"REMOANA"

"I'm sorry, Simon. It was the will of the British people"

PICK YOUR OWN FRUIT

Pre-Brexit

PICK YOUR OWN BLOODY FRUIT!

Post-Brexit

Daily Mail

Unelected Lord whose businesses are based abroad

Unelected editor who receives EU farm subsidies

Unelected openly heterosexual columnist

ENEMAS OF THE PEOPLE

How dare these three embittered and out-of-touch men offer their "judgement" on Europe by telling the British what to think and pour out toxic effluent which *(cont. p94)*

HOW THE BRITISH CONSTITUTION WORKS

1 The British democratic state is split into three branches – the Legislature, the Executive and the Judiciary

2 All three branches have equal importance

3 Unless you disagree with one of them, in which case they are completely undemocratic and should be ignored

4 Er...

5 That's it.

'I am the right man for the job' says Vaz

by Our Political Staff
Peter O'Bore

A delighted Keith Vaz was yesterday triumphant at being selected to join the Commons Select Committee on Justice.

Some MPs (and the entire British public) had expressed astonishment at the thought of the disgraced Leicester MP being voted on to any more Commons committees after being removed from the Home Affairs Committee for scandalous behaviour involving drugs and male prostitutes.

Vaz claimed at that time that this qualified him to remain as chairman of a committee that was looking into drug abuse and prostitution.

Today, he said, "I am even better qualified to serve on the Justice Committee because I've been successfully avoiding justice for years."

He continued, "A month ago, I was helping the police with their enquiries, now they are helping me with my enquiries!"

Mr Vaz was unavailable for further comment, as he was busy celebrating his latest appointment with two young Ukrainian friends he had met on the internet and who had promised "to help the party along by bringing some poppers".

Liz Truss – Tougher Sentences Needed

by Our Law Correspondent
Norman Stanley Fletcher

THERE were calls from several senior judges for Liz Truss to give out tougher sentences yesterday, in the light of the Brexit ruling.

"The sentence delivered by the Lord Chancellor is completely inadequate," said one old man in a wig, crossly. "Mumbling about the freedom of the press is a wholly inadequate sentence in response to those press barons calling us enemies of the people.

"Her sentences should be longer, tougher, and filled with proper punitive words like 'incendiary' 'incitement', 'mad' and 'bastards'."

Ms Truss insisted that her sentencing policy towards Mr Murdoch and Mr Dacre and others is completely proportionate, given the fact that it was only their first offence this week.

Jeremy Corbyn WRITES

Hello! It's me again. Well, I'm sorry to say I had to put on my stern face this week (not to be confused with my bewildered face, which is exactly the same face, except I wear my glasses further up my nose). I don't know if you saw this but an ITV reporter actually tried to ask me a political question! She asked me if I was looking forward to fighting an early general election, no less!

Fortunately, one of my personal aides managed to mace the reporter and wrestle her to the ground, while another grabbed me and bundled me to safety into my open-topped Corbynmobile. It wasn't until we'd got to Islington that they felt it safe enough to stop sitting on me and allowed me to get up off the floor. And the hated media complain about my clothes being crumpled, well it's their fault, as you can see!

I didn't see why I should be harassed in this way. If I wanted to go around spontaneously answering questions like that, I would have gone into politics.

I used to think ITV was one of the good ones, but, sadly, it's joined the BBC, Channel 4, the Guardian and the Independent, in that huge cabal of hated right-wing media outlets trying to humiliate me by forcing me to talk about things other than jam making, gardening, and how Tony Blair is a war criminal!

Now my aides have had a meeting, they think I am ready to answer a question about any future general election. I am certainly looking forward to it. My attitude is that any future election will be a reflection of my Brexit position. That is, I am prepared to ask very searching questions about the Government, before I decide to campaign to return the Conservative party to power.

I mean, Theresa May's not all bad, is she? At least she's against capitalism! So that's one up on Tony Blair!

Cheerio!

CEZANNE REVISITED

Fantoni *(with apologies)*

"A text from Emil... his horse has died"

"PSG have just gone one up"

OH NO! IT'S TRUMP!

TAKING POWER

> If you're famous, you can just grab it

TAKING ADVICE

> How do you rate Theresa May?

> She's a five, maybe a six if you're legless

TAKING OVER

> They're calling me a racist, fascist misogynist

> You're hired!

TAKING THE PISS

> You're going to be my First Lady

> No one is going to believe that!

The Eye's Controversial New Columnist

The columnist who can't decide whether he's more upset about wind farms or wind

This week I am very angry about Mr Donald Trump. Now it seems I am only the second most famous angry baby in the world and I am not going to take this quietly! Wake up, America! Mr Trump has been systematically ripping me off! Consider this: a month ago I threw a tantrum because a woman tried to spoonfeed me something healthy; suddenly, Mr Trump throws a tantrum because Hillary Clinton tried to spoonfeed him some facts. Coincidence? One time, I spent a day playing with my Lego, throwing bricks about, building a wall and causing misery for my ethnic nanny – just because I could – and the next thing I know Mr Trump adopts it as his policy! Another coincidence? I could go on and on. And I will. Beware, Mr Trump! You are not the only one who can sue. There is only room on the planet for one opinionated baby on the planet and that's *(cont. p94)*

STAGGERING VICTORY AS TRUMP WINS NEARLY HALF ALL VOTES

by Our U.S. Political Staff
Jim Naughtie-Even-Near

TWO weeks after the election, the final count has been completed, the truth is known. In an extraordinary repudiation of Hillary Clinton and everything she stood for, the Republican presidential candidate, Donald Trump, managed to win very nearly as many votes as his Democratic rival did.

If just one and a half million extra people had voted for Trump, he would have tipped over into actually having won even more votes than his rival for the presidency.

The "Trumpquake", which has shaken Washington in the last fortnight, proves the people of America overwhelmingly wanted Trump, apart from the larger group who wanted Hillary Clinton and got Trump anyway.

Nonetheless, the result shows that the tiny numbers of blacks, Latinos, and disabled trans-Muslim women who supported Clinton, managed to scrape together a mere 63 million votes, compared with the tremendous showing from The Donald's mighty alliance of laid-off rust-belt workers, which tallied 61.5 million *(cont. p94)*

EXCLUSIVE TO ALL NEWSPAPERS
94-PAGE TRUMP VICTORY SPECIAL

On other pages

● Why everything we said about Donald Trump during the campaign was wrong

● Why nobody knows anything any more, least of all us

● What's going to happen over the next ten years, by our top forecasters

● Why we are confident that Donald Trump will be completely different now he's in power

● Why you should read this paper even though *(cont. p94)*

AMERICA
THOSE CHANGES IN FULL

● White House to be renamed 'The Extremely White House'

● National Anthem to be retitled the 'Starlet-Spangled Banner'

● All bald eagles to be immediately given scalp surgery and luxurious golden thatches

● Immigrants who have worked in USA illegally to be kicked out, barring any who subsequently married the President-Elect

● Traditional Thanksgiving Turkey to be pardoned only after it's been waterboarded

Exclusive to all papers
AN APOLOGY

IN RECENT days, weeks and months, we may have given the impression that Hillary Clinton was unquestionably going to be the next President of the United States – not just because her poll lead was substantial, but because her decades of public service in Washington showed her true worth as a person: this was a strong woman, a woman who as President would bring stability in troubled times, who was unfairly criticised for her email protocols, who, as President, would defend minority rights and bring to the job a quiet dignity matched with a steely determination to maintain America's position as the leader of the free world.

We now know, in light of Trump winning the election, that nothing could be further from the truth, that Hillary Clinton was a terrible candidate, that the decades spent in Washington showed she was part of an out-of-touch liberal elite, that she was cold, a woman rightly pilloried for her email protocols, a politician who would rather talk to minorities than get out and meet ordinary, white, working-class Americans, a woman whose icy demeanour and inflexibility made it no surprise that America opted instead for Trump as President.

We apologise for any confusion caused and for any confusion in the future when Trump launches a nuclear strike after getting into a 3am Twitter spat with North Korea and it turns out that Hillary's email protocol isn't the talk of the fall-out shelters.

New J.K. Rowling franchise set to make gazillions

by Our Showbiz Staff
Val Dermort

There is global excitement as Potter-mad fans anticipate the latest addition to J.K. Rowling's literary oeuvre.

The news that J.K. is to put pen to paper to write a Christmas card to one of her family has been seized on around the world.

Publishers are lining up to buy the book rights to the Christmas card, working title *"Happy Christmas, Uncle Fred"*, theatre producers are working round the clock on a seven-hour musical version with special effects, and major Hollywood studios are involved

in a bidding war for a ten-movie franchise, based on the sentence "with Season's Greetings, Jo x".

Stars are already lining up and the names of Benedict Cumberbatch, Idris Elba and Jennifer Lawrence are being touted as possible Uncle Freds and J.K.s, with Sir Ian McKellen considered a shoe-in for the role of envelope.

It is thought Her Majesty the Queen may well be making a guest appearance as the stamp.

"This is the most magical thing ever," said everyone. "Not since J.K. was inspired to write a note to the milkman, asking for an extra pint of semi-skimmed, has the world of..." *(cont. Part 94)*

ADMIT IT— WE'RE LOST!

Britain gets tough with Putin

by Our Defence Staff
William Bootsontheground

IN a move that will terrify the Kremlin, Britain's defence secretary, Sir Michael Fallout, yesterday deployed the entire British Army to the Poland-Russia border.

"This shows that we really mean business," said Sir Michael from behind a pile of sandbags at the Ministry of Defence.

"I today ordered that all 150 men of the British Army, including reserves, should as soon as possible travel by train to a secret destination somewhere in eastern Poland.

"Obviously I cannot tell you where it is," he went on, "because we haven't yet been able to find it on the map.

"But rest assured, the defence of the little town of Czurrendernow will go down in history as the moment when the West finally called the dictator Putin's bluff."

As they were seen off from Victoria station by a Salvation Army band, there were men from every regiment in the British Army – the 17th/21st/49th/94th Guards Dragoons, the Black Watch and Wessex Fusiliers Light Infantry and the Duke of Wellington's Own Cyber Pioneer Corps.

Said a spokesman for the Russian Foreign Ministry last night, "We note with interest this latest initiative from West. I can tell you, all 30,000 Russian elite troops, equipped with nuclear missiles, will certainly be quaking in their boots. Ha, ha, ha! Just my little Russian joke!"

'Royal Navy To Send In Gunboat As Soon As It Is Built'

by Our Naval Staff **Tim Noshipman**

THE MoD is to back up its deployment of ground troops to protect the Baltic states against Russian aggression by sending a gunboat to sail up and down the Latvian coast in a stern and menacing manner.

"I can tell the Kremlin," said the First Sea Lord, Petty Officer Jim Floatsworth, "that as soon

as our new state-of-the-art flagship HMS Dinghy is ready to leave the dockyard, possibly as early as 2027, she will be on her way to preserve world peace and to demonstrate that Nato still has some reason for existence."

A Kremlin spokesman was not available for comment last night, due to a renewed fit of disbelieving laughter.

Sarah Ferguson sues for huge sum of cash over claims she wanted huge sums of cash

SARAH FERGUSON is suing Rupert Murdoch's News Group newspapers for every penny she can get, over their 2010 sting which painted her as a greedy woman who was desperate to acquire every penny she could get.

Her lawyer said, "It was absolutely outrageous that Rupert Murdoch's News Of The World printed stories claiming she wanted half-a-million quid to sell access to Prince Andrew. As a result, to prove that she is by no means a dim, grasping sort of woman, she is suing him for

£25 million, which is roughly the amount of money she could have earned for selling access to Prince Andrew between then and now. This sum should show beyond any shadow of a doubt that she is not remotely avaricious or untrustworthy, especially as £25 mill should keep even her going for a few years, at the bare minimum."

The Duchess was approached for comment, but refused to reply unless our reporter left £3,000 in a brown envelope down the back of the radiators on the third floor of Harrods.

POETRY CORNER

**In Memoriam
Sir Roger Moore, actor**

So. Farewell
Then Roger Moore.

You were the
Best James Bond,
Apart from all
The other ones.

You were also
Simon Templar and
Lord Brett Sinclair in
The Persuaders.

And yet some
People said you
Were typecast.

But now you are
The first Bond
To die.
*(If you don't count
Niven. Ed.)*

Sadly, you only
Live once.
(That was Connery. Ed.)

And you will not
Die another day.
(That was Brosnan. Ed.)

Unlike diamonds,
You are not
Forever.
*(That was Connery
again. Ed.)*

Your living daylights
Are over.
(That was Dalton. Ed.)

And with your
Passing, we need a
Quantum of solace.
(That was Craig. Ed.)

At least now you
Are the Saint.
*(Phew, you got one
right. Ed.)*

E.J. Thribb (0017½)

**In Memoriam,
Sam Panopoulos, inventor
of the Hawaiian Pizza**

So. Farewell
Then Sam Panapoulos,
Pizza pioneer.

You put bits
Of pineapple on
A pizza.

As achievements go,
It's hard to top.

E.J. Thribb
(17½ inches, deep pan)

THE BEARDED LEFT-WING REVOLUTIONARY WHO CHANGED THE WORLD

by Fidel Castro

FOR many of us around the world he was a symbol of hope, of the power of Marxist-Leninism to overthrow the old order and to defy the hated American imperialism. He never gave up the struggle and his ideology never wavered in all the long years he led his people.

With his trademark beard, his lack of cigar, and his plain uniform of anorak and sandals, Jeremy Corbyn was the unmistakeable face of an international movement that reshaped global politics.

Some critics claimed that he clamped down on his opponents and suppressed dissent in the party. Others said his macho attitude to women and his multiple lovers undermined his claim to be a champion of all the people.

But to me and those who first came across this romantic figure when we were teenagers, Jeremy and his Corbynista cadres embodied everything that we felt was possible in a new, socialist Utopia that Jeremy was ushering in before our very eyes. A world of bicycle clips, woolly jumpers, jam making, manhole covers... allotments... you can laugh at our idealism but you can't take the dream away from us.

And now the world mourns and Jeremy hasn't even left us for *(cont. p94)*

Millions celebrate Castro's death

by Our Cuba Staff
Miss Isla Crisis

All over the world, the death of Cuba's controversial former leader, Fidel Castro, was greeted with scenes of jubilation, as middle-class couples at last found a new topic of conversation for dinner parties.

"At long last, there's something different from Brexit to argue about," said one man, shopping for a bottle of wine that wasn't too expensive but didn't look too cheap either.

His wife, clutching a box of After Eight Mints, agreed, saying, "Castro's legacy will be enduring – it's such a relief to forget about the single market and instead fall out with that couple from down the road about whether you can ever strike a reasonable balance between political executions and 100% adult literacy. Personally, I think

Castro was misunderstood."

Her husband intervened, saying, "Oh come now, darling, have you been drinking? I think you've had enough!"

The fear is now, what will fill the vacuum when the memory of Castro begins to fade? Will it be a return to the bad old days of tired arguments about school catchment areas and house prices or will people seize the opportunity to start anew and discuss the impact of Ukip before descending into a fist fight?

EXCLUSIVE FIRST REVIEW OF THE GRAND TOUR, AS SEEN IN ALL NEWSPAPERS

The Grand Bore

Amazon Prime (All The Time)

Yes, it's back and it's being even more boring than ever before! They said that it wouldn't be nearly as boring on Amazon, but they were wrong!

It's **spectacularly** boring, with more boring cars, more boring explosions and top-level boring banter between the three bores who have lost none of their ability to bore for Britain!

Last night, critics were unanimous – *The Grand Bore* puts poor Chris Evans' attempts to be boring in the shade!

As Clarkson might have put it, "This is probably the most boring programme... **in the world!**"

Court Circular

**The Royal Lodge, Windsor
Official Residence of His Royal Highness The Duke of York**

Whilst his Royal Highness Prince Andrew is away from home on a fact-finding trade mission to Buenos Airmiles, his children Princess Beatitude and Princess Euphoria will hold a Free House Party and trash the place.

They will be attended by the celebrated popular singing virtuosi Mr Ed Beerdie and Mr James Bland who will provide musical entertainment.

There will be formal pre-lash drinks hosted by Her Former Royal Highness, Fergiana, the Duchess of Weightwatchers, in the George VI Drawing Room, renamed for the evening "The Fusion Xcelerator Food Emulsifier Sponsored Hospitality Suite". The Duchess will be accompanied by her new gentleman-in-waiting Sheikh Feikh of Mahmood.

Also in attendance will be the Rt Hon Charlie Ricketson-Snood, Jolyon St John Twitte, Count Vodka Von Binj, Major Hugo Jumpinlake, Lady Tara Rara-Boomdeeay and, representing the world of fashion modelling, the DeLa Very-Thigne sisters, Popsy, Flopsy, Cottontail and Cara.

Princess Beatitude will later attempt to invest Mr Bland into the Order of the Knights Bachelor by wielding a ceremonial silver sword removed from the wall, which was originally a gift to her father from the President of Bakhandia.

She will then dub Mr Bland with the sword, using the words "Arise, Sir You're Beautiful", but in so doing, will accidentally stab Mr Beerdie in the face, necessitating medical care.

That Procession in Full

1st Ambulance
Mr Ed Beerdie (Patient)
Ms Cherry Fizzypop (Girlfriend)
Mr Dirk van der Driver (Paramedic)
Ms Sheila Goolagong (Paramedic)

1st Moped
Slizi Papparazzo
(representing Oggli Magazine)

2nd Moped
Jean Luc Quic-Pic
(representing Paris Snatch)

1st Pooled Vauxhall Coarser
Sid Filth (Sun)
Ken Fags (Mirror)
Terry Photo-Lens (Mail Online)
Tom Peeping (Daily Star)
Roly-Poly Pudding
(Daily and Sunday Telegraph)

EVOLUTION OF WOMEN?

Kerina

Boris Johnson, the Secretary of State for Foreign and Commonwealth Affairs, writes exclusively for Private Eye

Cripes! Talk about jolly unfair – old Bozza sounds off about Johnny Saudi and how he's up to no good with his proxy little wars in Yemen and Syria... and then Mother May comes down on me like a ton of bricks.

For the very first time in my life I tried to tell the truth, and what happens? I end up being given a nutbagging by The One Who Wears The Trousers.

All I did was point out the bleeding obvious – that friend Salman and the rest of his Saudi towelhead gang have been using our weapons to arm their warlord chums and to bomb the hell out of a lot of unfortunate civilian chaps, not to mention women and children, who happened to be in the wrong dusty village at the wrong time.

Crikey, anyone would think I'd declared World War III. All Bojo had done was point out what everyone knows anyway, and Number Ten packs me off to the naughty step. I told Sheikh Shufti that Mrs T. had given me a rocket and he said, "Good. We'll take 50, plus some fighter jets and cluster bombs."

Well, no matter, I've learned my lesson. In future, Bozza will stick to his normal rule of telling porky pies because they're much more fun than the boring old truth.

So here's the first one that I hope everyone will print. I am totally loyal to Mrs May, and I am in no way plotting to oust her from her job as PM, which she is performing quite brilliantly!

Ha ha ha ha ha ha. Good one, eh?

Saudis furious at UK behaviour

by Our Diplomatic Staff **Hans Kuttoff**

The Saudi Ministry for Human Rights has issued a denunciation of the United Kingdom for the appalling way that British women are allowed to treat their men.

"To see Theresa May slapping down Boris Johnson was nothing short of shocking," said one Prince. "This sort of ritual humiliation carried out in public is simply barbaric.

"We know that Britain is living in the Middle Ages, with its huge Royal Family and its dodgy princes doing deals around the world, but it is still distressing to find out that their attitude towards women's rights to belittle the role of men in their society has not progressed since the times of Elizabeth the First."

He went on, "I am not sure that we can continue to do arms deals with such a backward country.

"I know we are helping their economy and we need their help with intelligence about terrorism, but do we simply have to stand by and watch a helpless blond Foreign Secretary being publicly whipped into line by a female leader who is only in place as the result of a coup?

"These proxy wars in the Tory party have got to stop!"

— VOGUE —

SAM LAUNCHES NEW FASHION RANGE

by Vogue's Deputy Editor **Sam's Sister**

Proving that she is at last her own woman, the ex-Prime Minister's wife has shown she's got the guts to go it alone – all the way to her little sister's office, to get me to write a piece about her new fashion range.

Okay, I'll do it, Sam. Stop going on at me. What? Photos as well? Alright then, just don't get mum onto me. Okay, here we go...

Samantha Cameron today revealed her new designer line of top fashion... Hang on, Sam, this stuff's a bit drab, isn't it? Bit county – bit tweedy? I mean, that one looks like sackcloth and ashes.

Who designed it? Dave after a bottle of Sauvignon?

Ow! Ow! Mum – Sam's kicking me in the shins!

Alright. It's fantastic.

It's a... what do you want me to say? Okay. It's a stunning debut from one of the most... Ouch! Sorry – **the** most exciting new name since... I don't know, I give up.

By the way, are we still on for Christmas? Just promise me the Goves won't be there.

NO SURPRISE AS WINNER OF SPARTS PERSONALITY OF THE YEAR ANNOUNCED

Winner McCluskey checks that the trains aren't running on time

by Our Media Staff **Ajit Prop**

IN THE end, the result was inevitable, as the dour veteran spartsman Len McCluskey stepped up to receive the supreme accolade once again.

After all, it was Len's year, as he had claimed the number one spart ranking and held onto it.

Sadly, he could not receive his award in person because all planes and trains were cancelled due to strike action, but in a video link he saluted his fellow spartsmen and said how honoured and delighted he was to be on a shortlist that included such legendary names as Sean "Spitter" Hoyle, the president of the RMT, Tosh McDonald, the president of Asleft and Dave Ward of the Communication Workers' Union who was hoping to win on postal votes but was defeated due to industrial action.

The Morning Star-studded event in the glitzy Amersham Arms in London's new Very Cross, was hosted by legendary sparts commentator Jeremy "Gabby" Corbyn, who congratulated *all* the nominees for a spectacular year of spart.

He told a cheering audience of three Momentum supporters and Diane Abbott, "Brothers and sisters, 2016 will go down in history as the year when the spart spirit triumphed, even though we haven't actually won anything."

"Only two shillings for delivering a parcel?! I suppose this is the bloody gig economy!"

DIARY

MELANIA TRUMP

Let me put this clear. Donald is who he is and that's who he is, he knows who he is and I know who I am so we both very strong, very independent, I entrepreneur in my own right, very successful, stand on my own foot, very independent, I offer him my opinion many many times in my own person, he say, what you think, I say, sounds great, we share a lot stuff together. And you know what? He always listens to me when we are in the same room.

Donald tell me last week, he say I never tell this to no one, Melania, but you my First Lady so I tell it you top secret exclusive. My plan, Melania, is to make America great again. That great idea, so I give my opinion, I say hey, Donald, that great idea you make America great again, because he always want my opinion, he listen to me, I say you going to be great President of our country and I will be very very gracious and elegant First Lady, top end of market, real hot.

@MelaniaTrump Donald saying he want to wound all heels. Loves mexicans latinos blacks muslims just not the filthy dirty lying crook rapist wrecker ones.

Donald and I so close, we so connected, he never looked at another other woman. Those ladies who say Donald had inappropriate hands are dirty filthy lying liars, they never even met him and so ungrateful too after all that money he give them.

Donald and I totally passionate about home decoration in style of #@KingLouis14. We share a favorite color and that is solid gold.

On the ceiling of our principal receiving hall in the Trump residence, we hired a costly artist paint classy ceiling of Sistine Chapel in Rome exact, only much bigger and better, with all the figures in designer clothing and guess who takes place of God reaching out to mankind? Is Donald in Armani, so elegant and powerful with beautiful long finger stretching out to man!

For our anniversary Donald get his people to go round Christie auction get me beautiful classic elegant Leonardo of Madonna and Child for many many millions of dollars, hundreds and hundreds of millions, and then he get top expensive artist to rub out Madonna's sad old face because so tired and plain, all wrinkles and lines, in those days they no have skin cream or moisturiser. Then he change it with my face, so now we are proud owner of Leonardo's Melania and Child, who is my son Barron, of course, in baseball cap and Melania in fabulous gold and diamond high-end necklace from Cartier so expensive but negotiated reasonable discount.

Donald is kind of guy who totally wants to hold out his hand to humanity, that's what people don't realise, but only if the man in the street has washed himself properly, you know, as President of the United States, you cannot be catching common germs from dirty filthy riff-raff you don't know where they been.

@MelaniaTrump Congrat to great team developing new #FirstLadyskincareline for QVC channel. Your passion, talent and dedication to #beauty is seen in your artistry&creations #anti-aging vitamin C.

Michelle Obama is such a gracious lady, elegant role model. I study her. When we visiting the President and First Lady at our new home, Michelle she greet me by saying, "So nice to meet you".

"So nice to meet you" I saying.

"And welcome to the White House" say Michelle.

"And welcome to the White House" I say.

We sit and have elegant cup of high-end luxury tea.

"What a beautiful day" say Michelle.

"What a beautiful day" I say.

Yes, we get on so great, I hardly believe it!

When Donald and I depart, Michelle say to me, "So nice to see you!"

And I say to Michelle, "So nice to see you!"

We being firm friends, Michelle and Melania, we gone through so much together. Next day, I get my people to send her courtesy gift Melania Trump Own Brand Gold Bracelet as seen on QVC ($2070) and Matching High-End T-Shirt ($599 or just $900 for two) with hand-written note saying "New Best Friend!"

I love to Tweet. Totally best place for Tweet is on Twitter. I am very feminist, very womanly, very warm and sensual so I love to tweet photographs of things that move me. I always make care to add a caption so to make it more personal. Next to picture of a sunset I put caption #"SUNSET", and to picture of flower I put #"FLOWER". Is makes it more personal so people can tell I am a human being just like them though maybe a little better.

I raise my son Barron Trump to be regular American kid. I make certain he connect with ordinary decent hardworking Americans, for instance a doorman or a chauffeur or a personal stylist.

When we visit the UK, the President and I will be sure to take Barron to meet The Queen #@Buckingham Palace, her desirable spacious luxury accommodation within walking distance of #@Harrods.com. Donald has already fixed on his top offer for this prestige slice of prime real estate and he confident #Her Majesty will grab bargain offer with both hands!

We go crazy for traditional old-fashioned English gentleman like Piers Morgan and Nigel Farage. So elegant and gracious! Nigel drop by our residence last week, he true gentleman, so posh, grin big grin at me and say, "You got a real cracker there, Donald!" He so posh and charming, like James Bond, Nigel know how to make woman feel great about herself. I tell him, Nigel, Donald really want you to work for him in White House, and Nigel he look so happy, just like schoolboy. And I say, You have driver licence? You be our top-of-the-range English chauffeur, Nigel, you make good money, smart uniform, cellphone, all come free!" Nigel he suddenly look all serious and say thank you, he think about it.

As told to
CRAIG BROWN

Forgotten Moments In Music History

"Will you all please get back to your places?" Gerry implored

Charlie and Craig were utterly fed up with train cancellations

Another busy day for Procol Harum

21

ENGLISH FOOTBALL
NEW ABUSE VICTIM STEPS FORWARD

by Our FA Correspondent
Ian Competence

TODAY yet another ex-footballer has been named as a victim of abuse.

At an FA press conference, the former England player Gareth Southgate told press, "I have accepted the role as the next person to be abused on a daily basis by the media and the public at large.

"As the new England manager, I am following in the footsteps of Turnip Taylor and the Wally with the Brolly, so it's only a matter of time before the press notice my resemblance to a root vegetable, or perhaps pick on an absurd habit like using an umbrella when it's pouring with rain.

"I look forward to headlines such as: 'It's all gone South–gate!', 'What's gone wrong? It's South–gate Gate!!', and 'Time for Gareth to exit via the Southgate!!!'"

CHURCH HEARS ABOUT ALLEGATIONS OF ABUSE IN FOOTBALL

THOSE BBC HEADLINES IN FULL

- ■ Football Abuse Story Escalates
- ■ Hundreds Report Football Abuse
- ■ Football Abuse Worse Than Savile
- ■ Football Abuse Far Worse Than Savile
- ■ Football Abuse Far, Far, Far Worse Than Savile
- ■ It Wasn't Us For Once!
- ■ Hooray! Back Of The Net!
- ■ Watch Hundreds Of BBC Programmes About Abuse
- ■ Nothing To Do With Auntie At All!
- ■ They Think It's All Over – We Haven't Started Yet!
- ■ Coming Soon: BBC Drama About Football Abuse
- ■ Breaking News: Football Abuse Story Escalates

"Look at you with your clean eating"

THE STRAIN OF PARENTING

by Her Royal Highness The Duchess of Cambridge

IT's the toughest job in the world and there's no point in pretending otherwise.

Looking for a full-time nanny is hard work and involves constant attention, endless patience and sleepless nights. Will you find the right person to look after your children? Are you doing the right thing, interviewing girls from Nobland Nannies? Will your husband do his fair share of nanny searching?

Like many, I have experienced all these problems and I wouldn't pretend to be an expert. But I do know this. Whenever I have agonised about what to do for the best for my children, I've always been able to rely on my mother to come round and find a full-time nanny for me.

© Kate Middleclass 2017

Grayling Gets Tough Over Rail Chaos

by Our Transport Staff
Michael Govia

TRANSPORT Secretary Chris Grayling last night lashed out at everyone involved in the crisis which has brought train services across a swathe of southern England to a complete halt for weeks.

Said Mr Grayling, "There is no doubt who is responsible for this unprecedented disaster.

"Obviously, the irresponsible unions are top of the list for blame. But so, let's face it, is the management of the train operating company, who have allowed this appalling situation to develop over many months."

Mr Grayling was also scathing about the role played in the crisis by millions of Southern Rail passengers who, he said, "have been turning up at stations expecting to get to work on a train, even though they must have known full well that it was rush hour and that no trains were likely to be running.

"These people have been milling about for hours, making an absurd fuss and suggesting that I myself should in some way be able to intervene to sort this out.

DOO DOO

"Surely commuters realise that I am only the Secretary of State for Transport? Just because the taxpayer is shelling out millions of pounds to compensate the passengers as well as subsidise the railway company, doesn't mean that the government should get involved.

"It is not my job to ensure that train services run on time. Who do they think I am – Benito Mussolini?"

Trump Cabinet 'Full of Ordinary Working Joe Billionaires'

by Our U.S. Staff
A. Hack

AFTER completing his cabinet appointments with Exxon CEO Rex Tillerson as Secretary of State, President-elect Donald Trump said he had given the elites a bloody nose just as he had promised during his campaign.

"Whereas Crooked Hillary would have appointed a cabinet full of Goldman Sachs bankers and big oil billionaires," Trump told a victory rally in Little Hope, Arkansas, "I have appointed a cabinet full of ordinary men and women who get up in the morning just like you, worry about how they're going to be able to afford to put fuel in their golden jets and trudge into work at Goldman Sachs and Exxon in their chauffeur-driven limos."

On the subject of his controversial new Secretary of State, who has been accused of being "too close" to President Putin, Trump insisted Rex Tillerson's appointment will have to be ratified by both Houses – of the Russian parliament.

Mr Trump refused to discuss his new Secretary of Health, who told journalists that "Leeches were good enough for the founding fathers and they're good enough for poor people", his new Secretary of Transport, who tweeted that "buses are for immigrants" and his new Secretary of Housing, who said in a blog that "homelessness is God's way of telling you that you're a loser".

School news

St Cakes

Zumba term (formerly Rugger Bugger term) begins today. There are no real boys left in the school, only loads of girls. R.J. Namby-Pamby is Head of Yoga. B.I.G. Girls-Blouse is Captain of Transcendental Meditation. The Master in charge of Rugby Football, Mr "Muddy" Oaf, has left the school, as has the senior cricket coach, the Rev. J.C. Flannelled-Fool. Their positions in the Holistic Centre (formerly the Games Department) have been amalgamated into one new post, viz Master of Mindfulness, and we are delighted to welcome Mr O.M. Omomomom who joins us from our sister school in Tibet, St Ricecakes. Tantric sex education will take place in the Sting Memorial Hub (formerly the Gymnasium). Exeats (or Extracorporeal Experiences) will be held on 19 Nov on St Pilates Day. The school Drama Society will put on a production of *Hello Dalai* in the Jeffrey Archer Theatre on 14 December. The Wellington Prize for Sporting Achievement will be replaced by the Wellness Prize for Best Aligned Chakras.

Universities To Replace Gender-specific Pronouns

STUDENTS have been told by their unions to replace the outdated gender pronouns *"he"* and *"she"* and to replace them with *"me"*.

A typical sentence should now be constructed as follows: "Me, me, me... it's all about me."

(Reuters)

Toby Young's Pocket Film Guides

I, DANIEL BLAKE
Doesn't ring true. A completely unrealistic depiction of life on benefits in Britain which suggests the unemployed aren't drunken scrounging freeloaders.

JAWS
Doesn't ring true. A completely unrealistic depiction of the hunt for a killer Great White Shark, would they really use that small a boat?

BRIEF ENCOUNTER
Doesn't ring true. Completely unrealistic depiction of how easy it was to find love on British Rail station platforms in the 1940s.

GODZILLA
Doesn't ring true. Tokyo supposedly flattened by the Monster. I've been to Tokyo. IT'S STILL THERE!!!

THE FULL MONTY
Doesn't ring true. If those men really did want to strip themselves totally of their dignity, surely they'd be writing terrible film reviews for The Spectator.

POETRY CORNER

Lines on the passing of actor Robert Vaughn, the last surviving member of The Magnificent Seven

So. Farewell
Then Robert Vaughn.
You were the last
Surviving member of
The Magnificent Seven.
(As well as,
Of course,
The Man From
U.N.C.L.E.)

For some reason,
I missed the news
Of your passing and
Wish to apologise
To readers
For this unusual
Oversight.

On a happier note,
You are now reunited
With Yul Brynner,
Steve McQueen,
Brad Dexter (who I
always forgot),
Horst Buchholz,
James Coburn, and
Charles Bronson.

As Keith put it
when I told him,
"Yes they are now
the Magnificent
Heaven."

All together now,
For the very
Last time,
Dum. Di-da-da-dum.
Dum. Di-da-da-dum.
Da-Da.
Di-da-DA-da.
Da-Da.
Di-da-DA-da.

E.J.Thribb (17½)

"These 'before-work drinks' are proving very popular"

Grizelda

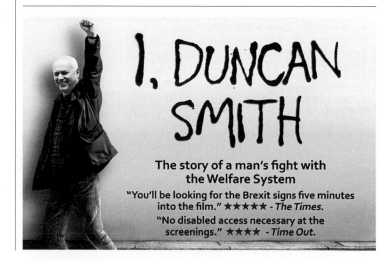

I, DUNCAN SMITH

The story of a man's fight with the Welfare System

"You'll be looking for the Brexit signs five minutes into the film." ★★★★★ - *The Times.*

"No disabled access necessary at the screenings." ★★★★ - *Time Out.*

THAT SHARED SOCIETY
What we will share

- Hospital beds
- Room in care home
- Seat on train (1 between 3)
- Book in classroom (1 between 40)
- Jobs (with robot co-worker)
- All our emails (with MI5)
- Sense of disbelief that anyone thinks these slogans actually mean anything

'We were wrong' admits Bank of England

by Our Economics Correspondent
Hugh Turn

A SENIOR economist at the Bank of England, Andrew Haldane, has admitted that the Bank of England had no idea that the financial crash of 2008 was coming and that this was a "Michael Fish" moment.

He said that their predictions regarding Brexit were also wrong and there was now a crisis in economic forecasting.

He then added, "However, I may be wrong about this and, in fact, economists may have been right about everything all along, there wasn't a crash and Brexit will turn out to be a disaster."

He continued, "But then I may be wrong about being wrong. After all, I'm a senior economist and we don't appear to know anything.

"However, the one thing I am sure about is that there is **no** hurricane on its way to Britain. January is gong to be hot, dry and sunny – so wrap up warm and don't forget to take a brolly!"

AMERICAN AIRPORT SHOOTINGS
THIS MUST NEVER HAPPEN AGAIN
by Our Firearms Correspondent **Ron Sequitur**

THE latest shootings at Fort Lauderdale airport in America have revealed a sad state of affairs. A mentally-ill man who had his gun confiscated just two months ago was able not only to get his gun back, but check it into his luggage, get on a flight, and then get his gun out in the baggage reclaim area, killing five and wounding several others.

It's plain to see that American airports are not equipped to deal with their firearms problem. The solutions are simple:

● More guns in baggage reclaim. Just ten heavily armed guards in every baggage reclaim area could mean we never see another shot fired, unless one of them goes mad, in which case

the other nine can shoot him.

● More guns at airport check-in desks. It's possible the check-in clerks would have noticed he was thinking about committing a crime and could have shot him before he even boarded the plane. Problem: solved.

● Everyone to be given a gun on entering an airport. If anyone walking through security is found to be carrying two guns, then security should get involved and take their other gun away.

● Everyone else to be given a gun. As the old saying goes: the only thing that can stop a BAD mentally-ill guy with a gun is a GOOD mentally-ill guy with a gun.

©NRA. Warning: anyone misquoting us to make fun of us will be shot.

DAILY MAIL EXCLUSIVE

So, what really happened the night George Michael died?

We don't know.

Was he a drug-addled pervert who was murdered by his openly gay boyfriend?

Probably not.

Was he a saintly figure whose life was devoted to helping the poor?

Probably not either, but we don't want to lose too many readers on account of the previous headline.

The Guardian   Friday November 11 2016

Why popular things are rubbish

by Our Clickbait Correspondent
Sucha Contrarian

SERIOUSLY people, what's all the hoo-ha about popular things all of a sudden?

I mean, pur-lease! If you think about it, popular things are really not up to all that much. Take your favourite television programme, for example. That's rubbish. And you're wrong for enjoying it. What are you thinking? You should like that television programme that no one watches because it's on a channel you can't find.

And that sport you like? How lame. That's only popular because it's not obscure and incomprehensible. If you click below, I've compiled a Top 50 list of overrated sports that are popular but are really lame. Your sport is at number three.

Am I annoying you? Are you going to retweet this article in outrage to encourage my web traffic? Not yet? Okay, you forced me to go there. That phone you have? I mean, come on. It's either embarrassingly out of date, or you're an idiotic sheeple for buying the latest one. Happy now?

"So, the idea is we leave it outside the gates on a bin day..."

24

WHY DIDN'T WE INTERVENE IN SYRIA TO SCREW THINGS UP IN A DIFFERENT WAY?

by Our Civil War Correspondent **Hans Wringing**

AS MORE details emerge of the slaughter of the innocents in Aleppo with the rout by Assad's forces of the final rebel enclave, the world is asking itself why it stood by and allowed the disaster to happen when it could have intervened and allowed a slightly different disaster to happen.

Recent Middle East history teaches us that the only thing worse than leaving innocent men, women and children in Aleppo to be slaughtered by a vile dictator is to intervene like we did in Libya, remove the vile dictator and facilitate the slaughter of countless other innocent men, women and children in the power vacuum we leave behind.

That is why the case for intervening over Aleppo, and at the same time not intervening, is so strong, as the UN demanded Western powers launch operation "Rock and a Hard Place" to solve things.

NICE TO MEET YOU! RIGHT AWAY, BOSS! GOOD MORNING! YES, I'D LOVE TO SEE A PICTURE OF YOUR BABY. KILL FUCK GO KNICKERSHATE NO ZZZ I CAN'T NO WHY URGGH WHY? NO. DIE NO. PLEASE LEAVE ME DEATH ALONE. KILL ME

W. McPhail

A&E DEPARTMENTS STRUGGLE TO COPE AS NEW CRISIS HITS

by Our Medical Staff **Seymour Patients**

BRITAIN'S hard-pressed Accident and Emergency departments were besieged yesterday by a flood of new patients suffering from a mystery illness.

Medics reported huge queues of people feeling nauseous, reporting to their local hospitals at all times of day of night. Explained one, "I feel physically sick. I don't know why, but it came on after I read the news that Jeremy Hunt was announcing another cut, namely his cut of over 14 million pounds from the sale of the 'Hotcourses' website."

Medical staff are particularly susceptible to an adverse reaction, with doctors being hit with depression and fainting in corridors.

"To think I spent five years doing a medical course," explained one exhausted medic, "when I should just have set up a crappy website about courses and frittered the rest of my life away being a useless government minister."

Mr Hunt defended his website, saying, "It provides lots of useful courses, including First Aid and Alternative Medicine, both of which may come in handy when you hear about my next round of cuts." He added, "Anyone who says there's a crisis in A and E is off their trolley. And must get back on it at once, because we haven't got any beds."

Sarah Vain

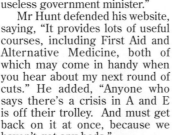

It's Me time!

WHAT have things come to when the designer stick insect, aka Victoria Beckham, is given an OBE? What for? Services to self-starvation?

The Honours list was already thin and then it suddenly got even thinner.

Surely they could find someone with a bit more weight to recognise, someone maybe who wasn't a needy self-publicist trading on her husband's success?

Barely a day goes by when we don't see "non-Posh" desperately appearing in the newspapers, so giving Ms Skinny Sour-Puss a gong makes a mockery of the whole rotten system.

Surely honours should be given to ordinary people doing important jobs for which they get little recognition and for which they receive no reward other than the knowledge that they have helped other people by offering informed criticism of the state of the nation in, say, a column in the Daily Mail?

I'm talking about the sort of normal woman who enjoys a glass of wine, a piece of cake and a good laugh at Z-list wannabes?

So, if PM Theresa wants to restore the reputation of the Honours list, there's one obvious role model for the Order of the Brexit Enthusiast – it's OB**ME**!!!

That New Police Degree Course In Full

Introduction: Hello, hello, hello!

Lecture: Don't do that again, sonny.

Tutorial: Anything you say will be written down and used against you.

Exam: What's all this, then?

SHOCK REPORT: EXPOSURE TO CAR FUMES AFFECTS MENTAL HEALTH

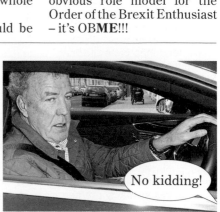

No kidding!

Nursery Times

THREE BEARS IN POP-UP BROTHEL SHOCK

by Little Boy Blue Movie

THE three bears were outraged last night when they returned home from a brief holiday "walking" in the woods to find that their charming cottage had been turned into a temporary vice den.

Said Father Bear, "Who's been sleeping in my bed?" "I don't think they've been doing much sleeping," added Mother Bear. Whilst Baby Bear said, "Could someone explain to me exactly what is a 'pop-up brothel'?"

The Bear family were shocked to discover a Goldilocks wig, some broken chairs and traces of what they initially thought was porridge all over their dream kitchen. (*You're fired. Ed.*)

Policeman Plod said this has been happening all over Nurseryland. Victims include the old lady who lived in a shoe who doesn't know what to do after a visit from foot fetishists. Old Mother Hubbard, returning home early to feed her dog, looked in her cupboard and found that it wasn't just the cupboard that was bare.

However, it is believed that the crooked man in the crooked house is helping police with their enquiries (*cont. p94*)

Late news

● Wee Willie Winkie banned from Tesco after running through town in dressing gown.

Press regulation: The case for Section 94

by Sir Maxwell Mosley

NO ONE is a greater defender of the freedom of the press than myself, having devoted a very considerable sum of my own money to set up the new regulatory body "Suppress".

The purpose of this body is to put an end to the tragic abuses which for so long have made the British press a scandal throughout the world.

Now at last the British government can lead the way in showing how a genuinely free press can be brought back to a proper sense of responsibility in the way it reports on the news.

Our politicians have rightly understood that this extension of freedom can only be achieved through a body appointed by the government, made up of wholly independent persons who themselves have every reason to understand the need for the press to be disciplined and brought to heel, and punished – yes, punished – by a severe spanking of the bottom by fierce young ladies speaking German. Jawohl, zey vill soon understand who is ze master, and who is ze servant who is crawling and begging for mercy!

At this point, Sir Maxwell had to lie down and take a brief rest, before continuing to speak for several hours about the need for all UK newspapers and magazines to sign up to his body Suppress. Sir Oswald insisted that newspapers should be forced to join, or that they would be made bankrupt by paying all sides' costs in libel actions, whether they lost or won the case. They would then be closed down under Section 94 of the Criminal and Courts Act which states that "all newspapers must in future cease from criticising anyone in public life, particularly members of Parliament and prominent sado-masochists who are not Nazis and wish only to be left alone to spend quiet afternoons in Mayfair in the privacy of their own dungeons".

On other pages

● Erdogan salutes Section 94 – "Mosley has right idea," says Turkish Prime Minister.

That Explosive EU Official's Goodbye Letter In Full

From Sir Ivan Hadenough, former UK Ambassador to the European Union

Dear Colleagues,

As you will by now have gathered, I have told Mrs May and her ministers that, frankly, I can take it no longer.

A more useless, muddle-headed bunch of ignorant no-hopers I have never had the misfortune to deal with in my entire career.

I will not name names, but none of the three prominent ministers involved has the faintest idea how the EU works and how unbelievably complicated it is going to be to get us out of it.

Again and again, I have tried to explain to these halfwits, as diplomatically as I can, that they are just a bunch of clueless twits, who couldn't even find their way out of a paper bag.

Night after night, for months, I've been putting together briefing documents, explaining in detail just how we might get out of this mess without landing ourselves waist-high in the brown stuff.

But none of these arrogant dimwits showed any sign of understanding what I was trying to tell them – in fact, I doubt whether any of them even read what I was sending them.

Anyway, the problem is no longer mine. I've done what I can and I'm now off... leaving you all to deal with that lazy, incompetent shower the prime minister seems to have surrounded herself with.

Yours,
Ivan

Our political editor writes

Even though it is couched in the careful and diplomatic language of a senior mandarin, we can see, by reading between the lines, that Sir Ivan is not wholly pleased or impressed by Mrs May's Brexit team.

He has not named names, but clearly feels that Messrs Davis, Fox and Johnson have been somewhat slow to appreciate some of the finer points that the forthcoming negotiations will involve.

Even for a seasoned political insider such as myself, it is difficult to avoid the conclusion that Sir Ivan foresees the possibility that trouble may lie ahead.

TRUMP BACKS ASSANGE ON RUSSIAN HACKING

You've gotta trust a fellow pussy grabber

● **Note to lawyers**: This joke works on the assumption that Mr Trump erroneously believes Mr Assange to be guilty of sexual misconduct, though, at present, the allegations have not been tested in a court of law, due to Mr Assange's unwillingness to leave the Ecuadorian Embassy and face Swedish justice.

"What do you want to be when you grow up? Boy or girl?"

DUMB BRITAIN

Real contestants, real quiz shows, real answers, real dumb!

Tipping Point, ITV

Ben Shephard: Snowdon is a feature of which mountainous National Park?
Contestant: The Andes.

Shephard: What well-known DJ's name is rhyming slang for something going wrong?
Contestant: Steve Wright.

Shephard: Which Labour leader was defeated by the Conservative Party in the 1987 and 1992 elections?
Contestant: Harold Macmillan.
Shephard: No, it was Neil Kinnock.
Contestant: Never heard of him.

Shephard: The Victorian era was named after which monarch?
Contestant: Pass.

Shephard: Name a country beginning with the letter Q.
Contestant: Kuwait.

Shephard: Mary Todd Lincoln was the wife of which US president?
Contestant: Roosevelt.

Shephard: In 1969, which poet and civil rights activist released her memoir *I Know Why The Caged Bird Sings?*
Contestant: Barbra Streisand.

Shephard: Which Elizabethan playwright had twins called Hamnet and Judith?
Contestant: The only playwright I know with twins in it is Cinderella. So I'm going to say Cinderella.

Shephard: Which brothers made the first manned powered aero flight in 1903?
Contestant: The Marx brothers.

Shephard: Which artistic movement, which originated in Italy in the 14th century, takes its name from the French word for "rebirth"?
Contestant: The can-can.

Shephard: A grenadier is trained to use which weapon?
Contestant: A spear.

Shephard: Miss Selfridge was originally the fashion department of which major department store?
Contestant: Debenham's.

Shephard: In which field of dance was Margot Fonteyn famous?
Contestant (*same one*): The tango.

Shephard: Which Australian state is separated from the mainland by the Bass Strait?
Contestant: Gibraltar.

Shephard: Gertrude, Queen of Denmark, is the mother of which Shakespearean character?
Contestant: The Merchant of Venice.

Shephard: A brickie is the informal name for a member of what profession?
Contestant: Plumber.

Shephard: In the periodic table, only two elements end with the letter "C". Arsenic is one; what is the other?
Contestant: Turmeric.

Shephard: A hi-hat is a type of which specific percussion instrument?
Contestant: I'm going to have to go for it because I really think he [her opponent] will know. I think it's a tuba.

Shephard: What stinging insect is an anagram of "swap"?
Contestant: Bee.

Shephard: In 1945, was the curtain that Winston Churchill said had descended on Europe (a) iron, (b) velvet or (c) invisible?
Contestant: I don't think he would have said iron. I think it must be velvet, Ben.
Shephard: Sorry, it was iron.
Contestant: Never heard of that, Ben.

Shephard: "England expects that every man will do his duty." Which naval hero said that?
Contestant: Napoleon.

Shephard: Which ancient British queen of the Iceni led a revolt against Roman rule in 60AD?
Contestant: Cleopatra.

Shephard: Who laid down their cloak for Queen Elizabeth I?
Contestant: King Henry the 13th.

Pointless, BBC1

Alexander Armstrong: Name any Commonwealth countries in the northern hemisphere.
Contestant 1: I think I'll play it safe, hopefully, and say New Zealand.
Contestant 2: I was thinking of Denmark.

Armstrong: We're looking for a 1941 film directed by Orson Welles, his directorial debut, starting with the letters "CK".
Contestant: Calvin Klein.

Armstrong: Name a country that ends in two consonants.
Contestant: Oh no, I did A level geography, but that's as far as it goes. Paris?

Armstrong: Which novel featured the characters Arthur Dent, Ford Prefect and Zaphod Beeblebrox?
Contestant: Pride and Prejudice.

Armstrong: In which of Shakespeare's plays is a Roman leader stabbed in the back by friends?
Contestant: *Gladiator*.

Celebrity Pointless, BBC1

Alexander Armstrong: We're looking for a chemical element that begins with a letter from the second half of the alphabet.
Arlene Phillips: Well, I know chemicals cause flames, so I'll say a flame.

Eggheads, BBC2

Jeremy Vine: How many wings does a butterfly have? Is it none, two or four?
Contestant: Ah, I think this is a trick question. I'm going to say none.

Fifteen to One, C4

Sandi Toksvig: Which British army officer, born in 1887, fought in both world wars and is best remembered for leading his Eighth Army troops to victory over the Germans and Italians at the battle of El Alamein in 1942?
Contestant: Rommel.

The Chase, ITV

Bradley Walsh: Samson lost his strength after what was cut off?
Contestant: His arm.

Walsh: Who was the last Tsarina of Russia?
Contestant: Peter the Great.

Walsh: Which 18th-century highwayman's surname is an anagram of the word "turnip"?
Contestant: Pass.

Walsh: The Eddie Stobart truck "Tammy" is named after which country and western singer?
Contestant: Dolly Parton.

Walsh: Twelve o'clock is noon and what other time?
Contestant: Midday.

Walsh: What Chinese city gives its name to a breed of dog?
Contestant: Poodle.

Walsh: The Yangtze river reaches the ocean near which major city?
Contestant: Los Angeles.

Walsh: Name the underwater tunnel linking Dover and Calais.
Contestant: The Suez Canal.

Walsh: Who was the only British king to abdicate in the 20th century?
Contestant: Charles Dickens.

Walsh: The inhabitants of which Scottish town or city are referred to as Dundonians?
Contestant: Cardiff.

Walsh: Elected in 1945, which Labour politician was known as the "red queen"?
Contestant: Clement Attlee.

Walsh: Which British prime minister was educated at Holton Park Girls' Grammar School?
Contestant: Winston Churchill.

Walsh: What's the only prime number between 85 and 90?
Contestant: 91.

Wave105 breakfast show

Steve Power: Name the composer of "White Christmas". I'll give you a clue: he shares his name with a German city.
Co-host: Frankfurt.

Tenable, ITV

Warwick Davis: Name one of the top ten most populated cities in France.
Contestant: I don't know if this place is in France, or even if it's a city... Andover.

The National Lottery: Five Star Reunion, BBC1

Nick Knowles: Jeremy Corbyn is the leader of which political party?
Contestant: Conservatives.

The Getaway Car, BBC1

Dermot O'Leary: Name any mammal you can see when you visit London Zoo.
Contestant 1: Mammoth.
O'Leary: I'm afraid that's not correct. Maybe 4,000 years ago, but not now.
Contestant 2: Eel.

The Washington Post-Truth

FRIDAY, JANUARY 27, 2017

Trump spokesman hits out at press

BY OUR WASHINGTON STAFF
CHERRY TREE

THE White House press secretary, Mr Sean Spice-Up, angrily attacked "media dishonesty" yesterday in a dispute over numbers which arose after the inauguration of President Trump.

The press had reported that the President's speech contained 25 statements that were untrue. Mr Spicegirl denied this furiously, claiming that there were "over a million lies" in the Inauguration Address and that the media were deliberately falsifying the figures, in order to "delegitimise" the President.

Said Mr Waste-of-Spicer, "Mr Trump produced more lies than any other president before or since. FACT."

The press spokesman was backed up by the President's campaign manager, Ms Kellyanne Conwoman, who said, "I entirely agree with Mr Spicerack, who has given alternative facts about the number of lies told by the President. There can be no doubt that Washington on Friday was filled with lies – almost as many as there were people who attended the inauguration ceremony."

The press, however, are refusing to back down, producing telltale pictures of Mr Trump with his mouth open, which, they say, prove beyond doubt that Mr Trump is lying.

THAT TRUMP/MAY SPECIAL RELATIONSHIP 🇬🇧 TRADE SUMMIT 🇺🇸 IN FULL

May: You say "Tomato"...
Trump: And I say "Keep your tomatoes out of America".
May: You say "Potato"...
Trump: And I say "American Potatoes First. Buy American. Hire American".
May: You say "Pyjamas"...
Trump: And I say, "Get 'em off, darlin'". ♪
May: Either...
Trump: Neither... ♫ ♫
May: Either...
Trump: Let's call the whole thing off.

©George and Ira Gershwin-win-for-America.

Rejoice! Mrs May is 'Front of Queue'!

Hooray! The British Prime Minister has today been honoured by being the first world leader to be granted admission to the Oval Orifice. Yes, Prime Minister May is at the very head of the queue to get inside President Trump's bottom, cementing the special relationship which British premiers have enjoyed since the Second World War – Harold Wilson, Margaret Thatcher, Tony Blair, all have enjoyed unique access to the seat of power. *(This is disgusting. Ed.)*

We should all be proud that, once again, Britain leads the way in being right behind the president. No ifs, no butts (except his, obviously) when it comes to international diplomacy. This is the bottom line and Theresa's got it licked. *(You're fired. Ed.)*

The Eye's Controversial New Columnist

The columnist who's had enough of 'experts' telling him he has to have a nap

This week, I am very angry about criticism of Theresa May's stance on Europe. Speaking as a baby *(see photo)*, I can tell you that asking for what you want and walking away when you don't get exactly what you want is a time-honoured negotiating tactic. For example, just the other day I wanted something other than diced carrot to eat. I refused to eat my diced carrot in no uncertain terms, and kept on refusing despite all persuasion. I banged the table with my Tommy Tippee cup and absolutely refused to eat my diced carrot. I made it clear that this was a red line, and that I would rather starve to death and put my parents in jail for child neglect than eat my diced carrot. And of course, the strategy worked. My parents left the table, had a conference in the kitchen (or I assumed they were having a conference – their conversation was drowned out by the blender) and they returned to the table with a counter-offer, a lovely mashed-up orangey soup-like substance that I found much more palatable. So you see, it's worth the UK's while to cry yourself purple and scream yourself hoarse, because you will eventually get *(cont. p94)*

THE Sun SAYS

How dare Vladimir Putin claim that Russia's prostitutes are the best in the world!

WHAT about our own brilliant British sex-workers?

The average hard-working British tart could knock spots off those Miserable Mishas and Awful Anastasias any night of the week!

We tell the boastful Russian dictator, "Sorry, Vlad, but Britain leads the world when it comes to sexy slappers – even if most of ours do seem to have come from Russia in the first place."

THERESA MAY SPELLS IT OUT

The British people have had enough of exports

A Global Britain

Notes&queries

What is a 'golden shower'?

● Keen to educate my grandchildren in current affairs, I made them watch President Trump's news conference and ever since they've been asking me "What is a 'Golden Shower'?" Can any of your readers help enlighten us?
Mrs Innocent Smoothie, Tunbridge Wells

● A "Golden Shower" was a type of lemon sherbet available in the tuck shop at my school, St Cakes, throughout the 1930s, accompanied by a liquorice stick which one could dab in the "golden shower" of sherbet for less than tuppence. The same price, incidentally, that you could purchase a Morris Minor before we joined the Common Market.
Sir Herbert Sherbet, Dorset

● Sir Herbert has, I fear, had too many sherbets. A "Golden Shower" is, of course, the first rainfall in the month of May when the sunlight passes through the raindrops, creating a dazzling light-effect, which was once captured by J.M.W. Turner in his famous painting, *Golden Shower in Margate with Mrs Kemp* 1832, exhibited in the Royal Academy but withdrawn for unknown reasons after a request from Mr Kemp.
David Hackney, Hockney

Nonsense, as any visitor to the great city of Manchester will tell you, the Golden Shower is a legendary Chinese Restaurant just off the curry mile. Established as early as

1989, and serving a wide range of fried chicken, pizzas and other traditional Chinese foods, the venue was very popular with the singing group The Stranglers who based their hit song, *Golden Shower* on this very establishment. Music fans will know that this was re-recorded by TV crooner Alexander Armstrong, with the word "shower" replaced with "brown", so that it could be played on Radio 2 without infringing advertisement regulations. From the Golden Shower's extensive menu, I can sincerely recommend the Number 1, but not the Number 2.
Lee Mak, Proprietor, The Golden Shower. 'All You Can Eat' buffet, Tuesdays 4-4.30pm.

● For heaven's sake, which century are you lot living in? As all my parishioners make perfectly plain to me, after attending evensong, when they say they are off for a "Golden Shower", they are simply referring to a perfectly normal healthy act of urination on another person for sexual gratification. Today's church needs to help society move forward and embrace such acts of love in a healthy relationship, rather than dwell in embarrassing ignorance like Messrs Smoothie, Hackney, Mak, and Sir Herbert Sherbet.
The Reverend Richard Coldshower

Next week:
Do butterflies like butter? What does the "i" in will.i.am stand for? Did anyone climb Lord Snowdon?

New Battle of the Sexes

Pussy Hat   **Dick Head**

Political Pundits Hail Distinguished Statesman in Oval Office

by Sky TV's **Kay Bully**

THERE was widespread relief throughout the world that a proven leader, orator and political thinker had been installed in the White House last week.

"It is deeply comforting," said commentators worldwide, "to know that behind the president's desk sits a figure we can all trust and who will go down in history as a defender of freedom, an opponent of fascism and champion of liberty.

"Unfortunately," these commentators continued, "he can't do or say anything because he is just a bust. But Winston Churchill, even in miniature statue form, is a reassuring presence, as we all go to hell in a handcart with the terrifying President Trump."

One observer concluded, "The two figures have little in common apart from the fact that they are both bronze coloured."

Daily Mail

FRIDAY, DECEMBER 9, 2016

SCANDAL OF THE UNELECTED JUDGES

OPENLY GAY   UNASHAMEDLY FEMALE   VOICE OF ESTABLISHMENT   LINKS TO EUROPE

Sky takeover shock

by Our Media Staff **Sonny Jim**

SKY Chairman James Murdoch has insisted that Rupert Murdoch's £11.7bn takeover of the company was independently scrutinised to ensure that Rupert was in fact his father.

"Before this deal could be agreed, rigorous independent checks were made to ascertain that I was definitely Rupert's son," James Murdoch told reporters. He continued, "The inquiry confirmed that I was indeed the son who was forced to resign in ignominy from News Group at the height of the phone hacking crisis, only for my father to get me this job.

"The deal was only approved by the board once they were certain that I hadn't paid the price for falling short of the conduct expected of a chief executive because Rupert Murdoch was my dad."

Welcoming the news, Rupert Murdoch said he was very relaxed at the prospect of Culture Secretary Karen Bradley referring the bid to the competition authority, adding, "After my recent private meeting with Theresa May in New York, I'm predicting that Ofcom will not give a Fox!"

HEIR OF SORROWS

by Dame Sylvie Krin, author of *Duchess of Hearts* & *You're Never Too Old*

"HE REALLY is... appalling." For once, Charles was NOT lost for words, as he attempted to describe the newly inaugurated President of the United States to his wife, Camilla.

"Mr Trump's attitude to our Muslim friends is appalling, his attitude to women is appalling and as for his stance on the whole climate change thingie, well it is absolutely..."

Camilla finished the sentence for him – "Appalling?".

"Yes," said the Prince, "that is the *mot juste*. If he comes over for this wretched State Visit, then I will tell him so at the State Banquet, you just see if I don't..."

"Come off it, Chazza," said his steadfast consort and adviser. "You know what your mater will say. It's all part of the job. Robert Mugabe, Matey Ceausescu, President Hu Hee, Mrs Thatcher... you just have to sit there and ask them what they do and whether they have come far..."

Charles sulked furiously. "Well, I do think there has to be a line drawn somewhere..."

"What about all those ghastly Sheikhs from Shady Arabia and the Emirs of Bakhanda who we suck up to when they come over here to buy gold-plated tanks from Harrods?"

Charles sighed. Sometimes he felt that Camilla's grasp of foreign affairs was a bit simplistic, but he couldn't face arguing with her at this moment.

"I am afraid I haven't got time to discuss this now – I have to go to a meeting with my publisher, Mr Ladybird, to discuss my new book, *The Royal Book of Five Go Global Warming*. Some of us are still trying to make a difference, you know..."

"You are not still annoyed because old Trumpy once boasted that he could have shagged Diana?" Camilla smiled innocently at her departing husband, but he refused to rise to the bait.

"That is beneath contempt... as is Mr Trump, whom I may have mentioned before is absolutely..."

"I do hope he doesn't try and grab your mother's hand like he did with Mrs May..."

or indeed grab her anywhere else..."

Sir Alan Fitztightly suppressed a snigger, as he shimmied into the room and helped Charles into his overcoat, an elegant Gieves & Wooster full-length Kashmir...

"Oh, do grow up," Charles offered as his parting shot. "Mr Trump really isn't funny. I'm going to see Mater to sort this out. This is a serious business."

"THIS IS a serious business." Charles stood alongside the elegant Louis the Roux State dining table where Her Majesty the Queen was already working out the placements for the Trump dinner, with the aid of the Duke of Edinburgh. "Protocol dictates that Mr Trump sits here between oneself and the Duchess of Cambridge..."

"Is that a good idea, old girl?" queried Prince Philip. "Putting Yankee Doodle

Randy next to the prettiest girl in the room? Er... I mean YOU, of course..."

The Queen allowed the gallant Duke a small but dazzling smile and he continued in the blunt, nautical manner that he had never lost since his wartime service on HMS *Irritable*...

"I mean, we can't have any small, roving hands under the tablecloth, can we?"

"No. Poor Kate might have to stab the President with a fish knife."

"Long as she doesn't do it during the soup course! You never know with the Middleclassingtons. Ha ha ha!"

Charles winced at his father's tasteless

class-based badinage and was delighted that his mother was having none of it.

"Philip! Behave! I shall move Kate and put the Archbishop of Canterbury there instead. Surely he will be safe?"

"Provided he doesn't turn up in a frock. Might confuse old Trumper..."

Charles was getting frustrated with his parents and interrupted testily, "Yes, yes, but where am I? Am I opposite Trump, ready to deliver a broadside over the Brown Windsor soup or a lecture over the lamb chops?"

"No, no," answered the Queen. "You are here with the First Lady Melanoma on your left and the President's daughter, Donaldina, on your right."

"But we're down near the kitchen," Charles protested. "I am miles away and won't be able to bend his ear on, you know, multi-faith issues and Arctic ice melting and..."

The Queen sighed and suddenly looked old – tired at the thought of the responsibility of hosting yet another unpleasant world leader.

"Sometimes it is all such a problem that I feel like handing it over to someone younger. In fact, that is exactly what I'm going to do."

Charles' heart leapt and his thoughts raced. Yes! At last, this was it. The Trump visit would have a silver lining and it would trigger his mother's abdication in favour of a new, fresh monarch who would usher in not a vulgar Golden Age but a Green One...

His mother interrupted his reverie. "I shall get Andrew to do it... he's very good at trade things and Mr Trump loves him..."

At that moment, the portly figure of the Duke of York, the Queen's favourite son, bustled into the room.

"Hi, parents. Hi, bro. Ah... placements. No problemo! We have the Donald opposite me for the business banter and inbetween my two girls Eugenix and Beautitude for the totty quotient... then we put some of his chief people next to you, Ma. So... Piers Morgan on your right and Nige Farage on the left... with Mr Klansman next to you, Pater. It's going to be a blast."

Charles put his head in his hands and sighed again. "The whole thing is going to be..."

(To be continued...)

KIM JONG-UN GOES BALLISTIC

"I'll have my people kill your people"

That BBC Coverage of the Great 2017 Flood Disaster

Clare Monger: And, as we've been warning you ever since yesterday morning, tonight Britain's coast will be hit by one of the worst storm surges since records began.

The Met Office tells us that, thanks to a unique combination of natural factors (plus, of course, global warming), we could be seeing waves 60-feet high engulfing huge areas of Britain, all the way from Yorkshire to East Anglia.

Let's go over now to Sandy Bagg, who is there on the frontline in Little Floodington on the Norfolk coast. Sandy, with only hours to go, how bad are things looking?

Bagg (*standing in the dark on beach with a few small waves gently lapping shore*): What we're hearing, Clare, is that the expected peak surge will hit this unfortunate village shortly after 10 o'clock – that's in two hours and 15 minutes' time.

The villagers have been told by the police and the army to evacuate their homes immediately and head for higher ground...

Clare: And that's pretty hard to find in Norfolk, isn't it, Sandy?

Bagg: Yes, indeed, Sandy, you're absolutely right. That's why several hundred of them are already bedding down in the local school, hoping that at least it will offer some protection against the giant tsunami that we're all expecting to hit us very soon.

Clare: Terrifying news from Sandy there in Norfolk. And now we go over to Patsy Lifejacket in Nearly-under-Water in Yorkshire, at the very epicentre of the approaching storm.

Is it safe for you to talk, Patsy?

Patsy Lifejacket (*also standing in darkness on beach with a few small waves, but with a helicopter preparing to land in the background*): You're absolutely right, Clare. Everyone on the ground here has been listening to this programme and they realise just how bad the situation now is.

In light of the latest update from the Met Office, I myself am being advised by the emergency services to evacuate immediately to safety inland before this colossal storm, bigger than anything we've ever known, puts this entire area under 100 feet of water.

(We see Patsy being winched up into helicopter to be safely returned to nearest BBC studio)

Clare: Thanks, Patsy, and as you can see, we are expecting large parts of Britain to be battered by an unprecedented weather event any moment now – and our teams across the country will be giving you the latest updates on the scale of the disaster throughout the night...

(At this point, viewers and listeners switch over to other channels to see if they are putting out the same terrifying story, only to discover that they are, plus commercials for home insurance)

Two hours later...

Clare: Well, there you have it. It seems that the Great Storm of 2017 was not quite as big as everyone predicted it would be.

Unfortunately, we can't go over live to any of our reporters on the coast because they all managed to escape before the disaster hit. But we've managed to ring up a few local residents, who tell us they stayed put, watching box sets of Game of Thrones instead of the telly and that everything was fine (*cont. Channel 94*)

(*cont. Channel 94*)

Jeremy Corbyn WRITES

HELLO! It's me again. Well, it's been quite a week for me, as you Corbyn fans well know!

Come the first week of February you'll always find me hard at work loading the empty jars in the dishwasher, ready to be packed to the brim with fruity goodness!

But of course, I also had to wash my hands, clip on a fresh tie and attend the Article 50 vote. I don't like to brag, but let's just get a show of hands here; who of you out there thought I wouldn't win a vote in Parliament? Well, I did it! Carried the vote with a thumping 384 vote majority! Who said Her Majesty's opposition wouldn't make an impact under my leadership? Well I think that result speaks for itself.

But of course every day of triumph is marred by a tiny soupçon of tragedy. I was gutted – gutted I tell you – that dear Diane Abbott was unable to go into the voting lobbies with me because of her migraine. There's been a little bit of unkind murmurings that Diane's headache wasn't genuine, but let me address those by furrowing my brow, and exhaling a world-weary sigh.

I can tell you that failing to vote because of a sudden illness is much more common than you realise. I've been up and down this country campaigning in by-elections, and I've been staggered by the amount of loyal Corbyn supporters who've suddenly had terrible headaches when it came to the big day and not turned up! Thousands of them, actually!

So if you do feel a headache coming on, please, please do stay at home and get well, because let me tell you, there are an equal number of loyal Corbyn supporters who stagger to the polls regardless, and have such terrible double vision, they accidently vote for the Lib Dem candidates! Strange but true!

So I'm sure Diane was genuinely ill – all the other Labour MPs believe it, because they got her a lovely funny "get well soon" card. It said "Being around Jeremy gives everyone a headache!" I'm sure their *best* wishes will have her up on her feet in no time!

Cheerio!

A Doctor Writes

Abbottsenteeism

AS a doctor, I am often asked, "Doctor, I've got to go to an important but difficult Brexit vote this evening, can you help?" The simple answer is, "Yes, of course, Diane".

What happens is that the patient experiences "a real headache" and displays symptoms of embarrassment, nervousness and mental confusion. This leads to a crippling migraine, a condition known as *Abbottsenteeism* or *Excusus Convenientus Suspiciens*.

The only cure is for the doctor to write a sick note, and give it to the patient's boss, and/or former lover, who will understand. If you are worried about *Abbottsenteeism*, you should consult a spin doctor immediately.

© *A doctor.*

"It's just a minor thing, but can you not refer to me as 'that Brie and condoms guy'?"

NEW US IMMIGRATION RULES

Full face covering
BAD

Full face covering
GOOD

Oxford Dictionary
THOSE NEW WORDS IN FULL

Post-Truth, *adj*. Relating to circumstances in which objective facts are less influential in shaping public opinion than emotional appeals.

Post-Truth, *adj*. Exactly the opposite. It doesn't mean this at all. Lighten up, losers!

Post-Truth, *adj*. I never said that, what's the matter with you? What part of post-truth don't you understand?!

Post-Truth, *adj*. Post-truth won! Suck it up, Lib-Tards, and get on with it!

Post-Truth, *adj*. Just because the post-truth won doesn't mean the post-truth argument shouldn't continue! Unless you feel it shouldn't.

Post-Trump, *adj*. Relating to era of the First President of the first post-truth era, or not. Depending on your emotional response.

Post-Trump, *adj*. Relating to era of global darkness, and rule by cockroaches, which began in 2017.

Post-Truth, *noun*. You were out when we called, and you will have to pick up your parcel from the depot which may or may not be open.

Post-Truth, *noun*. No, I wasn't – I was in the whole time. Why didn't you ring on the bell instead of just bunging a card through the letterbox?

Oxford Dictionary, *noun*. Publication that is not just trying to get publicity by sending out a press release about putting in words like "post-truth". No, honestly, it's not. It's a genuine lexicographical fact – that sales of dictionaries are not what they were, and we need all the help we can get in this post-truth era. Or possibly the opposite. We have no idea.

Your Country Needs You

But not all the time.

And not evenings and weekends obviously.

And not half-term.

And not if there's a war on.

And certainly not if there's any chance of you risking your life.

Apply now – if you can be bothered.

©The British Army, 2017

Nursery Times
Friday, Once-upon-a-time

OUTCRY AS JUDGE RULES OWL AND PUSSYCAT 'CANNOT DIVORCE'

by Our Legal Correspondent **Mr Piggy Wig**

NURSERYLAND was appalled last night as a senior judge refused to grant a divorce to the "deeply unhappy" pussycat who claimed that her marriage to the owl had "irretrievably broken down".

The judge told the pussycat that her complaints about the owl were trivial and did not constitute evidence of "incompatibility".

He dismissed her accounts of the couple bickering over "money and honey" and rowing about going on a holiday cruise in "a pea green boat".

The owl contested the divorce, saying his position of telling his wife "what a beautiful pussy you are, you are" had not changed and that he wanted them to spend the rest of their lives in the land where the Bong trees grow, "dining on mince and slices of quince".

The pussycat, however, said that she hated mince and quince and that most of their meals were spent in silence.

The judge finally ruled, in what some viewed as a deeply sexist judgement, "The owl is naturally the wiser of the two, whilst the pussy was just being typically catty."

POLICE NEWS

Edward Heath – was he a Europhile?

by Our Historic Abuse Staff **P.D. Phile**

A NEW investigation, involving several hundred officers from 28 police forces, claims to have unearthed shocking new evidence that former prime minister Sir Edward Heath secretly engaged in "Europhile practices" during the 1970s.

Key witnesses have come forward who remember seeing cartoons of the time, including several covers of the satirical Private Eye, which appeared to be suggesting that Sir Edward was guilty of Europhilia.

The police have discovered that, over several years, Sir Edward made regular visits to the Belgian capital Brussels, which has long been notorious as a magnet for men of similar inclinations from all over Europe.

The investigating officers, engaged in what is code-named "Operation Sprout", have even discovered incriminating photographs showing the former prime minister consorting on first name terms with other continental Europhiles such as "Gorgeous George" Pompidou and "Big Willy" Brandt.

Operation Sprout has already cost £2.5 million and is scheduled to last for at least five more years, or as one senior officer put it, standing outside Sir Edward's former home in Salisbury, "until we've got definitive proof of Heath's activities during those years", whichever is sooner.

Sir Edward is unable to help police with their enquiries, or to be raided at dawn with the aid of the BBC helicopter team, because, unfortunately, he is dead.

SUPERMODELS

KERBER

POETRY CORNER

**In Memoriam
Sir Ken Morrison,
founder of Morrisons
budget supermarket
chain**

So. Farewell
Then Sir Ken Morrison,
No nonsense,
Straight talking
Yorkshireman.

You are now
Past your sell-by date
And you have
Checked out.

I hope those jokes
Were cheap enough.

E.J. Thribb
(17½ tins of beans)

**Lines on the death
of Leonard Cohen,
singer-songwriter, who
should have won the
Nobel Prize instead of
Bob Dylan and would
at least have had a
decent reason for not
turning up**

So. Farewell
Then Leonard,
Or should I say
So long
(As in Marianne)?

Keith used to
Listen to you,
Sad and depressed
In his bedsit
In the Seventies.

He's listening
To you now,
Sad and depressed
In his comfortable,
Detached house
In the suburbs.

Hallelujah!
That was your
Most famous song.

I wonder if you are
Hearing it now,
As the angels do
Yet another annoying
Cover version.

E.J. Thribbute
(fellow poet, who
can't sing either)

33

Daily May

HISTORIC DAY OF HYPERBOLE

By Our Entire Staff

BRITONS be proud! Not since Agincourt, Waterloo, Magna Carta, The Battle of Trafalgar, and Lulu's victory in The Eurovision Song Contest with 'Boom-Bang-a-Bang', has this country displayed greater powers of exaggeration!

Today, this great nation rules the world of hype, over-statement and self-delusion, as we march unstoppably towards our glorious destiny, via a first reading of the Brexit bill in the House of Commons before the Committee stage, which if all goes well, subject to amendments, will result in a ratification of the legislative triggering mechanism of Article 50!

Rejoice! As Prime Minister Boris Johnson famously said during the World Cup of 1966, "Never has so much been said about so little by so many".

And how right he is, as we at the Mail salute ourselves at

Once more unto the Brexit, dear friends, once more!

this hysteric moment in our sceptred isle's golden future.

Long may May rule over us!

ON OTHER PAGES

■ Was there a plot by David Cameron to sack Paul Dacre? Possibly.

■ Was there a plot by Paul Dacre to sack David Cameron? Definitely. Yes, worked like a dream.

MORE GREAT NEWS FOR PROJECT CHEER
Pound collapses to new high

The John Hurt I Knew
⤝ By Sir Alien Chest-Burster ⤞

LET ME say this straight out… whatever else people said about Johnny being a hell-raiser or a difficult man, to me, he was always a marvellous host and an utter sweetheart.

Alien was my first acting job, of course, and I was understandably nervous, but darling Johnny took me under his wing, as well as inside his stomach. He would give me little tips, like how to "find the camera", and how to "draw focus" from your fellow actors by screeching and dousing them in blood.

And he was a thoughtful man too! When I was sweltering in his major intestine, waiting for simply hours for Ridley (Scott) to set up his shot, Johnny kindly drank an iced glass of water to cool me down.

He was like that. And the pranks! Such larks. Once I remember he nailed my egg shut so I couldn't leap out and fasten to his face! I got him back though – when he wasn't looking, I ate his make-up assistant! How we laughed.

When I got trapped by the dreaded typecasting, as was inevitable after the *Alien* franchise ended, he was always there for me, getting me work. I appreciated him putting me forward for Voldemort (alas, I was too tall for the cloak) but if *(cont. p94)*

JOHN HURT R·I·P

-Tayler-

Numéro 94
Dans le Love Nest

Mademoiselle Ferrutti: Ooh la la, Nige! Le Press est sur notre case!

Monsieur Farrago: Ne worryez pas, Mademoiselle Ferrutti! Personne suspects anything! Vous êtes une assistante de recherche pour un bona fide pense-tank.

Ferrutti: Mais Le *Mail sur Dimanche* dit que je suis une floozie – une waitress qui vous avez picked up en Brussels et installed dans ce bachelor pad ici!

Farranglais: Non! Non! Non! C'est absurde! Nous sommes juste de bons amis.

Ferrutti: Ça c'est le story, n'est-ce pas?

Farranglais: Oui et nous sommes tous les deux sticking to it.

Ferrutti: Et maintenant qu'est-ce que vous want me à faire, Grand Garçon?

Farrago: Je want vous à faire something très dirty…

Ferrutti: Ooh la la!

Farrago: Oui… take out les bins. C'est dimanche, le rubbish day – deux sacs, s'il vous plaît… l'un pour le recycling et l'autre pour la reste…

Ferrutti: Vraiement, vous savez how to show une jeune fille un bon temps! C'est no wonder toutes les women dans le monde veulent dormir avec vous…

Farrago: Vraiment! Je suis le parfait Ukip gentilhomme…

Ferruti: Bien sûr!

Farrago: Et maintenant je dois faire le Frexit! Je **quitte** par la fenêtre de la bathroom et je ne **remain** pas avec vous to face la musique. Au revoir!

(Farrago exit le love nest et confronts les journalistes et paparazzi)

Premier hack: Monsieur Farrago…!

Farrago: Oops! Pas de comment.

Deuxième hack: Trop late, Nige. Votre wife a spilt tous les haricots… votre mariage est fini. Et vous êtes aussi.

Farrago: Dans vos rêves.

(Continue à jamais…)

© Kilomètres Kington

END OF AN ERA, AS LLOYDS BANS BOOZY LUNCHES

by Lunchtime O'Booze

THE City of London will never be the same again, as the new Puritanism sweeps across the Square Mile and a culture of sobriety is recklessly inflicted on the insurance workers of Lloyds.

No more will we see boozed-up brokers staggering back to their offices after a liquid lunch. Things will never be the same again. In fact, it's hard to think now of any professions that remain whmere one can drink heavily whilst shtill performin an exshtreeemley

competentnt jobb analysching shoshial change.

And another thing, it'sh hard to think… well, that'sshh it really, it'shh hard to think… what a crying sshhhhame, that a chap can't be trushted to enjoy a worrrking lunch with a few drunks, or do I mean drinksh?

Anyway, where wasss I? Oh yes, in the old "Frog and Loss Adjustor" in Shhindicate Shtreet. Chhheerrs! Will thish do? Have you had enough? I know I havvv… *(continues, drink 94)*

GLENDA SLAGG

Yes, it's the gal with F*** News

■ JEREMY Paxman!!!??!?!!! What a disgrace!!?! You've got some questions to answer, Mr Interrogator-in-chief, namely why have you dumped your poor wife 'n' kiddies for a blonde bimbo who's half your age??!! Shame on you, Paxo, you shouldn't be going around stuffing birds in your position (Geddit??!). You should be setting a good example to all your viewers and holding the powers-that-be to account!!?!?!? Come off it, as you would say to some hapless minister on Nooznight, answer the question!!!?!!!! Are you a love-rat? Are you a love-rat? Are you a love-rat? Are you a love-rat? (Subs: repeat this 14 times.)

■ JEREMY Paxman!?!?!!!!??! Leave him alone, for gawd's sake!!?! Why shouldn't TV's Mr Sneery find love in his twilight years??!? OK, so she's young enough to be one of his children – but so what??!? What's wrong with a bit of May-December romance to cheer us up in dreary February??!! And as for the li'l lady left in the lurch with the abandoned kiddies – well, he never popped the big question to you, did he darlin' !??!! So why are you a-whingin' and a-whinin' and a-moanin' and a-groanin' about it???!?!!

■ YOUR starter for ten??! Which former national treasure is now a national laughing stock??!???!! Bzzz!!!! So, more questions on ageing lotharios... Which former Snoozenight presenter has been up to something fishy??!!??!? And I don't mean making a boring programme about angling!!?! Bzzz!!!!! Paxman, and no conferring with your fruity researcher!?!!?? Yes, it's you again, Jezza!!! And you've scored...again!?!!!! (Geddit??!?)

■ SHED a tear for poor old Paxo!!!!????! Just like he did when he was a-weepin' and a-wailin' on TV's "Who Do You Think You Are?"!!??!!? OK, so it looks like he's been a rotter, but he's only repeating the pattern of his cheatin' dad who left his mum to bring up the kiddies on her lonesome ownsome!?!???!! Jezza can't help it if it's in the genes!!!!??? Or it keeps getting out!!?!! (Geddit??!?)

■ PAXMAN!!?! Who do you think you are??!!!!? I'll tell you, you're a cheatin' love-rat who (Are you sure this is that big a story, Ms Slagg, and worth quite so many column inches??!!??!?)

■ HATS and trousers off to Paxo!!?! (You're fired, Ed.)

Byeee!!

The Eye's Controversial New Columnist

The Columnist who isn't afraid to say what everyone else is thinking, such as "I want a wee"

This week, I am very happy that I have been made editor of the Oldie. I do concede that I am slightly younger than the usual bearer of that illustrious job, but I can assure my readers that I am very much old at heart. I'm bald, I find walking difficult, and I often forget what I had for breakfast. But what does it matter if the Oldie is written by slightly younger old people like myself? Old old folks do go on about things from the past, besides which they always hang around the office to keep themselves warm because the libraries have all closed. After all, when all is said and done, what matters is good free-thinking articles and some good-natured irreverent humour and if I don't get those I will scream my head off and throw my *(cont. p94)*

"Unfortunately, the drugs he's on just now have only ever been tested on mice"

DIARY

PIERS MORGAN

Nothing should surprise one about David Beckham.

Sorry, but I saw through the guy years ago.

I'll never forget it. I went up to his table in Ralph Lauren's Polo Bar restaurant. I introduced myself, and made a well-timed quip about how he couldn't get a ball through a pair of goalposts even if he was wearing extra-strong specs.

How did he react? Well may you ask.

The guy said nothing – and just looked as though he wished I'd disappear.

Can't take a joke. Yet now he's begging for the proverbial knighthood.

"Arise, Sir Totally Humourless"?

No, I don't think so.

Or at least not after I've had a word with my good mate HM the Queen.

Amid all the tributes to the late, great, tragic Tara Palmer-Tomkinson, my mind goes back to something hilarious I said to her over a brilliantly funny dinner with old friends a few years ago at top West End eaterie The Ivy.

The air of sexual tension between the two of us was palpable.

I always know when this is happening with women, because they keep avoiding my eye.

But before long she just had to make contact.

"Could you pass the water, please?" called the fabulous Tara, who by now had moved so close to me that she was just two chairs away.

"I can see you've got the hots for me, love – and you'll be needing all that water just to cool down!!!" I quipped.

Classic! Once I had stifled my giggles, I generously entertained the assembled company of A-listers to tales of my highly amusing spats with the so-called "stars" of stage and screen.

"Did I ever tell you about the time I tweeted that Madonna was 'a scraggy-faced wizened old has-been'?" I said, fighting back the laughter. "Believe me, that took the old bag down the proverbial peg or two!"

In fact, it resulted in a Twitter-storm from Madonna's few remaining bat-winged "fans".

And, since we're on the subject, I added another 5,000 Twitter followers in the process, FYI.

On a more serious note, I'm not silenced that easily. I shall continue to fearlessly stand up against these revolting old gorgons who set the noble cause of feminism back a million years.

Piers Morgan @piersmorgan:
FACT: J.K. Rowling is one of the worst-selling authors of all time. And worst-SMELLING too. Ever heard of deodorant, love?!?!?

Piers Morgan Retweeted @BigBird: Brilliant take-down of that foul-smelling Rowling halfwit, Piers!

Piers Morgan Retweeted @DaftBloke: Respect to @piersmorgan. Continues to say what we've all thinked.

Why do bleeding-heart liberals keep whining on and on about my old mate President Trump?

Have they got nothing better to do with their sad little lives than attempt to wreck the presenting careers of those of us who don't regard him as somewhere to the right of Adolf Hitler?

I've known the guy for years now.

And I'm proud to count him as a close friend.

So I have been deeply upset by the insults hurled at him by all those pathetic has-beens and no-hopers.

If you ask me, they're just jealous of the sheer size of his massive achievement.

And – having got to know him in the TV locker room, I can tell you that's not the only massive thing about him!!!

When we were jointly starring in the hugely popular Celebrity Apprentice, we'd regularly enjoy a brilliant post-show shower together in an exclusive VIP cubicle.

We had a terrific laugh. First, I'd soap The Donald all over.

And then he'd return the favour.

Great times, great scrubs, great bloke. I wish my old mate President Trump every success in the job of a lifetime – even if he does have a few more Twitter followers than yours truly!

Why all the hoo-ha about former President Barack Obama? Career-wise, he's languishing in Siberia. Can't be long now before the long-suffering Michelle O. leaves him for someone a lot more famous and a lot more fun – like my best mate hilarious roly-poly Brit superstar James Corden, with whom she's been seen taking saucy "Karaoke" car rides. Remember – you read it here first!

As told to
CRAIG BROWN

The 75th Anniversary Desert Island Discs You Weren't Allowed To Hear

Guest David Beckham chose the following records

1 Knight Fever – *The Cee Bee Gees*

2 Summer Knights – *from Greasy*

3 O What a Knight – *The Fourteen Seasons*

4 All Knight Long – *Lionel Very Richie*

5 Hard Day's Knight – *The Bootles*

6 Let's Spend the Knight Together – *The Rolling News*

7 Knights in White Trainers – *The Moody Reds*

8 I Vow to Thee My Cunt – *sung by Dame Katherine Jenkins*

As his luxury, David chose to have all his money with him off-shore. His book was the one thrown at him by HMRC

It's a slippery slope I'm afraid

Moose

GLENDA SLAGG

Fleet Street's Trident Miss-ile!!!! Geddit???! She goes off in all directions!!!

■ SAINT BECKS??!? Don't make me laugh!!! Goldenballs has shown himself to be greedy, graspin' 'n' grubby with only one GOAL!!!?? (Geddit??!?) A knighthood!!! Arise, Sir Becks??!? No, let's give him the boot??!? Posh 'n' Becks??!?! Dosh and Becks, more like!!?!?

■ LEAVE him alone, Mister Newsman!!?!!? It's Saint David of Beckham I'm talkin' about, stoopid!!! Ok, so he's called hoity-toity blazered bores on the Honours Committee a bunch of c****!!! (And that isn't CLOTS, geddit??!?) He's right on target, as usual!!! After all Mr Bendit has done to make Britain great, can't we forgive him a couple of dodgy emails and a few dodged taxes??!?? Arise, Sir Becks and Lady Posh??!?? (And by that, I mean a PAY rise!!!?)

■ WELL, who'd have thought it??!? 50-year-old Kylie and the bearded toy boy half her age have split up!!! Pass the smelling salts, mister – NOT!!??!! The pint-size Princess of Pop has a dismal RECORD (geddit??!?) in the love department and I reckon she'll be SINGLE (geddit??!??) for ever!!!???!

■ POOR old Kylie!!!!?! Doesn't the Diminutive Diva from Down Under deserve a li'l bit of good fortune romance-wise??!? And isn't it a cryin' shame that her latest beau turned out to be a Pommy love rat!!! He should be so lucky?!?! (Geddit??!!??) Let's hope that beardy is miserable for ever and can't get her out of his head!?! (Geddit???!?)

■ BEYONCE! Put it away, love!!! I mean your bump, darling!!! Just 'cos you're up the duff double-time doesn't mean we all want to see you a-bulgin' and a-burstin' in the all-together!!?! Get your kit back on, for Gawd's sake??!?

■ AAAH, booty-ful Beyoncé is bloomin' marvellous!!?!!? With two babes on the way, this babe still looks like a billion dollars (which is what she'll make from the preggers pix??!?). Hats, coats, dresses, bras and thongs off to the most naked self-publicity in about-to-pop history!!!! (Geddit???!)

Byeee!!

"I hope you're not reading fake news?"

THE BREXIT BOOM: MAY'S PLAN TO CLOSE DOWN BRITAIN'S SHOPS

by Our Political Staff
Peter O'Boom and **Christopher Hopeful**

YES, it's all go for Britain's retail industry.

That is the message going out to a vast swathe of Britain's economy, as the Government unveils its brilliant plan to raise business rates by thousands of percent.

A typical small greengrocer's in Market Barkworth, Patel's Fruit, Veg & Fags, learned yesterday that its current rate demand of £8,500 a year will next year soar to £2,400,000.

Said the owner, Mr Patel, "We cannot possibly afford this – we will have to shut the shop after 30 years and tell our customers to go to Tesco."

And the story is the same up and down the country, as corner shops, hardware stores, bookshops, electrical suppliers and even charity shops are all targeted by business rate rises so huge that they will be forced to close.

"It's a key part of our strategy," said business minister Sajid Javid. "This way we will empty the high streets of useless and obsolete small shops, and everyone will

then have to do their shopping online with our friends at Amazon.

"This shows that post-Brexit, the UK economy will be leading the world with the new age of total digitalisation.

"And financially," continued Mr Rabid Vapid, "this makes perfect sense. Instead of having to go through the tedious job of collecting all these business rates, we only have to deal with Amazon who don't pay any tax at all. So what's not to like?"

So once again, Mrs May and her ministers are showing the world that Britain means business and, as the saying goes, "We are a nation of former shopkeepers."
(Is this right? Ed.)

PRESS FREEDOM

Go on, ask me anything I like

'I WAS THERE AT THE NUTTALL TRAGEDY' CLAIM HUNDREDS OF JOURNALISTS

by Our Football Staff **Jimmy Hillsborough**

A HUGE crowd of journalists in Stoke yesterday described how they had been present at one of the worst disasters in political history, when Ukip leader Paul Nutter (*surely "Nutcase?"*) had been horribly caught out by claiming that he had lost "close, personal friends" in the 1989 Hillsborough disaster.

As one journalist said last night, "I admit that Mr Nuttall was not a particularly close, personal friend of mine, but I was definitely there when his brief political life was crushed by the weight of evidence which showed that he was yet again making things up in a way which made him look a complete idiot."

The former Ukip leader, Mr Nigel Farage, was, for the first time in history, unavailable for comment last night because he was "too busy cooking lasagne" for his agreeable French housemate, Ms Phwoar Ferruti.

The backer of UKIP Mr Arron Banks, refused to condem Mr Nutter and said, "It was an accident, no one was to blame, and I'm bored of hearing about it. Why can't everyone stop going on about the so-called Nuttall disaster. It's time to move on and for everyone to get over it and vote UKIP."

Nursery Times

.... Friday, Once-upon-a-time ....

RATES HIKE HITS SMALL BUSINESSMEN

by Our Financial Staff **Big Bad Wolf of Wall Street**

LOCAL communities all over Nurseryland have reacted angrily to plans to increase business rates by over a squillion percent, sending firms to the wall and ruining the lives of small businessmen.

Seven particularly small businessmen today spoke of the damage it would do to their mining operation, Dwarfco.

"I'm grumpy," said one, whose name was Bashful. "The rate for small businesses has been established since once-upon-a-time, but these changes mean no one will live happily ever after again."

Equally small businessman, Grumpy, said, "I'm not happy. These new charges will severely damage the Hi-Ho Street." Bigger businesses, like Golden Egg plc, run by the greedy Giant, will be unaffected, as his premises are out of town and up a beanstalk.

One local resident, Mr Simple Simon, told of how he met a pie man, going to the fair, but was unable to taste his wares, because high overheads had forced the pie man out of the pie-making business.

Meanwhile, Dwarfco Head of Human Resources, Ms Snow White, tried to keep up the seven small businessmen's spirits by encouraging them to whistle while they worked, but instead they just marched off to the benefits office, singing, "Hi-rates, hi-rates, it's out of work we go!"

On other pages

● Gingerbread man runs, runs as fast as he can, but denies coach made him out of performance-enhancing ingredients **2**

● Maid in garden, hanging out clothes and suffers blackbird injury to nose, says "I'd never have been out there if my tumble-drier hadn't exploded" **27**

● Twee-del-dum has half-brother Twee-del-dee assassinated with rattle and toxic nerve agent **94**

Notes&queries

My ten-year-old was reading the Sun the other day and came across a piece about Prince William. As an ardent monarchist he is now curious to know what exactly are 'Slut drops'?
The Reverend Lucy Twerking

● As any boy who was at prep school in the Seventies will remember, slut drops were on sale in the tuck shop for a shilling a quarter. I can't tell you the Proustian rush I experienced when I heard the word Slut Drop for the first time in simply decades, and there I was back in the PE cupboard at St Yew Tree sharing a bag of these delicious sherbet-coated lemon treats with Perkins Major, Morris Minor and Mr Chips the Geography Teacher.
Sir Robert Baden-Powell-Dancer (Brigadier, retired).

● I fear the Brigadier's fondant memories are betraying him. Perhaps he should have been paying more attention in his history lessons. A Slut Drop, or to be more accurate, a Slute Droppe, from Chaucer's *Jouster's Tale*, refers to the simple act when a fair maiden, as a display of courtly love, drops her handkerchief, or "slute" to signal her favour for a particular knight. He might enjoy re-reading the passage about famous knight Sir Philip of Green and his fair lady Tina of Monaco, who did "slute droppe fayre exceeding welle and most untaxingly".
Professor Gang Nam-Style, University of Korea.

● Enough, fuddy duddies! Get with the modern age, Grandads and Mas, the Slut Drops, as anyone under the age of 300 knows, are the girl band who this year won no fewer than three Brit Awards for Best Band, Best Girl Band, and Best Band of Girls. Formed entirely of singers who came second in the last five series of the X-Factor, the Slut Drops were put together by Simon Cowell, and their first single 'Slut Drop to the Max!' reached number 37 in the Christmas chart. That's including downloads – for all you dead-tree media dinosaurs! *@crotch_grabber*

● Whoever Mr or Ms @crotch-grabber may be, their knowledge of geography is woeful. Slutt Drops is one of the finest geological features in the entire Arctic region. A thousand-foot cascade of frozen ice descends from the volcanic summit of Mount Slutt down to the Slappa Valley, a mere 50 miles outside Reykjavik. Seasoned travellers say that Niagara Falls has nothing on the Slutt Drops. Although, more recently, they have sadly become a popular destination for gap-year bungee jumpers, no doubt including the likes of @crotch-grabber.
Sir Peregrine Waltz.

Answers please:
Is George Smiley?
How do we make Geert Wilder?
Has anyone climbed Craig Mackinlay?

FOX, DAVIS AND JOHNSON

How they see themselves

How everyone else sees them

HOW TALKS WILL GO FOR THE NEXT TWO YEARS

● Someone raises the topic of Brexit over pudding at a dinner party.

● Everyone will agree how ghastly it is, that Theresa May doesn't even really believe in it, how impossible it'll be for us to get a good deal, and how we're depriving our children of the right to live and work in Europe.

● Geoff will say he voted Leave.

● The whole table will go quiet.

● Geoff will also mumble something about the Greek debt time-bomb, the Italian banking crisis, Brussels' pampered fat cats and taking back control.

● His wife will not speak to him in the car all the way home.

● Er...

● That's it.

I didn't tap Trump's phone, I was too busy tapping Mrs Merkel's

Ukip 'doesn't need Carswell' by Our Political Staff Noah Seats

Ukip leader Paul Nuttall has denied the party is in turmoil after the loss of its only MP, Douglas Carswell.

"Douglas was never really one of us. Unlike Nigel and myself, he didn't manage to never get elected to parliament, which is a key prerequisite for all Ukippers.

"Besides, we have a vast pool of talent to draw from, even without Carswell: there's the bloke with the squiffy eye who's been banned from coming within 50 feet of his ex-wife; the old woman with the gammy leg who reckons all Easter Eggs are Halal these days, and the bloke who calls all foreigners 'Gollywogs from Tally BungBung Land', and if you have a problem with that he'll set his Rottweiler on you.

"Ukip, under my leadership, will be as successful as Manchester United were when I managed them to three Premier League titles between 2007 and 2010."

NEVER TOO OLD

A love story by Dame Sylvie Krin, author of
Heir of Sorrows and *Duchess of Hearts*

THE STORY SO FAR: Rupert Murdoch, the octogenarian media mogul has had his Sky takeover bid referred to the British regulator Ofcom by Culture Secretary Karen Bradley...

THE sweat poured down Rupert's wrinkled brow, as he clocked up another mile on the Bradley Wiggins Team Sky-cycle exercise machine in his penthouse gym on the 94th floor of the Snewscorp Tower in Manhattan.

"What the bloody hell do they mean, I'm not a fit and proper person?" Rupert gasped, as his beautiful supermodel bride, Leggy, offered him a refreshing glass of isotonic Vegemite smoothie.

"Now, don't you go botherin' yerself, y'all Rupee, you hear me now?" she cooed in her Southern Belle-from-Beauty-and-the-Beast drawl. "Why, you're the fittest near-nonagenarian news tycoon in the whole wide world."

The lycra-clad billionaire clambered creakily onto the next piece of equipment, the Virtual Reality Zimmerlator Walking Machine, which enabled him to walk at a sensible pace around any location in the galaxy.

"I'm as fit as a fiddle... and I don't mean my tax position!" joked Rupert, as he

strolled around a CGI Pluto, looking for real estate to invest in.

"I'm fitter than a dingo chasing a koala bear up a gumtree in Crocodile Dundee Creek that I once saw on Anzac Day in 1925 when..."

Leggy cut short her billionaire's youthful reminiscences. "Of course you are, Rupee..."

But Rupert was on a roll, "...and mentally, I'm 150 percent all there. The only things I forget are the things I **remember** to forget! Like when old Limey Leveson tried to outfox the Digger, heh heh heh!"

Leggy looked idly at the advertisement in the newspaper which urged UK citizens to sign a petition to stop Rupert from owning "everything in the world, for ever".

"But, honeybunny, it says here in this li'l ol' pressure group campaign literature that you have an improper influence over Government..."

"What a load of billabollocks!" retorted the world's most powerful man, as he stepped onto his yoga mat and adopted the Potus position.

"That's not true. And I'll get little Govey to write a column in the London Times denying it. Then Fox News will pick it up, Sky News will lead on it and even the Libflakes at Auntie Beeb will have to report it in the interests of balance."

Rupert wheezed with mirth at the thought of the newscycle which he manipulated like the Machiavellian mastermind that he was.

"And why then, Ofcom, Karen Bradley and ol' Missy May herself will have to roll over and give in!! You sure are a piece of work, Rupee!"

"The only thing that puzzles me," continued Rupert, as he contorted his ancient frame into the Useless Sun Salutation position on the mat, "is how did they get 300,000 signatures on the petition against me?"

At that moment, Rupert's Nokinon 89 Smartphoncy trilled with its distinct *Waltzing Matilda* ring tone and he heard a familiar voice cackling down the line.

"Check signatures, glandad! 300,000 say 'Wendi Deng'! You ruse, Lupert! Levenge is sweet. But sour for you!"

Outside the dark clouds gathered ominously, as ice storm "Anna Wintour" swept into New York, turning it into a frozen wasteland...

(To be continued...)

COMPLEX BREXIT NEGOTIATIONS BEGIN

Tally ho! Gibraltar, here we come!

"One of the upsides of plastic ocean pollution is not having to provide your own beach toys"

GOTHS

Goth **Visigoth** **Hi-visigoth**

Ariss

The Armed Forces AN APOLOGY

IN recent weeks we may have given the regrettable impression that Britain's armed forces were in some way compromised by budget constraints, equipment failures, recruitment issues and the lack of an aircraft carrier until 2020. Headlines such as "PATHETIC WEEDY BRITAIN SACKS ALL MARINES", "OUR WARSHIPS COULDN'T BLAST THEIR WAY OUT OF A PAPER BAG" and "WE'RE SITTING DUCKS FOR LITERALLY ANYONE WHO WANTS TO INVADE" may have added to this impression.

We now realise, in light of Michael Howard suggesting Britain might go to war with Spain over Gibraltar, that nothing could be further from the truth. Britain's armed forces are well-equipped, braver than anyone else and ready to defend against any attack on British interests. We have tried to make the proper situation known in our more recent coverage, including our pieces headlined "MAJESTIC BRITISH LION READY TO TRAMPLE PATHETIC DAGOES", "BRING ON THE SECOND SPANISH ARMADA IMMEDIATELY" and "NUKE SPAIN NOW, MA'AM, AND THROW IN BRUSSELS, JUST IN CASE".

We hope this clears the matter up.

OSBORNE COMEBACK AS NEWSPAPER EDITOR

He's not a total banker, just part-time

Hold the Front Bench!

It's the lead tory!

There's no conflict of interest – he's not interested in journalism

Read all about twit!

DEVIL TO EDIT BIBLE

by Our Media Staff **St Matthew Parris** and **St Mark Lawson**

IN A controversial move, Beelzebub has been given the job of editing the top heavenly free-sheet which covers the goings-on in the celestial city.

Critics have suggested that Mr Beelzebub is unsuitable for this prestigious job, having been firmly criticised in the Bible for his controversial role in the Fall of Man.

But supporters of the Devil (he has many names, including Satan, Lucifer and Gideon) point out that he has an unrivalled contact list, including some of the most evil people in history.

However, there are still concerns that editing the Bible, which is "a job for all time, not part time," may prove incompatible with representing his constituents in Hades, which many feel should be his prime occupation.

And then there is the matter of Mr Beelzebub's connections to the banking industry.

Said one archangel and media observer, St Peter O'Borne, "It is one thing having the Bible edited by the incarnation of evil, but when the editor is connected to a Hedge Fund in the City, then we really have to admit that things have gone to hell in a handcart."

Falling standard

Mr Beelzebub has no experience of editing, since his former job largely involved torturing sinners and he is perhaps best known for his youthful membership of the Papal Bullingdon Club where he *(cont. p666)*

Jeremy Corbyn WRITES

HELLO! It's me again. There's no point denying it any longer. These are momentous times for our nation. You know it. I know it. There is something that we as a country need to address. We all know what I'm talking about here.

Buses without Wi-Fi.

I first learned of this appalling state of affairs only last month, when I wanted to tweet a picture of myself lying down in the aisle of a bus showing that I had failed to secure a seat. But guess what? No Wi-Fi! And to make matters worse, there was no one on the bus able to help me get to my feet! What a waste of my extremely valuable time!

So, having had a conflab with my marketing department comrades, we declared 29 March a national "Let's Get Wi-Fi On Some More British Buses Right Now Please, But Not If It's Too Much Of A Faff Because We Don't Want to Annoy The Transport Unions Too Much" Day.

Which, I think, is a very snappy slogan! I'm glad I was persuaded to have it edited down.

Of course, our momentous (geddit!) PR campaign came to nothing, scuppered by the Hated Mainstream Media, which cynically concentrated on some ridiculous non-story about Prime Minister's 50 articles, or something like that! I hardly think a puff piece about the PM's extensive wardrobe takes precedent over the blight of our internet-free buses!

Conspiracy? Of course! Much like the traitor Blairite press's ignoring the other big news of the week, namely my triumph in finally getting rid of Teresa. Yes, she's gone and it's one in the eye for all those doubting Thomases (Watson) who said I didn't have the oomph to see her off.

The fact that it's Teresa Pearce, my minister for Local Government, rather than Theresa May the PM, in no way diminishes my achievement. Nor does the fact that nobody, including me, had heard of Ms Pearce before yesterday. Still, whoever she is, I wish her great success in her new job, whatever that is. And welcome aboard her replacement, whose name escapes me. Cheerio!

THE TIMES OF LONDON
MAY 21ST 1928

Fascist Only Comes Second In European Elections – World Can Relax Again

by Our Continental Correspondent **Will Ders**

GREAT news for all those who until recently were worried about the rising tide of intolerance sweeping across Europe! This election, the weirdo with the bad hair, Adolf Hitler, has been soundly defeated at the polls. His Nazi party didn't perform anywhere near as well as expected. So, what does this mean for Europe?

Well, the good news is that this shows that Europe is clearly a long way from the risk of falling into chaos and conflict again, as it did so tragically and so recently. This is also a very strong indicator that Europe simply isn't ready for lunatics with extreme political views, and that the sensible majority opinions of tolerance and decency will always win at the ballot box, against the ugly policies of fear and division.

In short, there is no reason to feel at all worried, and we can now go about our business content in the knowledge that unpleasant, divisive and racist views have no place in modern pluralistic European society.

What a close shave that was, and how nice to bask in the sunshine of liberality and maybe have a short nap, safe in the knowledge that the long-term underlying structural problems that have split the continent will probably melt away!

AMUSING VIDEO GOES VIRAL

AN amusing video recently did the rounds on the internet, and everyone who saw it agreed that it was very funny and silly.

ON OTHER PAGES

● Why you're a racist if you assumed the woman in the video was the nanny

● Why you're a bleeding-heart pathetic luvvie if you thought the woman in the video was the wife, even though she was

● Why I, as a journalist, also have an amusing story about my children

● Why the traditional patriarchal narrative of a working father and domestic mother must be called out

● Why half-Korean children are so well-behaved compared with British brats

● Why British parents aren't even allowed to shove their kids any more, due to PC madness

● Why can't we just laugh at a funny video without commissioning a thousand opinion pieces about it?

● Why North Korea's missile program threatens us all (cut for reasons of space)

Court Circular

Veriboozier, Monday

His Royal Highness Prince William, the Duke of Cambridge, will attend a Bachelor Companions skiing holiday weekend at the Chalet Huré Henri. The Duke will be accompanied by Mr Charles "Charlie" Ricketson-Smythe, Mr Guy "Bolly" Pellinger and Mr St John "Pongo" Van der Cutzam-Flotzam-Jetzam-del-Strawberry-Zebedee.

The Duke's party will proceed down the Piste Encore via the Piste Comme-Un-Newt to the Floozy Bar where the Ducal ensemble will be introduced to the Australian model and events organiser Ms Sheila Fruity, 24, and her associate, Ms Totty Challay-Gurrle.

The party will be served traditional alpine refreshment viz 48 Jagerbomb Bastardo Vodka 'n' Schnapps shots with lager chasers, after which Prince William will propose the formal toast of "Bums up! Downton in one!" before paying an official visit to the next après-ski hostelry, the "Pussy Bar". Here, there will be time for unscheduled "Bantz", possibly involving the de-bagging of Mr Pellinger to the accompaniment of the in-house band *Oompah*, who will be playing a medley of Abba hits.

The Party will then form a procession up the mountain for luncheon at the renowned Swiss restaurant La Toblerone. The procession will be constituted as follows:

First Chairlift
The Duke of Cambridge;
Ms Sheila Fruity;
Ms Totty Challay-Gurrle;
DCI Colin Undercover,
Royal Protection Squad

Second Chairlift
Signor Slizi Papparazzo, Ogle Magazine; Monsieur Bleurie Photo, Paris Snatch; Mr Ken Filth, The Sun; Mr Nicholas Witchell, BBC

First T-Bar
Mr Guy Pellinger

Second T-Bar
Mr Guy Pellinger
(having fallen off the first)

Third T-Bar
Mr Guy Pellinger (again)

First Bloodwagon
Mr N. Newman (knee injury)

London, Tuesday

HRH Prince William will appear on the front page of The Sun newspaper where he will be formally granted the title of "Workshy Willy" and will be presented with 1,000 words attacking him for failing to attend the Commonwealth Day Service in Westminster Abbey *(see above)*.

HRH the Duchess of Cambridge, on seeing the newspaper, will suggest the Duke pays a formal visit to the spare room and *(cont. p94)*

Let's Parlez Franglais!

Numéro 94 Le LBC Interview

Nigel Farright: Bonjour listeners, this is Le Nigel Farright Show avec moi, Nigel Farright, et mon guest speciale ce matin, la très sexy politicienne froggy, Mademoiselle Marine La Plume.

Le Pen: C'est Le Pen, vous idiot.

Farright: Et maintenant, Madame La Tante, j'ai un très important question politicale pour vous...

Le Pen: Shootez.

Farright: Voulez-vous coucher avec moi?

Le Pen: Non.

Farright: Ce soir?

Le Pen: J'ai dit que non!

Farright: Mais nous avons so much en commune. Vous êtes très wing-droite. Je suis extrêmement wing-droite. Vous êtes bonkers et moi, je suis bonkers. Ensemble, nous pouvons become littéralement 'les bonkers'.

Le Pen: Avez-vous been drinking?

Farright: Naturellement! C'est dix heures au matin.

Le Pen: Vous êtes un dodgy fag-fumant xenophobiste populiste artiste de piss.

Farright: Est-ce que c'est un 'yes', then?

(Continuez à 94 KHz...)

© Kilomètres Kington

How dare you, Prince Boring?

ONCE again, our work-obsessed Royal Prince is out do-gooding, when he could be getting bladdered with his mates in a ski-resort.

While his more responsible brother is providing valuable tabloid fodder and keeping the paparazzi in work in Verbier, dull Prince Harry is at the Wood Pasture Restoration Project in Epping Forest.

For heaven's sake, Harry – you're a disgrace to the name of the Royal family. The sooner you drink ten Mojitos and fall out of a nightclub naked but for an iron cross over your privates the better.

The Royal family has a job to do and that's to fill our pages with drivel. If you don't dirty up your act, pull up your socks and pull down your trousers, we're going to have to have Brexit on the front page, and start providing our readers with genuine news. Take a leaf out of work-shy Wills' book and get back on the Piste!

GARDENERS' QUESTION TIME

Q: How do I grow a 'Garden Bridge'?

Bob Flowerdew: What a great question! We're seeing a real trend for these. What you need first is a river which already has lots of bridges over it. The next thing you need is hundreds of millions of pounds. Now, this should be in cash, and it should ideally be taxpayers' money, but really any large bundles of unmarked £50 notes should do.

The next step is to pile the £50 notes up on the area you've chosen for your bridge. Then – make sure you're not doing this on a windy day, so it goes right – set fire to the money. This will provide the soil with the nutrients it needs. When you've done that, burn some more money on top of it, and then some more money. You need to make sure the money is thoroughly burned, so there's no chance of it ever being spent on anything more useful, like a school or social care for the elderly.

Once this is done, you'll have the perfect bridge for your garden! But be careful – you won't be able to cross it at night, or without your paperwork!

SECOND REFERENDUM?

You'd be crazy to want to leave the Union!

NICOLA STURGEON'S HISTORY GUIDE TO THINGS WE CAN BLAME THE ENGLISH FOR

Number 75: The Introduction of the Midge

Mr Greedy to the rescue

"I'M fed up with people calling me greedy," said Mr Greedy, tucking into his fifth plate of jellied eels and caviar on his luxury yacht *Lying-Fart*. "What can I do to rescue my reputation?"

"You could do the decent thing," said Mrs Greedy.

"What? Fall off the boat like Mr Maxwell?"

"No," Mrs Greedy replied, shocked and tucking into her sixth plate, "why don't you give back some of the money we 'borrowed' from Mr Old and Mrs Poor and Miss Destitute?"

"Good idea. Then maybe they'll let me keep my title," said Mr Greedy.

"What title is that?" asked his wife.

"The world's greediest man, of course! You daft, Monaco-based muppet."

So, with his arm twisted behind his back, Mr Greedy looked down the back of his sofa, and came up with £363 million – rather than the £500 million that would have filled the pensions black hole.

All the Mr and Mrs Men cheered, saying, "Hurrah for Mr Greedy, he hasn't been quite as greedy as he was going to be. Although, to be honest, he's still f***ing greedy!"

Sorry, children – it's time for bed! The language seems to have gone a bit blue, as opposed to Green.

"I wonder what the people who aren't screaming on Twitter think..."

Daily Mail, Friday, April 21, 2017

ENERGY FIRMS
An Apology

In recent years, we may have given the impression that we somehow disapproved of caps being placed on the profit margins of energy firms, as proposed by Labour's Ed Miliband.

Headlines like 'Loony Ed Will See The Lights Turned Out As We Go Back To 1970s Hell', 'Mad Miliband Wants To Choke The Life Out Of British Industry With His Weird Commie Fingers' and 'If Labour Win, All Pensioners Will Have To Burn Their Own Homes To Pay For Fuel' may have added to this impression.

We now realise, of course, in the light of Theresa May's plan to, er, introduce price caps on the profit margins of energy firms, that actually such a move would be a pragmatic, sensible step, which would help many of those in poverty to make their money go a little further.

We have tried to show this with this week's coverage, including 'Thank God Someone Is Finally Taking On Greedy Fuel Bosses' and 'Thatcher Rises From Grave To High-Five PM Over Brilliant Energy Move' and 'If Labour Win, Prices Will Rocket And Pensioners Will Be Burned As Firewood'.

We would like to apologise for any confusion, particularly as in normal circumstances we would be opposed to government intervention in free markets, but *(cont. p94)*

Banker who does something wrong resigns

THERE was a horrified reaction in the City today as Charlotte Hogg resigned as Deputy Governor for failing to reveal her brother worked for Barclays.

"Clearly she's done something wrong... so surely that means she should be promoted?" said one banker, snorting cocaine off a prostitute's tits.

"She has blackened the name of banking, clearly... so where's her million-pound bonus?" said another fund manager, buying a £52,000 round of drinks in a City bar.

"This sends out a terrible message to the City that people could actually be held accountable for what they do," said another trader, rigging a series of trades to make himself a cool half-million in an afternoon.

Bank of England Governor Mark Carney came to Charlotte Hogg's defence, saying he hoped that her honesty in holding her hand up and accepting responsibility for the wrongdoing wouldn't stop her having a career in the corporate banking world.

He added, "Charlotte's paid almost as heavy a price as the taxpayers did for cleaning out the family moat, which her father Douglas Hogg claimed on expenses."

THE INCREDIBLE TRUTH ABOUT THAT DISASTROUS OSCARS ENVELOPE

Someone opened the wrong one.

On other pages

PricewaterhouseCoopers apologises

For making Oscars ceremony less boring than normal.

"I don't understand the opprobrium! After all, furnishing our clients with misleading results for public consumption is what we excel at!"

'TODAY WE TAKE BACK CONTROL OF OUR LAWS' SAYS MAY

by Our Legal Staff
Great Repeal Bill Deedes

PRIME MINISTER Theresa May today unveiled the most historic piece of legislation ever put before the British Parliament.

"The Great Repeal Bill marks the moment," she said, "when Britain once again regains its proud sovereignty.

"From now on, every law the British people have to obey will be one passed by their own elected parliament.

"Never again," she went on, "will we have to kow-tow to the diktats of an unelected foreign bureaucracy.

"The moment we leave the EU," she continued, "my Great Repeal Bill will at a stroke restore the supremacy of British law.

"We are doing this by a bold and very simple four-point plan:

1. We repeal the hated European Communities Act which for 44 years has been the supreme symbol of our subservience to laws passed by those over whom we have no control.

2. We then incorporate all the 19,000 EU laws into British law.

3. Hey presto! All that nasty, oppressive, unaccountable foreign law has now been transformed in a matter of seconds into benign, responsible, much-needed British law, as approved by our very own sovereign British Parliament.

4. The hated EU red tape has become patriotic red, white and blue tape."

Mrs May then concluded, with a broad smile, "You know, this Brexit thing is turning out to be much easier than I thought."

Envelopegate
Day 94

The story continues...

At a special ceremony to announce the replacement for PricewaterhouseCoopers as regulator of the Oscar Envelopes, there was shock and disbelief as Warren Beatty opened the envelope containing the name of the winner of the contract.

Beatty, 94, raised his eyebrows (which Faye Dunaway was unable to do), and passed the buck (surely card) to his co-host. Dunaway's face then fell (or it would have done if it could) as she read out the name of Britain's "Royal Mail".

A representative from Royal Mail began his speech saying, "If anyone knows how to deliver the wrong envelope to the wrong person, it's us. We're delighted and honoured to take on this incredible responsibility..."

But he was interrupted by Warren Beatty, who said that there had been a horrible mistake and the winner was in fact Amazon, who had left the correct envelope with Mr Beatty's neighbour, who'd forgotten to give it to him.

Faye Hadsomework-Dunaway is still 21.

The Secret DIARY OF SIR JOHN MAJOR KG aged 77¾

Sunday

This evening, at the end of a not inconsiderably long weekend, I surprised my wife Norman by keeping the bedside light on well past nine o'clock, as I dotted the 't's and crossed the 'i's on my landmark speech for the next day about Brexit (which has one 'i' and one 't').

As I read the climactic 157th paragraph out loud, I apologised to Norman for keeping her awake. "On the contrary," she replied from underneath her BOAC eye-mask (a present from yours truly, following one of my many trips to Maastricht), "keep talking and I'll be asleep in no time."

Undaunted by this in no small measure playful quip, I returned to the heart of my argument in which I warned my audience of the pitfalls of an acrimonious separation from the European Community.

"We are in grave danger," I said gravely, "of underestimating the not inconsiderable challenges that lie ahead, by putting long-standing relationships at risk and betraying those closest to us." A snore – or was it a snort? – emanated from beneath Norman's floral-patterned 10.5-tog duvet.

"In short...," and here I paused for dramatic effect and polished my glasses on the sleeve of my Winceyette pyjamas... "In short, I say, we should think twice before making a historic mistake."

"You'd know all about historic mistakes," exclaimed Norman, suddenly rather more awake than I had previously imagined, as she picked up my mug of cocoa and accidentally poured it all over my head.

Monday

Last night, perhaps because of the regrettable cocoa incident, I slept badly and went downstairs to watch television, which was only showing the, in my judgement, very trivial news about the Oscars ceremony. Eventually, I fell asleep and dreamed about Mr David Dimbleby.

It was the night of the Referendum result and, just after he had announced on the BBC that "Leave" had won, he apologised, and explained that he had been given the wrong envelope.

In fact, he said, "Remain" had won the vote. We all cheered and began to sing and dance, just like in *La La Land*.

But then I woke up. Oh yes. Or rather, oh no.

Lookalikes

Kate   **Lorraine**

Sir,
Watching the daughter of famous air hostess Carole Middleton arrive in Canada, I was struck by her resemblance to Lorraine Chase, whose name is inextricably linked to Luton Airport. Might they be related?
ALISON HOWARD,
Tunbridge Wells.

Roman Republican   **Andrew Neil**

Sir,
I note from this 1st century BC bust in the Getty Museum that Mr Andrew Neil has been posing as a serious man of affairs for much longer than we thought.
MARK YNYS-MON,
Glasgow, Scotland.

May   **ET**

Sir,
I hope that this image portrays just how much trouble and effort the vexatious issue of aliens returning home is causing Mrs May and her twin sister, ET.
GRAHAM GLASSON,
Wells, Somerset.

Bentham   **Dylan**

Sir,
I'm wondering whether the recent award of the Nobel Prize for Literature was a case of mistaken identity, and the intended recipient was the philosopher (deceased but still present at University College) Jeremy Bentham.
ALISTAIR WYLIE,
Chepstow.

Harry as Charles   **Sir John as Chilcot**

Sir,
Has Sir John Chilcot replaced Harry Enfield as Prince Charles in 'The Windsors'? I think we should be told.
SIMON GROVES,
Via email.

Honey G   **Cameron**

Sir,
Is our ex-Prime Minister enjoying a new career as a rapper on X Factor?
ROTCIV WERDLEM,
Via email.

Ingrams   **Hockney**

Sir,
Seeing the picture of David Hockney in your Pseuds Corner column reminded me forcibly of Richard Ingrams, former editor of your esteemed organ [and author of the recently published biography of Ludovic Kennedy, "Ludo and the power of the book"]. Are they by any chance the same person?
JOHN WILFORD,
Horsforth, Leeds.

Melania   **Lady Penelope**

Sir,
Lady Penelope's twin's face is almost as expressive, but a little less warm somehow...
GEORGE AWTY,
Via email.

Angry bird   **Alex Salmond**

Sir,
I couldn't help but notice the similarity between these two characters. Is Alex Salmond (still) an Angry Bird? I think Nicola Sturgeon should be told.
JON PARROTT,
West Linton, Scotland.

Gareth Bale   **Grommash Hellscream**

Sir,
I wonder if perhaps you have noticed the similarity between a famous footballer and a lead character in a recent film release?
ALAN COCKAYNE,
Romford.

GCHQ

Apple HQ

Sir,
Ironically, the internet has brought to my attention two interesting buildings.
One is the headquarters of an organisation that has access to the private communications of millions of ordinary people across the world with the potential to exploit this data for their nefarious purposes. The other is a British Intelligence Agency.
JUSTIN REES.

Crayfish   **Stephen Fry**

Sir,
In Beijing recently, when visiting a crayfish restaurant, I was surprised to find Stephen Fry appears to be the model for a different kind of fry.
ROD,
Via email.

Scherzinger **Amenophis IV**

Sir;
Is there any evidence of trout pouts in the 1300s BCE?

D. THOMAS.

Arlene **Paul**

Sir;
Now that the "other bloke" on HIGNFY has taken over the poisoned chalice of Acting NI First Minister, how about getting Arlene Foster lined up?

PHIL SHARPE,
Lichfield, Staffs.

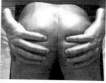

Ad **Art**

Sir;
I wonder whether this German advert for haemorrhoids was the inspiration for Anthea Hamilton's Turner Prize entry?

IAN CAMERON,
Via email.

Elton John **Nicola's mum**

Sir;
Is Elton John Nicola Sturgeon's secret mother?

BRENDAN MARTIN,
Broadstairs, Kent.

Gary **Pope**

Sir;
Has anyone else noticed the similarity between Diego Velazquez's Pope Innocent X and Gary Lineker?

J. CHEESEMAN,
Via email.

Victor Meldrew **Jeremy Paxman**

Sir;
Am I alone in spotting a similarity between the irascible old gits, Jeremy Paxman and Victor Meldrew? You never see them on screen together.

JOHN NAULLS,
Via email.

Media giant **Giant tortoise**

Sir;
I wonder if any of the other attendees at Sir Tom Stoppard's widely reported 80th birthday party noted the resemblance between these two non-native species, introduced from overseas many years ago and enjoying astonishing longevity?

ENA B. GALAPAGOS,
Via email.

Graham Norton **Père Tanguy**

Sir;
Does Graham Norton have a long-lost French cousin, a certain Monsieur Père Tanguy painted by Van Gogh?

GORDON JOLY,
Via email.

Eddie **Kellyanne**

Sir;
Is there some family relationship between a topical alternative reality spin-doctor and Eddie, the Iron Maiden mascot? I think we deserve to know, y'know... before it's too late and stuff?

G. WILLICKERS,
California.

President Business **President Elect**

Sir;
Given the uncanny resemblance of Donald Trump to Lego's President Business, should we be concerned about the structural integrity of the forthcoming border wall?

GORDON SHURE,
Via email.

David Davis **John Inman**

Sir;
Has anyone noticed the similarity between Britain's Brexit negotiator, David Davis, and Mr Humphries from Are You Being Served? To paraphrase young Mr Grace, "He's not doing very well..."

ENA B. WILLIAMS.

Pippa **Meghan**

Sir;
Have you noticed the remarkable similarity between Pippa Middleton and Meghan Markle? I think that Prince Harry should tell us.

JAMES NICHOLSON,
Goudhurst, Kent.

Greg Davies **Ronaldo**

Sir;
I couldn't help but notice the resemblance between the new bust of footballing giant Cristiano Ronaldo, and the cheerful features of the giant comedian Greg Davies. I'm sure this is a happy coincidence.

DAVE LOVE,
Kesgrave, Suffolk.

Presenter, Phil Airtime: ...and let's go over live to Westminster for the latest update on the horrific events outside the Houses of Parliament...

Reporter, Philippa Slott: Well, Phil, I can tell you that what I'm reading on my iPhone is that the police are now regarding this as a possible terrorist incident. It seems that quite a few people have been injured, and just now we heard the sound of shots from somewhere near the Palace of Westminster.

Phil: Well, thanks for that, Philippa, and for those of you who've just joined us and don't realise that I've been saying all this for the past hour, what we're hearing is that a number of people have apparently been involved in what may be a terrorist incident on Westminster Bridge, involving one or more attackers, and sounds of a possible shooting have been heard from the Palace of Westminster. I think it's now time to play again the extraordinary phone footage, filmed by a member of the public, where we can see other members of the public running along the road, clearly unsure as to what is going on.

(Cut to 94th repeat of iPhone footage showing members of the public running away from, or possibly towards, the scene of the alleged incident)

Phil: I'm afraid I've got to interrupt those remarkable pictures, because we've now got a helicopter on the scene which can give us much better pictures of the horrendous scenes unfolding below, and of course the extraordinary and heroic work being done by the emergency services.

(Blurred shot from helicopter of various vehicles parked by the side of the road)

Phil: ...and now there's been another truly unprecedented development, as we are gathering that Westminster is in a state of total lockdown.

Hundreds of MPs are trapped inside their offices and one of them has sent us this incredible message from right at the epicentre of the crisis. This is what Simon Suit MP has retweeted from behind the locked door of his office: "We've been stuck in here for an hour and we haven't a clue what's going on. Can anyone help?"

Phil: And now, over to Philippa for some breaking news...

Philippa: Thank you, Phil. I've just picked up this remarkable tweet on my phone, from one of the MPs trapped in the lockdown. Apparently, no one's been telling them what's going on, and they're hoping that someone will soon tell them what's happening.

Phil: Thanks Philippa. But now we've got a security expert here in the studio, Professor Jim Padding from the Institute of Strategic Terrorist Studies at the University of Neasden. Professor, we know it's too early to speculate about what's going on down there at Westminster, but would you say this has all the hallmarks of an attack by terrorists on the heart of Britain's parliamentary democracy?

Padding: Well, it is obviously much too early to speculate, but since you've asked me to come along here to fill in some time on your programme, my own guess is that it looks like some lone nutter who's only become a Muslim in the last five minutes so that he can work out his resentment of the modern world in an act of futile and violent stupidity.

Phil: Yes, well, that's one theory but, as we say, it's too early to speculate and until we've got a few facts to go on, we'd better just have another look at those shots of people running along the pavement while we wait for a senior policeman to come out and tell us that he can't tell us what's going on for operational reasons.

(Continued for many hours until a few facts do actually emerge and there is some real news)

WESTMINSTER TERROR ATTACK
WE MUST CARRY ON AS NORMAL

ON ALL OTHER PAGES: Headlines, pictures, news reports, opinion pieces, graphics showing how this paper is not carrying on as normal.

©All newspapers

Exclusive to all UK newspapers

SICK TERROR TIPS EASILY AVAILABLE ON GOOGLE

by **Clare Monger**

THIS paper has discovered, as part of an extensive campaign, that there are shocking websites which contain information about how to MURDER people, all accessible via Google. The website reveals that:

1. People can be run over by CARS.
2. People are VULNERABLE to knives.
3. People die when they are SHOT.

There is a real risk that sick Isis thugs will be able to piece these obscure pieces of information together and combine them to carry out attacks on normal people going about their business and then we'll all be DEAD and *(cont. p94)*

Exclusive to all US newspapers

BRIT CAPITAL CLOSED — TERRIFIED LONDONERS FLEE TO SCOTLAND

by **Katie Hopkins**

A DEFEATED and demoralised Britain was last night demanding that all police officers be armed, as well as all civilians, to fight the rising menace of millions of Islamic extremists, radicalised in the ghettos of Tunbridge Wells. *(Is any of this right? Ed.)*

HAPPY, DARLING?

DIARY

JACOB REES-MOGG

Calling in on my tailor for my second fitting for a new pair of swimming trunks in navy blue pinstripe, I had the great pleasure and privilege of discussing with him our departure from the behemoth that is the European Union.

"It has long been my belief that a robin feathering his nest has very little time to rest while gathering his bits of twine and twig," I told him, as he placed his measuring tape cordially around my waist. "Though quite intent in his pursuit, he has a merry tune to toot. He knows a song will move the job along."

"If I could just ask you to stretch your leg out, sir," said my tailor, a request with which I duly complied.

"Just a spoonful of sugar helps the medicine go down" I continued, "in the most delightful way."

"Indeed, sir," he said, moving on to the area that I believe is known as my "inner thigh".

"We are, I sometimes fear, in grave danger of forgetting these most ancient and wise of all maxims," I added.

"Excellent! We should have your trunks ready in a fortnight, Mr Jacob," he replied.

"Acta est fabula, plaudite!" I said, with a chuckle, as I left. It is my experience that ordinary, decent people respond to such observations in a way that the panjandrums who constitute our political establishment, for all their modish talk of "egalitarianism", have yet fully to appreciate.

@JacobReesMoggMP: A burger is a flat round cake of grilled minced beef served in a bread roll. One learns something new every day.

No one has more respect than I for the plucky little fellow who is prepared to shin up chimney with brush and broom in exchange for a couple of bob and a nutritious slice of bread-and-dripping. I have long clung to the age-old belief that a sweep is as lucky as lucky can be.

Needless to say, the European Union – in its infinite wisdom!! – has deprived these enterprising children of this luck, and has prevented them from pursuing this most agreeable and far from unremunerative profession. Meanwhile, many thousands of chimneys the length and breadth of our nation have been forced to languish unswept.Quis est iste in omni sensu? Where is the sense in all this?

At the same time, the most atrocious moving staircases, or "escalators", continue to be installed in many large buildings without consultation with local communities. Only last week, I visited a shopping arcade and witnessed countless of these "escalators" wreaking their modernistic havoc.

The British people are not enamoured of these monstrosities. They much prefer to walk up and down stairs on their own two feet, under their own speed, rather than have a faceless mechanic do it for them.

Great Britain's historic rejection of the European Union will put paid to these devilish contraptions. We have turned our back on the escalator, as we have on the cuckoo clock and the croissant. Robert Peel never ate a croissant in his life, yet he is remembered to this day as for his enormously successful step in repealing the Corn Laws. Vivat, Shanks Pony! Salve, festa dies!

@JacobReesMoggMP: Was it Catullus who first observed that with tuppence for paper and strings you can have you own set of wings? Wise words, indeed.

I am only too well aware that I am regarded by many as the fuddiest of duddies when it comes to matters pertaining to the modern world.

Much as one is loath to awaken one's critics from their slumbering prejudices, I feel it my duty to point out that I am much taken with one of the "conveniences" of modern life.

One morning shortly before Christmas, an esteemed constituent introduced me to the delights of "frozen food". This exemplary character was good enough to present me with a brightly coloured box containing 12 frozen "fishy fingers" cooked by a retired naval officer who rejoiced in the most excellent name of Captain Birdseye.

I duly returned home with the "frozen fishy fingers", and we presented them to our children for luncheon that day.

Yes, the Rees-Moggs may be rather more used to hot or warm food, but there was something delightfully stimulating about picking up these splendidly rigid "frozen fishy fingers" in one's fingers and licking away at them, just as one might an iced comestible on a stick. Not the tastiest of experiences, perhaps, but huge fun and wonderfully convenient. Never let it be said that I am not a man of the people. Salutant nos digito circum piscosos! We salute the fishy finger!

@JacobReesMoggMP: The triggering of Article 50 will ensure the return of the steam train, the Penny Farthing, Corned Beef and gristle. Exultate!

It goes without saying that President Trump is held in enormous respect by the people of our nation. We welcome his wit and wisdom. He may not speak the Queen's English, but fair play to the fellow: he is, through no fault of his own, an American, and need make no apology for it. An open, warm-hearted individual, he is clearly as honest as the day is long. I have no doubt that his forthcoming state visit will be greeted with celebrations on all sides of the political divide, particularly from members of our cheery working-classes. "Good luck will rub off, when I shakes 'ands with you!" as one of my constituents put it to me the other day.

Her Majesty, in particular, will be greatly looking forward to his appearance on our shores. The President has the grace of St Anselm and the wit of St Boniface and his wealth, though not princely, is considerable. Moreover, he is a keen supporter of Brexit, and fully cognisant that Britain's future lies not with Europe, but with the United States of America, which, though not an old country, continues to exhibit considerable pluck and stamina. And this is why I, for one, will be the first to dance to the President's tune when he urges us all to, in the words of the bard: "Flap like a birdie, step in time! Never need a reason, never need a rhyme! Flap like a birdie, step in time!"

@JacobReesMoggMP: …And after just two short years, Startbursts will once again be known as Opal Fruits.

As told to

CRAIG BROWN

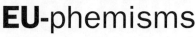

TRUMP BOMBS SYRIA THEN BROADCHURCH

by Our Defence Correspondent **Tommy Hawk**

A PROFOUNDLY moved President Trump last night ordered a massive attack on the English seaside village of Broadchurch after he had seen harrowing footage of a murdered child.

Using his executive powers as President, Mr Trump bypassed Congress to send a message to "the guys in charge in Broadchurch" that they had "crossed a red line".

The Prime Minister, Mrs May, supported his action, saying she'd been fully informed of Mr Trump's "proportionate and responsible act" at least five minutes after he'd done it.

This latest move is in line with the new Trump foreign policy doctrine of "seeing bad stuff on TV and lashing out".

There are now fears that the next target for an intercontinental ballistic missile strike might be the White House in Washington DC, as the President has been catching up with the new series of House of Cards on Netflix and the "appalling behaviour by American leader Frank Underwood who is abusing his powers and is one bad dude. Totally. #Bombsawayloser".

Apparently, the President was dissuaded at the last minute from bombing "Africa" in spite of a tearful call from his daughter Ivanka, who had seen a lion savaging a baby antelope in an unprovoked attack while a callous and uncaring David Attenborough looked on.

DONALD TRUMP'S FOREIGN POLICY IN FULL!

1. Shoot
2. ~~Ask questions~~

Thank God Trump now resembles the great presidents of the past, says everyone

THE world has breathed an enormous sigh of relief as it has become clear that instead of being a withdrawn, insular president not willing to police the world, Donald Trump is going to be a mad, shortsighted warmonger, willing to blow things up based solely on his substantial gut and his nightly television viewing.

"We thought he was going to be withdrawn, like his predecessor Barack Obama. In fact, he's going to take us back to the glory days of presidents like LBJ and Richard Nixon, when the US Air Force travelled the world blowing shit up at the drop of a 42-megaton weapon," said one military source.

Citizens around the world have been hugely relieved to know that the missiles and bombs which will end their lives will be fired not by mad terrorists from an armoured truck, but by responsible pilots carrying out the whims of a mad president. *(Rotters)*

Bye-bye, world!

A Sports Doctor Writes

AS A sports doctor, I'm often asked, "Doctor, can I have some corticosteroid triamcinolone for my allergies?"

The answer is, "Of course you can, Bradley."

What happens is that the patient experiences symptoms of extreme anxiety brought on by fear of not winning a race, ie an allergic reaction to losing.

This is known as Wiggins Syndrome or, to give it the full medical name, *Thereapeuticus usus exemptione normalis non suspicius at allus*.

There may, however, be unpleasant side effects for the doctor, such as a camera crew arriving on your doorstep, asking you why your colleagues have spilled the beans on you.

If you are worried about Wiggins Syndrome, you should seek professional legal advice at once or get on a bike and cycle very fast up the furthest mountain you can find.

© *A sports doctor, 2017*

Man dragged off flight by American authorities

by Our Aviation Staff
Brian Air

THERE was international outrage last night after news spread on social media that a passenger on his way to Russia had been dragged, kicking and screaming, off the plane by American security staff.

The passenger, a Mr Johnson, claimed he had an urgent appointment with the Russian foreign minister and absolutely had to get on the plane, but the Americans refused to take him seriously.

Video footage showed Mr Johnson protesting violently that he was a very important person and lives were at stake, as the Americans threw him out of the door on to the tarmac at Heathrow airport.

"You're going nowhere, buddy," said Mr Tillerson, who took Mr Johnson's place at the last minute and flew off to Russia himself.

The Middle East
AN EYE UPDATE

'Who's Fighting Whom?' It couldn't be simpler, says our defence expert Sir Michael Fallible

(based on a brief by the Ministry of Defence)

1 We are backing the US over Syria.

2 The US is backing the "rebels".

3 Saudi Arabia is also backing the "rebels".

4 The "rebels" are al-Qaeda under the name of al-Nusra.

5 The US is against al-Qaeda but in favour of al-Nusra, so long as no one notices.

6 Al-Nusra are against Isis, as are Assad, the US, the Saudis, the Russians and everyone else.

7 The Russians are for Assad and against al-Nusra, al-Qaeda and Al Gore. *(Is this right? Ed.)*

8 The Turks are against Assad, Isis and also the Kurds.

9 The Russians were against the Turks when they shot down a Russian plane, but seem to be warming to the Turks now that President Erdogan is becoming more like President Putin.

10 Quite where the Russians stand on the Kurds no one seems to know.

11 Oh, we nearly forgot about the Iranians. The Iranians are backing Assad and are also backed by the Russians.

12 The Americans used to be in favour of the Iranians but are now against them. Except in Iraq where we and the Americans are fighting with the Iranians against Isis.

13 We also have to remember Yemen, where we are supplying arms for the Saudis to support some of the Yemenis against other Yemenis who are supported by the Iranians.

14 On second thoughts, don't even go there.

15 Yemen, we mean... or Libya for that matter, or the Middle East in general.

16 We did try it once, and that's what caused all the trouble. But be careful not to mention that bit.

17 Er...

18 That's it.

THE PRESIDENT'S 'SITUATION ROOM'

Why are we watching reruns of The Apprentice?

WIKIPEDIA FOUNDER TO ENSURE NO FAKE FACTS ON THE INTERNET

ON OTHER PAGES
● Foxes to ensure safety of hens kept overnight in henhouses

● Arsonists to spearhead campaign to reduce number of house fires.

PRAVDEYE

21 April 2017 — Three roubles

AN APOLOGY

IN RECENT times, in common with all other Russian newspapers that have not yet been banned, we may have given the impression that we viewed the election of President Donald Trump as the most positive step for Russo-American relations since the Great Patriotic War.

We may have reinforced this impression with such headlines as "Comrade Trump is a man we can do business with", "Presidents Putin and Trump form undying alliance for world peace" and "We applaud Trumpski's pledge to keep out of Russian sphere of influence in the Middle East".

We now realise that there was not a word of truth in this unfortunately mistaken and deluded view.

As recent events have shown, Trump is no more than a crazed imperialist war-monger whose only desire is to undermine the great humanitarian work for peace that Russia has been undertaking in Syria, by giving way to the lunatic urgings of the far-right US military-industrial-intelligence complex which, thanks to Trump's nakedly aggressive intervention with his Tomahawk missiles, is now threatening to plunge the world into a nuclear armageddon.

We hope that today's front-page headline will help to give a more correct perspective: "Fascist running-dog Trump will unleash new Great Patriotic War which, under the calm and wise guidance of Comrade Putin the Terribly Good, we shall undoubtedly win".

We apologise to readers for any confusion that our previous articles in praise of Mr Trump may have caused.

The so-called chemical weapon attack – what actually happened

*by Our Defence Comrade **Putin Perspektiv***

THERE has been much misunderstanding, thanks to Western propagandists, regarding the alleged "Sarin gas attack" last week in the Syrian town of Khan Sheikhoun.

Contrary to the blizzard of fake news to which the world has been subjected by the CIA, the FBI and the much-hated WHO (World Health Organisation), the 90 people who allegedly died were not in any way the "victims" of the Syrian air force.

They were, in fact, all actors, paid for by the Saudi government, to appear in fake footage, pretending to have been gassed.

Any Sarin gas that might have been involved in any incident only escaped when the canisters were deliberately blown up by the jihadists of al-Nusra.

The fact that this coincided with a peaceful fly-past by the Syrian Red Arrows aerobatic display team has enabled the cunning lie merchants of CNN and Channel 4 News to fabricate one of the greatest lies in the history of the world.

"Alexa – cancel the cat food, and double the bird seed order"

From The Message Boards

Members of the online community respond to the major issues of the day...

MP in Nazi row

In The Year Of Our Lord Two Thousand And Seventeen, The Right Honourable Roger Burgon, being Shadow Secretary Of State For Justice and Shadow Lord Chancellor and Member of Parliament for Leeds East, did no more than record an album with rock band Dream Tröll, who allegedly did no more than use Nazi iconography. But others claim they did no more than pay tribute to Black Sabbath, whose album bore 'lightning bolts' in place of the letter S, resembling the insignia of Hitler's SS. Yet others did no more than declare it worse, for Black Sabbath were Satanists. Inasmuch and insofar as they did so do, then they did no more than Jesus, who 'saw Satan fall like lightning from heaven'. (Luke 10:18) – *Mr Salmon*

As a fellow Yorkshireman and a WWII re-enactor holding the rank of SS-Gruppenführer, I am disgusted by this disgraceful and inappropriate use of Schutzstaffel insignia. The Siegrune symbolises victory, a concept that is thankfully alien to this Labourite buffoon. It was adapted for the Leibstandarte Adolf Hitler by Sturmhauptführer Walter Heck, who was a graphic designer, and his stylish device resembled twin lightning bolts. As well as standing for SS, it was also a rallying cry: Victory! Victory! The symbol became so popular that it was typeset using runes rather than letters, and a special SS key was added to German typewriters. I need hardly add that my word processing programme, which incorporates every other trademark, logo, and foreign symbol known to man, has no such facility. – *Legion of the Damned*

Interesting how the mainstream media has focussed on this sideshow, while ignoring the twin lightening bolts in the logo of Kiss, whose cosmopolitan NEW York roots are brazenly flaunted in the rhyme therein. More fake news and deflection from the ZOG/NWO/Isisrael axis, and their puppets in the yellow press. – *new user name*

not bein funny but i dont really follow politic's but i no this guy is labor and there the party thats antismitic. wat i dont get is he say's he is not a nazi so is he one of them nearnazi's who are nearly nazi and nearly normal like them russian's that beat up are fan's in the euro's? – *Hayley 321*

Leaving aside the politics, Hitler is a great role model. Like Bobby Moore he only had one bollock but he became a hero to millions. – *West Stand Chap*

If this Labour idiot's heroes had won the war he wouldn't enjoy the freedom to display his SS paraphernalia at all. – *Dave's Dad*

Time to end the disastrous democratic experiment – *Sword of Truth*

HOW THE ELECTION COVERAGE WILL LOOK FOR THE NEXT SIX WEEKS

Daily Mail
JEREMY CORBYN IS UTTERLY RUBBISH

The Sun
JEREMY CORBYN IS BLOODY RUBBISH

The Daily Telegraph
Jeremy Corbyn Is Terribly Rubbish

THE TIMES
Poll shows Jeremy Corbyn is rubbish

theguardian
Jemery Corbny is only slightly rubbish

DAILY EXPRESS
DID RUBBISH CORBYN HAVE SOMETHING TO DO WITH MADDIE'S DISAPPEARANCE?

"I've got that projectile vomiting bug, doctor"

ELECTION ROUND-UP

Poll of poll of polls

A SHOCK new poll has revealed that despite polls being totally discredited in the 2015 General Election, the 2016 Brexit vote and the 2016 American Presidential Election, 100 percent of news organisations still have complete faith in them.

"There was a widespread expectation that after these votes, where the polls proved to be about as accurate as playing darts blindfolded in a wind tunnel, the media would stop putting their faith in them," said all voters.

"But as soon as Theresa May called the snap election, polls showed that 100 percent of headlines contained the word 'Polls'. These included: *'Polls Predict Tory Landslide', 'Tory Lead Halved In Shock Poll', 'New Poll Contradicts Poll We Had Yesterday and the Day Before'.*"

Fallon: 'Trust us on defence'

DEFENCE secretary Michael Fallon said the public shouldn't entrust Britain's armed forces to a dangerous pacifist like Jeremy Corbyn after his lukewarm comments on renewing Trident in an interview on the *Today* programme.

"Only the Conservatives can be trusted to run the armed forces into the ground, as we have during the last seven years," said the defence secretary.

"No aircraft carriers, no new fighter jets, tens of thousands of regular soldiers axed... that's what safe and stable management means – don't risk that by voting for Corbyn."

Labour sources later clarified that despite the Leader's comments, the party remained committed to Trident, as the nuclear option could be the only way to remove Jeremy Corbyn as Opposition Leader after the Tories win by a landslide.

LABOUR REVEALS SECRET ELECTION WEAPON

Vote Tory!

Let's Parlez Franglais!

Numéro 94
Le controversial meeting between Monsieur Juncker et le Pape Francis

Monsieur Drunker *(pour c'est lui)*: Bonjour, Madame. J'aime votre dress blanche. Très sexy!

Le Pape: Non, je suis un bloke.

Monsieur Drunker: Oh, oui! Et je suis the Pope!

Le Pape: Non, je suis le Pape.

Monsieur Drunker: Zut alors! Et qui sont les autres cutie-pies dans les robes rouges?

Le Pape: Ils sont les cardinals. Je crois que perhaps vous avez une drink problème?

Monsieur Drunker: Absolument. La problème est que je don't have a drink! Une grande one, pour moi! Mademoiselle la barmaid...!!

Le Pape: Non, c'est un nun.

Monsieur Drunker: Ok, un Bleu Nun!

Le Pape: Il n'y a pas de Bleu Nun.

Monsieur Drunker: Puis I'll have le Chateauneuf du Pope. Une bouteille, s'il vous plaît. Juste pour moi!!

Polish MP: Monsieur Drunker, vous êtes un disgrace.

Monsieur Drunker: Non, **vous** êtes le disgrace. Both of you!

Le Pape: Poor Monsieur Drunker a besoin d'un long rest.

Monsieur Drunker: I'm déjà having one – je suis head de l'EU!!!

© *The late Kilomètres Kington 2017.*

'I <u>will</u> get the numbers down!' May's shock pledge

by Our
Political Staff
Peter O'Bore

Theresa May last night shocked her followers by promising that she would bring down the Tory majority at the election to "low single figures".

"I do not need thousands nor indeed hundreds more Tory MPs coming in to tell me how to run the country. I am doing it perfectly well on my own, with the help of Nick Beardy, and as far as I'm concerned, a majority of half a dozen is all that we need."

She continued, "For that reason, we have decided that our best strategy is to propose a whole lot of Labour policies, like capping energy bills and giving workers a whole lot of new rights, and then to perform some embarrassing u-turns."

Mrs May concluded, "That should do the trick and, before you know it, the figures will be slashed to zero."

Guardian to move to Slaford

by Our Media Staff
Miss Print

As a result of a financial crisis due to being based in London, the long-established Grauniad Newspaper is to move up North to try and save money by relocating to cheaper premises in Alsford.

Said the editor, "The business rates in King's Cross have become punitive in the last year, and the deteriorating commercial outlook for the newspaper has made it necessary to make a drastic decision to uproot the entire operation and start anew in Lasfrod."

● *If you are reading this piece online, please, please feel a bit guilty about it, and give us some money because, let's face it, it's your fault that we've got to leave our lovely offices in London. If you give us enough money, we'll be able to employ some good, local spell-checkers in Munchester.*

Justine Greening Guide to
The New Grammar Schools

1 The new Grammar Schools will emulate the success of the Grammar Schools of old which used the 11-plus exam to select an intake of the brightest and most gifted students from all backgrounds.

2 To ensure no one is left behind, the new Grammar Schools will scrap the 11-plus exam, as selection tended to discriminate against the less bright and less gifted, preventing them from enjoying the fruits of a Grammar School education.

3 Having removed the element of selection, the term 'Grammar Schools' will be shortened to the much catchier name: 'Schools'.

4 These 'Schools' will then be open to all students, regardless of ability or background.

5 Er…

6 That's it.

Boris Johnson, the Secretary of State for Foreign and Commonwealth Affairs, writes exclusively for Private Eye

CRIPES! Poor old Bojo has had a rotten stinker of a week!

First off, as soon as the election was declared, some nincompoop locked me in the toilets! And I couldn't get out! Can you imagine? Mr Electoral Asset himself, the victorious Bozza, stuck in the khazi unable to get out on the stump and win the election single-handed as per!! It's almost as if Mrs T told someone to lock me in the FO bogs deliberately!

Still, after a couple of days banging on the door of the crapper some civil service bod finally turned up and let me out.

Hoorah! Time to get to work, thought I, so I immediately leapt into action and made a cracking speecheroo calling Comrade Corbyn "a mullet-headed moggchump" or words to that effect, which had the desired effect of making someone look an idiot!!

Next up, I tried out a bit of diplomacy on the hoof, to wit backing friend Trumpy-Pumpy 100 percent and promising to press the jolly old nuclear button whenever he told me to without worrying about boring old parliament!

Blow me down if I'm not hauled in front of the beak, ie the Sainted Theresa, for a roasting for talking out of turn.

"Zip it!" she says and adds, "And I don't mean your trousers!"

Talk about ungrateful. Just when I was setting the election on fire and making the headlines again I've been put in purdah.

So here I am writing from inside the toilet where I appear to have been locked in again.

Craps!
And Double Craps!
Bozza.

PS: Little sis has gone stark staring bonkers and joined the Lib Dems! Mega-embarrassing for yours truly, as I was thinking of growing a beard, buying some sandals and doing the same thing if it all went belly-up with the Tories and Mrs May Queen gave me the old heave-ho! Watch out Rache, you rotter!!

HEIR OF SORROWS
A Short Story Special

by Dame Sylvie Krin, author of *Duchess of Hearts* & *You're Never Too Old*

THE STORY SO FAR: Charles has been sent an advance copy of a new biography of himself by the famous lady historian, Sally Bedchamber-Smythson. It is called "The Passions and Paradoxes of a Puzzled Prince". Now read on...

"THIS really is..." For the third time in as many minutes Charles put down the book in despair.

"What is appalling now, Chazza?" asked Camilla sympathetically, as she took another sip of her strong Gordonstoun gin and tonic. She could feel that it was going to be a long evening.

"This American woman says that I am thin-skinned, petulant and can't take criticism," replied Charles furiously, "which is absolute rubbish. And stupid. And ill-informed."

"I thought that this was meant to be a sympathetic portrait?"

"Well, it isn't. She says that I am pampered and spoilt and that I take my own salt when I go to dinner with other people."

"Well, that bit is true. You do."

Charles reddened and insisted, "No, I don't. Sir Alan takes it. In a silver case with my initials on it .Which is very different. No, this book is really..."

"Well, I dunno, Chazza, it doesn't seem too bad..."

Charles stood up.

"I had rather hoped for more support from you," he said huffily, as he dropped the book and left the room.

Camilla looked at the page... "He tends to leave the room if anyone contradicts him in argument..."

CHARLES lay in the soothing waters of his Victorian cast-iron Kermode & Mayo bathtub, but somehow his turmoil increased. The Duchy Original Essence of Badger Relaxing Bath Oil was not having the desired effect. What if that awful woman was right? What if the wait to become King

had turned his mind and driven him as mad as King George III?

He asked Sir Alan Fitztightly to turn on the sturdy Andrew Roberts radio to find some distraction. Perhaps Radio Four Extra Extra had a repeat of the Goons on again?

"The wireless, sire? Is that a good idea, sire?" asked the Royal Aide-de-very-camp, wary of previous radio-based misunderstandings in the bath.

"Not you too, Sir Alan?" replied Charles testily, as he guided his plastic replica Arctic research ship, the Boaty McBoatface, through the bubbles towards the taps. "I am not a child, you know – I think I can cope with whatever is on the radio."

"Right you are then, sire. Just don't say I didn't warn you – as Backstairs Billy used to say to the young footmen when he invited them into the broom cupboard in the days of your dear old Nan..."

"Yes, thank you, Sir Alan," said Charles, cutting short the reminiscences of the Squeezer of the Toothpaste Royal. He lay back in the bath and listened to the soothing voice of the newsreader...

"Friends and colleagues are mourning the man who was for many people King Charles III and who was taken from us too early mid-way through his work on that role. He will be greatly missed and no one who saw him performing will forget..."

Sir Alan Fitztightly hurried to reassure his master, but it was too late. Charles had leapt from the soapy water and was running down the corridor naked, wildly shouting,

"I have died! King Charles is dead! Long live the Queen!"

Sir Alan let the water out of the bath slowly, as the news continued with its obituary of the actor Tim Pigott-Smith, who had become famous in TV's *Jewel in the Crown* and who had recently played Charles so convincingly on stage...

Perhaps one day he would talk to the American lady historian and tell her the real story...

(To be continued...)

HOW THEY SAW IT

WEDNESDAY, MARCH 22, 2017

IRISH MASS MURDERER DIES AT LAST
Terrorist serial killer goes to grave unrepentant

by Our Entire Staff

THE British people breathed a sigh of relief yesterday when it was announced that the former IRA commander Martin McGuinness had finally died and gone to hell.

No one will mourn the passing of a psychopath in a balaclava who was personally responsible for the killing of hundreds of innocent people.

In later life, McGuinness started a new career as a politician and played a small part in Northern Ireland's so-called "peace process".

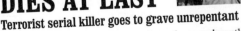

Wednesday 22.03.17

'Irish Mandela' sadly taken from us
World hails the death of the 'Great Peacemaker'

by Our Entire Staff

World leaders, headed by former President Bill Clinton, were heading for Northern Ireland yesterday to say farewell to Martin McGuinness, one of the greatest statesmen the world has ever seen.

We can all mourn the passing of this outstanding political leader, who single-handedly brought peace and reconciliation to Ulster after decades of sectarian violence.

In earlier life, Mr McGuinness had a different career, as an active campaigner for human rights and social justice in his native Northern Ireland and it was alleged that he played a small part in the so-called "troubles",

Father Ted.

Farther Ted.

Donald Trump's First 100 Days

THE PRESIDENT REVIEWS HIS ACHIEVEMENTS

What I promised!

What I delivered!

How The Policies Worked Out In Full

My Non-Entanglement With the Middle East Policy

1. SYRIA. Bomb it
2. AFGHANISTAN. Bomb it
3. NORTH KOREA. Bomb it soon. Is that in the Middle East?

My Normalisation of Relations With Russia Policy

1. Announce talks with my old friend Vlad, a man I can do business with.
2. Bomb Syria.
3. Accuse tyrant Putin of committing war crimes against Syrian people.

My 'China is America's No. 1 Enemy' Policy

1. Accuse of fraud, cheating and rape of US economy.
2. Discover China is only hope of solving North Korea problem (*see above*).
3. Invite my new friend President Xi to agreeable chocolate cake tea in Mar-a-Lago.

My Building a Mexican Wall Policy

1. Put wall on temporary hold.
2. Ask son-in-law to get estimates for fence.
3. Ask Ivanka to get estimates for large sign saying "Keep Out" in Mexican.

My 'Putting America First' Trade Policy

1. Put Europe first.
2. Put Britain last.
3. Build wall between America and Canada.
4. Renegotiate NAFTA deal with Canada.

My Scrapping Obamacare Policy

1. Try getting Congress to scrap Obamacare.
2. Fail, due to outdated and obstructive American constitution.
3. Rename existing system "Trumpcare".

My 'Lowering Taxes For Everyone' Policy

1. Lower taxes for the very, very rich.
2. Job done.

MELANIA TRUMP WINS DAMAGES CLAIM FROM MAIL OVER BASELESS 'ESCORT' CLAIMS

How dare they suggest I would sleep with a man for his money

THE ☙ TIMES

SUMMER 1788

BRAVE ROYAL COMES CLEAN OVER MENTAL HEALTH ISSUE

OUR COURT CORRESPONDENT MISTER ALAN BENNETT

FOR THE first time, a member of the Royal Family has talked openly about his struggles with mental illness. His Royal Highness King George III surprised the nation last week by discussing his condition openly with a tree in Windsor Great Park, under the impression that the oak was in fact the King of Prussia.

Onlookers applauded what they called "His Majesty's bravery, honesty and humility" which they said had changed the way they thought about such problems.

Said the Prime Minister, William Pitt, "In the old days, we would have treated this sort of madness in a very barbaric way, but nowadays we know that it is best to strap the king to a chair and apply caustic poultices to draw out the evil humours."

He continued, "In the meantime, we'll lock him up and run the show without him. Whoops."

'No, it's not a sin' Farron hits back

by Our Theological Staff **Gay Search**

The world of Westminster was rocked to its foundations last week by the latest twist in the ongoing controversy over Tim Farron's religious beliefs. In an interview on the Andrew Peston show (*surely Robbie Marr show? Ed.*) Farron came out with a restatement of where he stands on one of the great issues of the day.

"Look," he insisted, "let me make this absolutely clear. I do not believe it is a sin to be a Liberal Democrat.

"I admit that I have long been struggling with how to reconcile my faith with being a Lib Dem and it is not easy being a Lib Dem at a time when most other people look on us as just a weird minority."

When pressed by Channel 4's Kathy Neill to explain how he could be both a practising Lib Dem and a Christian, he replied testily, "I'm getting really tired of answering all these silly questions.

"When I said earlier that we are all sinners, what I meant was that we are all Lib Dems, but most people don't want to admit it because of the prejudice they would face from the intolerant majority."

Mr Farron went on to point out that the Bible was not entirely clear in its attitude to people who have Lib Dem inclinations.

"But I like to think," he concluded, "that when Jesus told his followers 'I am the way, the truth and the life', what he really meant was 'I am the third way', etc, which would obviously indicate that he was neither Conservative nor Labour.

"The one thing Our Lord didn't say," Farron added, "was 'I am the gay'."

Within seconds this outspoken clarification of his position provoked a colossal Twitterstorm which lasted (cont. p94)

HAVE YOU SEEN HOW INCREDIBLY THIN GRAPHENE IS?!

BITCH!

BERNIE

Pippa Middleton's Guide to Marriage

1 It's often a good idea when getting married to find someone to marry.

2 Make sure you're single first. This is a common mistake.

3 Get a well-known party planner to organise everything. I can recommend Middleton Party Planners for all your party needs.

4 Choose a page boy and bridesmaid. It is a good idea if they are heirs to the throne.

5 Invite any other heirs to the throne you know, especially if they are your brother-in-law.

6 Make sure you're not upstaged by a woman in a tight white dress. I suggest wearing an even tighter one.

7 Remember to say "I do". Don't say "I don't". It won't do.

8 Congratulations! You're now married and don't need to do it again for, like, ages.

"This is completely unacceptable"

Cinema highlights

Not Coming Soon...
Bridge over the River Thames

Classic big-budget British extravaganza in which crazed upper-class twit Boris Johnson (Alec Guinness) attempts the impossible feat of building a bridge across the River Thames in order to attract Japanese investment.

But a crack unit, led by Sadiq Khan (William Holden) is sent on a mission to sabotage the madcap scheme. Will the budget for the bridge get blown up out of all proportion? Yes.

Don't miss the cameo from veteran Japanese actor Sesui Hayakayawi as Joanna Lumley, the woman who is determined to build the bridge "at all costs".

Watch out for the final explosive scene where Boris and Sadiq grapple with the banks of the Thames, who are financing the scheme, and Boris utters the final words "Madness, madness" before the Garden Bridge Scheme collapses completely.

Includes the stirring theme tune performed by whistleblowers, *"Major Cockup"* (surely "Colonel Bogey"? Ed.)

THE EYE'S NEW TECH COLUMN

AMBER RUDD SOLVES ALL YOUR COMPUTER PROBLEMS

HELLO, EVERYONE! My inbox has been full to bursting with questions about computer thingies, but until I find out how to open my inbox, and what an inbox is, I'll make a start on your postal letters!

The first one comes from a Doctor in Kidderminster...

I seem to have a problem accessing all my patient records. Can you help me sort out my gremlins?

Thank heavens, an easy one to start! Well, the best way to deal with gremlins is to turn your keyboard upside down, give it a vigorous shake and hope the little gremlins fall out! I would shake the keyboard over a Tupperware container or shoebox, to stop the little green nasties climbing back inside, and all will be peaches and cream!

The next one is from a Nurse in Great Yarmouth...

My computer screen has completely frozen, and I need to get on with my work. Can you help?

Of course I can! I would say the best way to unfreeze any computer screen is use much the same method as I use to defrost prawns. Just dip it in boiling water for twenty minutes and it'll be fine. Alternatively, if it's a very small computer, like those eyepuds, you can zap it in the microwave for 30 seconds and it should be completely hunky-dory in no time!

Finally, a plea from a Consultant in Crawley...

My firewall is completely breached. Is there any way you could help me get a new one?

Ooh, I couldn't say. I'm not sure what that is. Is it like a fireguard? Because they do lovely ones in Oka! Actually, I just asked Jeremy Hunt if he had a firewall, and he said that I was his! So my expert advice is call up your nine-year-old nephew who's a whizz with anything electronic and ask him what to do. That's how I aim to solve the NHS Trust cybercrime crisis!

GEORGE TO BE PAGEBOY

Ya, I'll be front page, middle page, every page!

Huge arse hits headlines

by Our Media Staff
Philippa Bikini-Bottom

AN enormous arse has been dominating the pages of the world's newspapers amidst fears that it is out of control.

Said Kim Kardashian's bottom, "Donald Trump is now beyond a joke.

"He should not have been allowed to become so enormous. He looks weird and ridiculous," continued the reality TV star's posterior and *(cont. size 94)*

"I love what you've done with your hair!"

THOSE CONSERVATIVE 2017 ELECTION POLICIES IN FULL

FOREIGN AID	**THE NHS**	**THE ECONOMY**	**SOCIAL CARE**	**TRIDENT**
Jeremy Corbyn is Labour leader	Jeremy Corbyn is Labour leader	Jeremy Corbyn is Labour leader	Jeremy Corbyn is Labour leader	Jeremy Corbyn is Labour leader

The Eye presents its own list of the Corbyn-inspired new bank holidays that will liven up Britain and send us all back on a three-day week

- **St Michael's Day** (patron saint of underpants at a reasonable price)
- **St Trinian's Day** (patron saint of naughty girls' boarding schools from the 1930s)
- **St Ivel's Day** (patron saint of yoghurt and associated dairy products)
- **The Saint's Day** (patron saint of wooden actors who played Simon Templar)
- **St Moritz's Day** (patron saint of menthol cigarettes)
- **All Saints' Day** (patron saint of girl bands)
- **Saint And Greavsie's Day** (patron saint of football pundits)
- **Saint Jeremy's Day** (the patron saint of lost causes)

Very good, have the day off – St Paul of Dacre (patron saint of swearing).

"I hate films with pubtitles"

Manilow shock announcement

by **Gay Search**

THERE was astonishment in Tinseltown this week, as flamboyant crooner Barry Manilow came out and announced, "I've got some surprising news for everyone. You're not going to believe this, but I think now's the time to tell you – the Pope is a Catholic! We've all had our suspicions for a while... I mean, let's face it, his clothing has always been a touch ecclesiastical, and his music always had a very select group of fans."

The colourful songwriter continued, "The Pope always seemed the kind of guy to keep his personal faith to himself and I had absolutely no idea that he was an out-and-out Catholic." Mr Manilow added, "That's not all – I found out something about bears and their lavatorial habits that you are not going to believe..." (*That's enough showbiz news. Ed.*)

Bank holiday plan

THERE has been widespread condemnation of Jeremy Corbyn's plan to introduce four new bank holidays if Labour win the election.

"Who wants another four bank holidays where we set off for the seaside with the kids, only for it to start chucking it down when we're almost there, meaning we end up having to eat fish and chips in the car, then the wife and I have a massive row, meaning neither of us speak the entire way home?" said one miserable-looking dad.

"Four more bank holidays mean there's no way I can dream up enough excuses to get out of doing all the DIY work round the house I've been successfully putting off for the last three years," said another disgruntled bloke being marched round B&Q.

"It means finding something for the kids to do, so they don't start moaning that they're bored by 11am. Why can't they just be in school?" said one frazzled mum, counting down the hours until she could get back to the office on Tuesday.

The British Chamber of Commerce said four extra bank holidays would be extremely costly to productivity, as everyone would spend the following Tuesday in the office updating their Facebook and Instagram statuses, in an attempt to fool the world that they had had the most brilliant long weekend ever.

IVANKA'S DIPLOMATIC MISSION

Hands up all those who've been ogled by Donald Trump

"Oh, not Mendelssohn again!"

WHY 'THE CROWN' LOST AT THE BAFTAS

1. Netflix spent far too much money. Had they won, the BBC would have had to bankrupt itself staging lavish period drama crowd scenes which involve more than three bored extras and a shire horse.

2. Episode one didn't end on a nail-biting cliff-hanger where George VI was left to die in a filthy basement after a savage beating at the hands of a masked assailant.

3. Following her coronation, the young Queen didn't engage in an epic battle of wits with a sadistic serial killer taunting Her Majesty, in order to stop him before he killed again.

4. Nor are any paedophiles brought to justice in a nail-biting bloody final episode where shifting loyalties have you on the edge of your seat.

5. Er…

6. That's it.

DAVID CAMERON

Do you ever sit in your shed thinking about your disastrous decision to hold a referendum on the EU?

Well, the great thing about the shed is that it was a very reasonable £25,000 from the Reclaimed Bijou local firm in the Cotswolds, and…

Why did you run off to your shed, leaving everyone else to deal with the mess you left behind?

Actually, yes, it is rather spacious inside – there's room for a sofabed and desk inside it, meaning we can…

What was the point of your whole premiership, apart from giving you the money to buy a pointless shed?

I personally love the design. Samantha insisted the whole outside was in the Heron's Smudge colour, which looks really…

Will your memoirs, written from the shed, acknowledge you bollocksed the whole thing up?

Of course, the beautiful wheels were hand-crafted, I believe, and it creates a really pleasing sense of elevation from the ground when you're…

Why spend thousands of pounds on a shed when millions of people are struggling to make ends meet, thanks to your policies?

We did have a bit of a row about who got to spend the first night in the shed, actually, which was a bit of a pickle…

Has anything amusing ever happened to you in connection with a shed?

I'm glad you ask me that. As a matter of fact, there was one…

Oh, shut up.

NEXT WEEK: *Jodie Marsh, "Me And My Marsh".*

THOSE FILMS BRAD PITT MADE WHEN DRUNK

Ocean's 11 Pints

Ocean's 12 Pints

Ocean's 13 Pints

Tight Club

The Curious Case of Benjamin Button's Whisky

Meet Joe Rum and Black

The Big Shorts

Mr and Mrs Squiff

Troy-llied

Inglorious Bar Stewards

12 Years a Slave to the Bottle

Legends of the Fall Over

EMMA WATSON WINS FIRST EVER GENDER-NEUTRAL AWARD

I'd like to thank my… er… parent. And my… other parent…

BAFTA Frocks Shocks! with Philippa Page

✔

You're top of Bafta's **Poll-dark** *(geddit?)* **Eleanor!** And it's good to see it's not just Captain Ross Poldark who shows us his chest!! **Demure-za** you ain't, **Ms Tomlinson**, but you're a winner on the **red-head** carpet. *(This is rubbish. Carry on going. Ed.)*

✘

Foy what a scorcher! No **Crowns** for **Claire**, as the young queen in Netflix's Royal romp loses out! *(It's a picture of Charlotte Riley from Charles III! Ed.)* Ok, I'll have a vowel, please, Ms Riley! *(That's Countdown's Rachel Riley, you fool.)*

✘

Oops! Sorry **baby** (iguana), but you've made a fashion faux pas turning up naked for the Bafta big night! Forget the **snakes**, us tabloid fashion editors will eat you alive!! Your career is definitely on the **rocks**, love. *(They won a Bafta, you complete idiot! Have a pay rise. Ed.)*

DIARY

LUCY WORSLEY'S HISTWEE LESSON

Lucy Worsley: Lots and lots and LOTS of people remember their histwee lessons from school as being about Kings and Queens

cut to Lucy dressed in crown and robes

    – and battles

cut to Lucy dressed in chain mail, swinging a sword

    – and dates.

cut to Lucy dressed up as a raisin

    You might think histwee is a record of what happened – but actually it's not that AT ALL! As soon as you do a bit of digging –

cut to Lucy in wellingtons with a spade, pretending to wipe sweat off her brow

    – you discover it's more like…

Lucy pretends to be looking for the right word

    …a TAPESTRY woven by whoever was in power at the time!

cut to Lucy dressed up us Queen Elizabeth I, weaving a tapestry.

INTERIOR. LIBRARY

Lucy Worsley: Here I am in a DUSTY OLD LIBRARY talking to a man with a beard who really knows lots and lots and lots about the WARS OF THE ROSES!

    So, man with a beard, am I right in thinking that the WARS OF THE ROSES was not actually a series of battles between one rose –

Lucy produces a red rose in one hand

    – and another rose?

Lucy produces a white rose in her other hand, and then bashes them together

Man with beard: That's right, Lucy. The Wars of the Roses were in fact between the House of Lancaster and the House of York.

Lucy Worsley: Fascinating! But are we talking about two ACTUAL HOUSES MADE OF BRICKS AND MORTAR fighting each other –

cut to Lucy wearing boxing gloves, dressed up as a house, with her head where the chimney would be

    – or are we in fact talking about something REALLY RATHER DIFFERENT?

Man with beard: Yes. Very different.

EXTERIOR. LUCY STANDING ON TOP OF WHITE CLIFFS OF DOVER DRESSED UP AS A BLUEBIRD

Lucy: So there we have it, in a nutshell –

Lucy dips into a packet of pistachio nuts, and starts shelling them

    – the so-called WARS of the ROSES were VERY, VERY DIFFERENT from what we've been taught!!!!

    They were in fact like a real-life Game of Thrones, or Emmerdale Farm, but without a tractor –

cut to Lucy driving a tractor through a field

    – because back in the olden days, they didn't have tractors – they had horses and carts!!!

cut to Lucy dressed as Tudor milkmaid driving a horse and cart

    So now let's take a look –

cut to Lucy dressed up as Admiral Nelson, taking a look through a telescope

    – at how William Shakespeare, the greatest storyteller of them all, portrayed King Richard III!

cut to Lucy dressed up as King Richard III, with hunchback, etc.

Lucy: "Now is the winter –"

snow starts falling in studio, Lucy as King Richard builds snowman

    "– of our discontent, Made glorwious summer –"

cut to Lucy sunbathing on a summer beach in Victorian swimsuit

    "– by this sun of York"

cut to Lucy in a cloth cap, feeding a Yorkshire pudding to a whippet.

EXTERIOR. BOSWORTH FIELD. LUCY WORSLEY DRESSED AS KNIGHT IN ARMOUR

Lucy: But what, you may ask, was the TRUE HISTWEE of the Battle of Bosworth? Alas, there was an awful lot of bloodshed –

cut to a pool of blood

cut to a garden shed

    – that day. First the Yorkists were chased –

Lucy runs along the field, a look of mild alarm on her face, as she continues talking to camera

    – all the way to this hedge. And then the Lancastrians started to massacre them, so that they all fell over –

Lucy falls over

close up of Lucy with a little bit of mud daintily smeared on both cheeks

    – and the slaughter was HORRENDOUS

close up of Lucy putting on sad face

    – and the battle was lost!

INTERIOR. MEDICAL LAB. LUCY DRESSED AS MORTUARY ATTENDANT

Lucy: I'm now holding an old skull from the battle.

Lucy puts on "yucky" face

Lucy: And so, Dr Tompkins, I suppose this proves that whoever this skull belonged to is now dead?

Dr Tompkins: That's right, Lucy. And he's probably been dead quite some little while.

Lucy: Super! Smashing! Goody, goody gum-drops!

INTERIOR. TOWER OF LONDON

Lucy: Here I am dressing up as a real-life Yeoman of the Guard!!!! Golly gosh, what an awful lot of buttons there were to do up! What you never see in the histwee books is that in the olden days there were no such things as zips – which is probably why all those Kings and Queens were always losing their tempers!!!

    So, Keith, you've been a Yeoman for these past forty years, is that right?

Keith the Yeoman (*proudly*): That's right.

Lucy: So could you do me up at the back, please? Super!

EXTERIOR. TOWER OF LONDON. LUCY IN HER YEOMAN'S OUTFIT WITH HER HEAD ON THE EXECUTIONER'S BLOCK

Lucy: So what we've learned is that, as far as histwee goes, there's really an awful lot at stake.

close up of a steak and chips

    Next time, I'll be explorwing the Legend of Robin –

close up of a little bird

    – Hood.

close up of Lucy in a hood

    And we'll be asking ourselves – who was the REAL FRIAR TUCK?

dressed as Maid Marian, Lucy mounts a white horse, and gallops away into the sunset, looking over her shoulder, whimsically.

As told to

CRAIG BROWN

DESPERATE BUSINESS

JON & MICK / MODERN TOSS

hello, we've come to repossess your buttock implants

alright if I store some of my rubbish in your garden till the next bin collection?

I was going to apply for a small business loan but I couldn't be arsed with all the paperwork

what do you reckon then?

yeah it looks a bit smaller than it did on your affordable homes website

nice dog mate

yeah it's a foodle, it's a cross between a fish and a poodle

'Too close to call' – Election sets Snoresbury alight

by Our
Political Staff
Peter O'Bore

No constituency in Britain can tell us more about the public mood than that comprising the rural industrial Midlands North Eastern market towns of Snoresbury and Dullsville.

Standing yesterday in Dullsbury high street, there was a deceptive air of calm, as nothing appeared to be happening and no one was there.

However, as I soon discovered, knowing that I had 1500 words to write, this was deceptive.

Away from the empty high street, I soon found plenty of evidence that this key marginal constituency was the best possible clue as to how dramatically Britain's political landscape has been transformed since the last election.

In 2015, Snoresville's result was a cliffhanger five-way split between Cameron's Tories, Miliband's Labour, Clegg's Lib Dems, Farage's Ukip and Sturgeon's SNP.

This time around, however, my soundings from reading the local paper, the Snoresbury Messenger (incorporating the Dullsville Advertiser) indicate that the result on June 8 could be very different.

For a start, it seems clear that the Ukip vote has collapsed, because their candidate, Dave Loon, has rejoined the Tories, saying, "I no longer have faith in the new leader, Paul Nutcase".

Equally on the back foot, it seems, is Labour's Patsy Jacket, a former Blairite, who now says she has no faith in Jeremy Corbyn as her party leader and has joined the Tories.

Hopes of a Lib Dem resurgence seem to be faltering, as their veteran candidate, Gay Sandals, has publicly admitted that he has no faith in his party leader Tim Farron and is thinking of defecting either to the Greens or the Tories.

As for the SNP's Alistair McGonagall, he has yet to surmount the problem of living 350 miles from his constituency, but he has also said that he is no longer quite so keen on his party leader Mrs Sturgeon, and is thinking seriously of joining the burgeoning revival of the Scottish Tory Party under Ruth Davidson.

This appears to leave the way clear for the Conservative candidate, Steve Selfie, a former Remainer-turned-passionate Hard Brexiteer, who says, "I have total faith in my party leader, Mrs May, who is the only one who can offer Britain stable and strong leadership – whoops, is that the right way round?"

My prediction, from careful reading of the runes *(surely you mean the Dullsbury Courier, incorporating the Snoresville Clarion? Ed.)* is that in the interests of making this article sound remotely worth reading, I had better say that this one will go down to the wire and at present looks too close to call.

"You've met someone else, haven't you?"

ME AND MY TEAM
by Prime Minister Theresa May and My Team

I want you to know just why I think it is so important that everyone in Britain votes for me and my team on 8 June. This is because only me and my team can offer a strong and stable leadership rather than a coalition of chaos.

Who are my team? Let me introduce them:

 ■ Firstly of course there is the prime minister, the person who is overall in charge of everything. And that, of course, is me.

 ■ Then there is the person in charge of the economy. I'm afraid Mr Hammond has rather let me down as Chancellor, so this again has to be me.

 ■ Then there is the person in charge of foreign affairs. Again, I'm afraid Mr Johnson has really let me down, by being even more embarrassing as Foreign Secretary than I thought he would be. So it's me again in charge of that one.

 ■ As for the person in charge of home affairs, since I myself was Home Secretary for longer than anyone in history, it would be ridiculous to think that Amber Rudd would know what to do. So, I'm afraid, that's me again!

 ■ And the most important job of all for my team, of course, is Brexit. This is so vital that it would be irresponsible to leave it to Mr Davis, who obviously doesn't know what he's doing, let alone– God help us – Mr Fox. So I'm afraid, once again, there is no alternative but for me to take on the mantle of responsibility.

That's what we call real teamwork in the new Toresa Party! REMEMBER! ON 8 JUNE – VOTE FOR MRS ME!

The Nottingham Herald
Friday 19 May 1194

Radical Manifesto Leaked

by Our Political Staff Richard Little John

THE self-proclaimed outlaw and champion of the common man, Robin Hood, last night launched an investigation into the leaking of his controversial manifesto in which he laid out his policy of "stealing from the rich to give to the poor".

The manifesto has been widely condemned by the Sheriff of Nottingham, who said, "Robin is trying to turn the clock back to the bad old days of the 1170s".

He continued, "It's a total shambles. Hood and his coalition of chaotic but merry men have not costed any of their proposals and his definition of what constitutes a rich person will lead to unjustifiable attacks on anyone carrying a large bag of silver and riding through Sherwood Forest."

The sheriff said that hard-working professionals would

be targeted, including "lawyers, merchants, money lenders, apothecaries, bishops and, in particular, sheriffs".

He concluded by promising that only he and his team offered strong and stable feudal oppression and that he would have no alternative but to hold Maid Marion hostage until Hood "came to his senses".

Hood (formerly Robin of Triple Locksley), however, defended his manifesto, saying that it was hardly radical to try and bring about a redistribution of wealth in a country where the poorest serf earned less than 0.0000001 percent of a king's ransom.

He promised to continue fighting until he got his message across – probably attached to an arrow hitting the Sheriff of Nottingham in the head.

Sarah Vain
Putting the 'I' in 'The Mail'

DID you see that amazing interview on the One Show with the brilliant Mrs May and her lovely hubby, Phil?

I tell you, it's definitely the worst job in the world being married to the prime minister.

And I should know, because I nearly was.

The May marriage sounds very much like life chez Gove.

Michael does the boy jobs, like writing boring columns for the Times, and I do the girl jobs, like writing about Mrs May's gorgeous legs in the Daily Mail.

They were a lovely couple and I hope that if Mrs May reads this, she will remember "my Philip" in her post-election reshuffle.

Then I can once again write pieces about how I am married to a famous and powerful politician.

***

DID you see that Joanna Lumley say that she dyes her own hair, rather than having it done professionally? So do I, but I don't feel it necessary to tell the world about it.

***

DID you see that the new thing in the celebrity fashion world is rib cages? I've got one of those. But I've also got a brain, which means that I don't have to waste my time going on about women's rib cages. Honestly!

Philip Retires From Public Life

HE's been by her side through thick and thin, in moments of national crisis he's been her rock, but now it's time to call it a day. Philip is to step down from appearing in public after entertaining us all for literally minutes in a truly toe-curling *One Show* appearance.

His role was to stand in the shadows and make her look good, which he did right royally, but for any self-respecting husband there's a limit to how many inane interviews you can sit through, and that limit is one.

He's earned the right to a spell out of the limelight, and so we say to you, "Philip, thank you. You've done your bit and we now know everything we want to about you – if anything, a little too much. Whilst your

wife goes around the country waving regally at ordinary people held back behind security barriers, you can enjoy your well-deserved retirement from the spotlight. We certainly will." God Save The May Queen!

And now the end is near and so I face the final curtain ...

Rohny Balle

ASSANGE – SWEDISH POLICE DROP RAPE INVESTIGATION

59

Exclusive to all media (again)

THE ONLY PROPER RESPONSE TO TERRORISM IS THAT WE SHOULD CARRY ON AS NORMAL

THIS IS why we are devoting 24-hour coverage/ 94-page special editions to the Manchester terrorist atrocity, including deeply distressing interviews with victims and relatives, footage you may find disturbing (particularly when we repeat it six times an hour)

and wild speculation from dozens of experts who all say that it's too early to speculate but that everyone should be very, very afraid.

Which unfortunately leaves no time or room for coverage of any other news or anything else that would normally be normal.

"I see Corbyn's left a tribute"

R&J

EYE TERROR UPDATE

1 BBC To Suspend Manchester Coverage For Respectful Pause To Report On The Election

2 "Bomber Is A Terrorist Not A Muslim" Says Everyone, Hopefully

3 Prime Minister Announces 'Operation Stable Door' To Prevent Further Attacks Of The Type We Haven't Been Able To Prevent

4 Prime Minister Renames Operation 'Strong And Stable Door' To Reassure Public That It Is Non-Political

5 "We Can't Afford To Keep An Eye On All The Suspects", Says

Government That Spends £35bn On Defence Annually

6 Public Shocked To See Armed Police On Train – "We Haven't Seen A Train For Years" Say Passengers

7 Rail Commuters Fear Attack In Quiet Carriage – "How Would We Raise The Alarm?"

8 Ring Of Steel Around Theresa May – Security Level Raised To "Crick"

9 "I Was Thinking Of Going To Manchester Some Time This Year But I Didn't" Says Lucky Survivor

10 Much, much, much, much, more …

YOUR facebook GUIDE TO MAKING A BOMB

1 Set up Facebook
2 Get billions of subscribers
3 Rake in advertising revenue
4 Fail to moderate terrorist content
5 Show how to make a bomb
6 Make a bomb
7 Er, That's it

ARMY PRESENCE AT FLOWER SHOW – PUBLIC REASSURED

SOCIAL MEDIA TERROR ROUND-UP

Why does she get attention?

■ THERE was total disbelief on social media at all the attention Katie Hopkins was getting after she posted two highly offensive tweets following the Manchester bombings.

"Why is this vile woman trending all day on Twitter?" said all Twitter users, retweeting her tweets with demands that Twitter users ignore her.

"It's almost as if Katie Hopkins' whole career is based on her posting offensive tweets to maintain her media profile, knowing we'll spend all day talking about how we shouldn't be talking about her," said all Twitter users.

Hopkins insisted her demands – that vile extremists who preach hatred be removed – were now clearly being heard, after LBC promptly up and sacked her from her radio show.

Why aren't you talking about another atrocity?

■ THE online outpouring of grief about Manchester was condemned by some Twitter users who managed to find another atrocity in another country that wasn't being as well reported.

"Why isn't there the same

outpouring of grief for this other atrocity you haven't heard about? It's almost as if you people are only concerned about the atrocity on your own doorstep (which you have heard of)."

It was later confirmed beyond a shadow of a doubt that these individuals are the sort of people who tell you the ending to movies you've yet to see, and who leave passive aggressive notes in the fridge at work.

Person on Twitter 'has all the answers'

■ THERE was a joyous reaction amongst world leaders grappling with the problem of IS and the terror threat to the news that a Twitter user with 874 followers had all the answers to stopping ISIS.

"We have grappled with this seemingly intractable problem for years," said all Western leaders, "but then along came TruthSpeak345 with his answer all neatly wrapped up in 140 characters."

"In fact, that's wrong," said TruthSpeak whose tweet solving everything had been Rt'd over two hundred times. "I actually needed only 66 characters to solve everything."

That Tweet In Full
We must come together now as one community to hate the moose limbs.

60

THE ENEMY WITHIN

Those subtle, hard-to-spot indicators that your neighbour may be an Islamist terrorist

1. Quiet, studious type who keeps himself to himself

2. Apart from putting Isis flag in window

3. And tendency to scream "Death to the West" as he puts out bins

4. Complains he has been banned from local mosque for being too extreme

5. Frequently shows you holiday snaps from Libya and Syria

6. Members of his family are known Jihadis

7. Orders bomb online from Ocado and flies into rage when strawberries are delivered as nearest substitute

8. Friends regularly warn you that they are alarmed by his obvious radicalisation

9. Establishes caliphate in back garden

10. Is not detained at any point by MI5 who declare him "below the radar", "known up to a point" and "only reported to us as dangerous by US intelligence".

FORTRESS BRITAIN IN TOTAL LOCKDOWN

by Our Terror Staff **Phil Withdread**

AS Britain battens down the hatches and calls the army onto the streets, a state of national emergency has been declared.

With the terrorism threat at its highest possible level, the entire nation is gripped by panic. The mood across the country is one of extreme fear and anxiety, as the public stay outside, take off their tops and go sun-bathing.

Inside, the pubs are silent and empty, as everyone is on the pavement, knocking back their pints, and dining al fresco.

In newspaper offices the

atmosphere remains tense and foreboding, as editors insist on wall-to-wall fear and misery, despite what appears to be a population that is refusing to over-react to terrorism unlike all the newspapers *(You're fired! Ed.)*

"I'm afraid it's my trombosis again!"

A Viss

LIB DEMS BACK WEED

Hello!

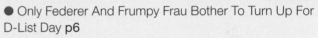

Jeremy Corbyn WRITES

HELLO! Well, here we go again! Who couldn't have predicted that when I started talking about international defence that the hated mainstream media would smear me by quoting words I've said?

It's the usual "He's just a pacifist!" and "He'll never commit to any conflict because he's against war!" nonsense. Yawn!

As I claimed this week, I am not a pacifist, and just because, at that precise moment, I couldn't name a British war I approved of post-1945, doesn't mean to say I can't come up with a few, given a few days thinking time mooching around my allotment.

So here is my list of justified UK wars...

1) Robot wars It's clear that the house robots, Sir Killalot, Sergeant Bash and Matilda are the clear aggressors here. So, even though I would look for a peaceful solution with NATO first, I fully approve of the Jenkins family from Croydon pitching their home-made, colander-based effort in the arena. There's something about their futile struggle against impossible odds that really strikes a chord with me!

2) War by U2 A great effort by our boys. The great thing about this war was that it was concluded without any casualties (though I think Bono's feelings were hurt during the NME offensive in '83).

3) The Northern Irish War Is this a war? I know, in terms of British troops killing the IRA, it was "cold-blooded murder of freedom fighters during an occupation", but let's not forget when it was the other way round it was actually "a terrible miscarriage of justice", so let's mark that one up as a half!

4) The Civil War in the Labour Party. This one's my favourite! I know I deplore any conflict with casualties, but as most of them are Blairites, I think it's a price worth paying that they lay down their political lives so that I can prove I'm right!

Anyway, apart from that, not a bad week, apart from running over a BBC cameraman! He shouted "foot!" at me, but at least for once he didn't mean Michael.

Cheerio!

The Eye's Controversial New Columnist

The columnist who not only addresses the elephant in the room, he is also prepared to hug it until it squeaks

This week I am very angry about the news that twin girls have been born to the Clooneys. Every news story I have seen has described them as "babies"! Speaking as a baby *(see photo)*, I know how frustrating it is just to be pigeonholed this way. Just because I am extremely young, have no hair and wear nappies, I am immediately referred to as a "baby" in coverage, rather than a columnist, wit, raconteur, novelist, Twitter pundit, intellectual and close friend of royalty. I sincerely hope that these girls' parents, the ruggedly vacant actor Mr Clooney and his glamorous clothes-horse wife, Mrs Clooney, take this seriously, and take time out from their busy schedule of wearing sunglasses, posing for pictures and making speeches about things they know nothing about, to protect their children from such mindless pigeonholing from the lazy mainstream *(cont. p94)*

Parallel lines give you headaches

by Our Medical Staff **Anna Din**

A NEW study into the causes of migraines has shown that prolonged exposure to parallel lines can give you the most appalling headache.

The survey was conducted amongst commuters at Haywards Heath, who were forced to stare hopefully at a set of parallel tracks for hours and hours without any interruption, causing 90% of them to cry out in agony, "For God's sake, where's my train?"

The symptoms include headache, nausea, hypertension, and writing a stiff letter to Southern Rail asking if it would be possible to get compensation for the non-arrival of the 7.37 Brighton to Nowhere. *(That's enough. Ed.)*

From The Message Boards

Members of the online community respond to the major issues of the day...

Sgt Pepper's 50th anniversary

Guys, Sgt Pepper is fifty, the same age as yours truly! My parents bought it when it came out and I took it to boarding school years later. This didn't go down well with the Genesis fans and rugger rags, and when they weren't flushing my head in the lavatory (hence the nickname!) they were trashing my Beatles records. My copy is thus adorned with a cartoon penis and the legend SGT BOGBRUSH LONELY TWAT BAND – the title by which my daughter Charlotte still refers to it! – *Bogbrush*

remember i posted befor about my copy of sargent pepper in the sleeve of dawns greatest hit's wich I got at a car boot for 50p? well i recken your copy is even more rarer bogbrush ive never seen one with them rude thing's on it? mite be worth a few bob 👍 – *record fan*

As I've told you before, there is nothing collectable or valuable about this sort of thing. You might consider yourself a 'record fan', but you are a laughing stock on all the serious collector forums. – *PCS 3042*

soon as i heard about the terrist attack i posted a video of myself singing all you need is love wich say's it better than word's ever can. some people said it was unapropriate and it was too soon but i wanted to give something back to the comunity – *special one*

Your behaviour WAS inappropriate. 'All You Need Is Love' was not on Sgt Pepper, whose anniversary we are officially celebrating. It was also too soon, as its own anniversaries are not until 25 June (when it was performed live on the 'Our World' broadcast) and 7 July, when it was released (Parlophone R 5620). – *PCS 3042*

The anniversary box set features a so-called 'reproduction' of the original sleeve. Using a magnifying glass, compare the full stops in 'E.M.I.' and 'Gramophone Co. Ltd.' on the two versions, and you will see that their size has been altered by about 10%. Some people will no doubt say I am nit-picking, but it ruined the whole thing for me. – *The Music Man*

In 1967, I wrote to The Beatles Monthly Book to say how pleased I was that Strawberry Fields Forever failed to reach number one. Why? Because the Beatles had cheated by taking drugs, and in my opinion they should have been stripped of all their gold discs, like they do with athletes. I was glad to see a clean singer like Engelbert Humperdinck top the charts instead, even if he was foreign. – *Sandra*

Humperdinck was from Leicester, which wasn't a foreign city last time I looked at a map. – *Gerard*

go there now mate and see what you think – *uk toilet of the world*

Great stuff guys! – *Bogbrush*

"Don't worry, Mum, you'll make friends soon"

DEMENTIA TEST

Do you know who the Prime Minister is?

It's too close to call

The correct answer to this question is: "Paul Dacre"

A Doctor Writes

AS A doctor, I'm often asked by the Prime Minister, "Doctor, do I have dementia? I keep forgetting simple things, like the fact that older people do not like having all their money taken away from them..."

The simple answer is yes, she does appear to be exhibiting signs of memory loss which form a worrying pattern, ie the patient forgot that she was a Remain supporter, she forgot that she had promised not to have an election, she forgot she had promised not to raise national insurance, etc, etc.

This condition is known as "Maggielomania" (or *Dux Potens Hubristicus*, to give it the full Latin name).

If you are worried about dementia, you should leave all your money to the government by making a will, in which Mrs May inherits everything. This is called "The Will of the People" and your savings will be donated to Mrs May's new charity "Dignitas In Old Age".
© *A real doctor.*

SOCIAL CARE
THERESA MAY REVEALS NEW CAP

D

"Right – let's post that up on mylifesbetterthanyours.com"

Despot calls Qatari black

by BBC24's **Qatty Qay**

THE world of pots and kettles and also the Middle East was plunged into chaos last night, when the King of Saudi Arabia, Salman al-Rushdi, lashed out at his fellow Gulf State ruler, the Emir of Qatar, for using his country's colossal wealth to sponsor radical Islamist terrorism across the region:

"It is outrageous for this despotic hereditary ruler, who is supposed to be a leader in the fight against terrorism, to be now sending huge sums of money to fund ruthless Jihadis. That is my job."

LATE NEWS

Qataris accused of having financial links with dangerous international organisation called FIFA.

YES, IT'S 1789 ALL OVER AGAIN AS REVOLUTION ROCKS FRANCE

by Our Entire Staff
Jean-Paul Dacre

FRANCE was hit last night by the most sensational political upset since the Parisian mob stormed the Bastille.

The country will never be the same again, as the population delivered a death blow to the sclerotic political establishment which has ruled it for more than half a century.

Both of France's major political parties were wiped out in a deliberate rejection of everything they had stood for – the rule of a tiny self-perpetuating elite which had totally lost touch with the concerns and interests of the French people.

Above all, millions of ordinary, hard-working French patriots rose up as one to say "non, non, non" to the moneyed and privileged denizens of the Parisian bubble who had contemptuously ignored and patronised them to the point where they could take it no longer.

That is why they now look set to elect as their President a complete outsider, who can lead France into a new and very different world.

Emmanuel Macron is quite unlike anyone who has ever stood for president before. He was educated at the Ecole Nationale d'Administration, he was an investment banker with Rothschild, served as Economy Minister under President Hollande and is 100 percent a supporter of the EU.

Yes, last night they were singing in the streets of Paris the new National Anthem *"Allons Macron pour la patrie, le jour de gloire est arrivé".*

⚑⚑ French Election ⚑⚑
THE GAP NARROWS

by Our Paris Correspondent **Philippe Espace**

FRANCE was in a state of shock last night, as it was revealed that the age gap between the French presidential candidate, Emmanuel Macron, and his wife, Brigitte Trogneux, is a mere 25 years.

Said one French expert, "It is nothing. For us French people, this is no big deal. It is hardly a gap at all. You English are so... how you say... buttoned up and repressed. She is what we call 'a cougar', and he is a europhile candidate of the centre-left attempting to redefine French

politics. What is your problem?"

Political sexperts see the gap narrowing as they get older. They point out that, at the moment, Madame Trogneux is nearly twice the age of her spouse. But in 40 years' time, he will be three-quarters her age, which is very different.

Marine Le Pen commented that it was unfair to bring people's elderly relatives into the election. She said, "Can you imagine if people remembered that my father is 88 and a convicted anti-semitic fascist?!"

63

 HUSBAND

POETRY CORNER

In Memoriam
Edward Albee, playwright

So. Farewell
Then Edward Albee.
Your most famous
Play was *Who's Afraid
Of Virginia Woolf?*
About a married
Couple having a
Long argument.

I thought it was
Brilliant, but my
Partner was too
Stupid to get the
Point and was very
Rude to me.

Honestly. Women.
She can't see the
Point of anything
And just goes on
And on, contradicting
Everything I say.

She even thought
That Richard Burton
And Elizabeth Taylor
Were overrated in
The film.

Honestly.
I give up.
(Curtain)

Edward J. Thribbee (17½)

In Memoriam
Adam West, TV's Batman

So. Farewell
Then Adam West,
The first
And greatest
Batman.

Your departure is
A real blow.
KAPOW!!!

Your outfit was
Mainly pants.
OOF!!!
But you were not.

Now you have a
New set of wings.
FLAP!!!
"Holy Trinity, Batman!"

Altogether now:
"Dinner, dinner, dinner,
Dinner, dinner, dinner,
Dinner, dinner, Batman!"

E.J. Thribb,
aka Bardman (17½)

GLENDA SLAGG

Chelsea Flower Show's Not-So-Shrinking Violet!!?!!?!

■ KNEES-UP, Mother Macron!!??!! Sacré bleu, Brigitte, don't you think you're a bit old to go flautin' your pins in a short skirt? It's the G7 summit darling, not the Folies Bergère!!?!! Put them away Ms Ooh-La-Leggy – your toy-boy-teacher's-pet may want an eyeful tour (geddit?!! Like "Eiffel Tower"), but we'd prefer Notre Dame to cover herself up!!!?! Geddit????!!!

■ HATS and trousers off to beautiful, pouting, sexy Brigitte Trogneux?!!!?! Or Brigitte Bar-olegs, as I call you. (Geddit???!!! Like "Bare Legs"!!??!!) At last, there's a mature madame who's not afraid to show that she's got legs that go all the way to the top – ie the President of France!!!??!! OK, so she's 97 *(subs, please check)*, but she's still the Bee's Knees (Geddit??!!?!) and the sexiest sextagenerian at the G7 summit??!!!?!?

■ ORLANDO Bloom – what a bloomin' nerve more like!??!! Tolkien's Legolas got his legover (Geddit??!!) with a fruity waitress at the glamorous eaterie The Chiltern Fire Brigade *(subs, please check)* and guess what??!?? As soon as he's got her in the sack, she gets the sack!!?!!?! And he swans off back to LaLaLand with another notch on his elfin bow!!?!?!

■ ORLANDO Bloom – what a bloomin' marvel!??!! There aren't many A-list celebrities who ring up and apologise after they've got you sacked for getting them in the sack!!??! *(You've done this, Ed.)* Orlando is a true English gent, like the character he plays in the Pirates of Penzance *(subs, please check)*!!?!! As for the willing waitress, here's a tip from Auntie Glenda!!??! Try keeping your knickers on, love, until after pudding!!??!!!

■ Seen Pirates of the Caribbean 94???!??? Me neither. Zzzzzzzzzz.

Byeee!!

That Harvard Honorary Degree Citation In Full

SALUTAMUS JUDI DENCHUS GRANDISSIMA DAMA THEATRICA ET STELLA CINEMATICA VICTOR BAFTARUM ET OSCARUM MULTORUM, PER EXEMPLUS REGINA ELISABETHA PRIMA IN "SHAKESPERIUS IN LUVVI", SED CELEBRITISSIMA "M" IN FRANCHISI INTERMINABILE JACOBUS BONDUS VIZ "OCULUS AUREAM", "QUANTUM SOLATIUM" ET CETERA ET CETERA ET FINALITER "CAELUM CADENZA" , TREASOR NATIONALIS ET HOSPES REGULARA IN COLLOQUIUM GRAHAMI NORTONI IN TELEVISIONE. AMAMUS DAMUS JUDI NUNC DOCTOR ARTIS IN UNIVERISTATUM HARVARDIS! GAUDEAMUS IGITUR!

© Universitatum Harvardis 2017.

Notes & queries

My grandson follows President Trump on Twitter and asked me what is the meaning of 'covfefe'?

The Reverend G. Whizz, Santa Barbara, Cartland.

● As a proud Greek American and honorary secretary of the All-American Hellenic Baking Federation, I have to say the answer is obvious! A covfefe is a delicious Greek pastry made with honey and almonds, somewhat like Baklava, but flavoured with a dash of Notaxa brandy. It comes originally from the Cycladian island of Argos and is said to have been served to Odysseus himself by the Argossians after the weary travellers had been tempted by the famous Argos catalogue of irresistible cake-style delicacies. We here in Pumpernickel, New Dworkin, still produce the finest covfefe this side of Mount Olympus-Trip. *Milos "Miley" Cyros, Maryland.*

● Mr Cyros is sadly mistaken and may have eaten too many of his own brandy-laced pastries! Covfefe, as anyone with the most basic knowledge of Washington politics would know, is an acronym for an extremely important government security organisation, similar to the British COBRA. The President was clearly calling an urgent meeting of COVFEFE, the Committee of Very Frightening Events Facing Everyone, which is held in a secret bunker five miles underground, beneath the Pentagon. Those attending are hand-picked representatives of the most important people in the United States, who would guarantee the post-apocalypse survival of American life and culture. They include the leaders of Congress, all the Chiefs of Staff, Bill Gates, Tiger Woods, Ronald McDonald and the cryogenically frozen head of the late Walt Disney. Covfefe is so secret that only I know of its existence. *Professor Al Trite, Editor of the Washington Post-Truth.*

● I hope the good Professor takes more care fact-checking his own newspaper! Covfefe is, of course, an insult in Yiddish and has long been incorporated into American inner-city slang. You will remember the scene in Woody Allen's early, New York-based comedy *Fake Jews*, where the hero, Woogy Hallen, says to the art gallery owner, Alan Woodee, "You're such a covfefe, already!". It means something like a "schmuck" or a "Louise Mensch", but is not as offensive as a "trumpf". The President clearly meant to cast aspersions on the ability of the press to tell the truth as he sees it. *Rabbi Al Obama, Banjo-on-Knee, Louisiana.*

Answers please:

Is a Macron bigger than a Micron? Is Fergal Keane? How Holy is Moly?

"Yeah, I'm pretty old school"

Election Special

MAY FINALLY UNITES BREXIT BRITAIN

Leave! Leave! Leave! Leave! Leave! Leave!

Exclusive to all newspapers

INCREDIBLE, BRILLIANT GENIUS CORBYN GETS ONLY NINE SEATS FEWER THAN DISASTROUS NEIL KINNOCK DID IN 1992

On Other Pages

● Useless Loser May Gets Only Two Million More Votes Than Brilliant Moderniser David Cameron ● Political Pygmy Farron Only Wins Four More Seats Than Serious Political Figure Nick Clegg ● Washed-Up Nicola Sturgeon Only Wins More Than Half Of All Seats She Stood For

"Obviously, it's been a disappointing night..."

WHAT WILL HAPPEN NEXT?

by **Someone Who Got It All Wrong Last Time**

MAKE no mistake, this is a seismic shift in British politics which I, for one saw coming but didn't think I'd mention.

The signs were there for all to read but nobody to actually remark upon, and that's how we've got to where we are. It's easy to look back with hindsight and say "I got it all wrong", but that doesn't help anyone – it's the future we've got to focus on, as I did in the past when I used all my experience to predict a hung parliament with a majority of just 100 seats for the Conservatives. And a Labour collapse ending in Corbyn's resignation, and a new SDP-style Party run by Peter Mandelson, Nick Clegg and a fully vindicated Tony Blair.

But now let there be no doubt Theresa May is in it for the long haul *(subs, please check if she's resigned)*. Her skilful deal making will allow the DUP-Tory Alliance to negotiate a Brexit deal which will be hard/strong/stable/weak/wobbly/chaotic/cancelled *(subs, please delete as appropriate)*.

Senior insiders in Downing Street ask me privately, "Do you know what's going on? Because we haven't got a bloody clue." My other sources in the opposition camp confide "We haven't got a bloody clue, do you know what's going on?"

However, my detailed research, involving asking a number of my children if there's anything on social media that I should have read, points to an amusing meme of Mrs May to the music of Stormzy.

So in my considered view, we are in for a rough ride, a period of stability, and the resurgence of a Centrist, far-right, left-wing coalition led by Nigel Farage, Vince Cable and Laura Kuenssberg.

It may be time for me to have a holiday, but one thing's for sure, by this time next week I will still be here, writing something completely different while pretending I know exactly what's going on. And that prediction, trust me, will be 100% right. *(You're fired. Ed.)*

Nursery Times

.... Friday, Once-upon-a-time ....

PIED PIPER CAPTURES YOUNG FOLLOWERS

by Our Youth Culture Correspondents **The Brothers Grime**

THERE was shock in Hamelin this morning, as the self-styled saviour of the city led his band of young supporters on what he described as a "new and exciting journey".

The Pied Piper of Corbyn defied expectations by attracting young people, much to the surprise of the city elders. Said one, "I can't believe the kids fell for him, he's just playing the same old tunes, but with a grime beat, and offering them a brighter future, without tuition fees. I mean it's a total fairy tale."

The Pied Piper had previously been successful at ridding the town of rats, or "Blairite Scum", as his followers called them, but had not been given his due reward. As a result he has targeted the young. Said one fan of the Piper's music, "Corbynzy's the best! He's decent! He's authentic! And he makes great jam! Which he assures us we'll have tomorrow."

Said another, "We'll follow him wherever he goes – I don't know how this will end up, but the Pied Piper promises us we'll all live happily ever after."

A Message from Boris Johnson Prime Minister (whoops – steady on folks – slip of the proverbial pen) Foreign Sec!

CRIPES, nobody saw that coming. By which I don't mean another chance for yours truly to have a crack at the top job. Heavens, no. Nothing could be further from my mind. Haven't given it a second's thought. Me at Number 10. Imagine! Bozza as boss man! No way Jose (Prime Minister of Italy, I think)!

No, time for everyone to calm down and get a grip on that knife. I mean get a grip! Just because Theresa performed disappointingly on the night.

It happens – I should know. Everyone's gone doolally saying that she's the most disastrous PM in history and there's only one person who could possibly save the party and we don't mean Amber Rudd!

Now listen, to repeat such suggestions would be utterly disloyal, as would be to retell the story of Cincinnatus, the great Roman who assured everyone he didn't want to be leader and then was recalled from ploughing his neighbour's wives. Or was it fields? I forget.

Anyway, the point of the story is that the noble Roman may have stepped into the breach and answered the call, and saved the day, but there's no obvious comparison between him and Boriatus Maximus, who succeeded the Empress Mayhem on the grounds of being a safe pair of trousers.

So just because my first recorded words were "Boris for Prime Minister!" doesn't mean that yours truly is on the blower to everyone trying to organise a coup.

Now is not the time for a leadership challenge. Next Tuesday would be much better because I've got to go to a barbecue this weekend and then I've got a cricket match, so Bozza might be bladdered for a couple of days rather than focusing on my first PMQs.

PS. May I be the first to welcome with open arms my old friend and sparring partner, Michael Gove, aka The Govester, Govey-Boy, Judas! Just kidding Michael, there's only room for one disloyal shit around here. And that's The Bozmeister, Bozza-Boy, Judas!

"Theresa May's been running through the wheat again"

IT'S THE SUN WOT HAD NO EFFECT AT ALL!

YES, folks, you read it here first. Your lovable current bun has absolutely no influence on anything at all.

Hang on! Bloody hell! Why am I spending all this money then? We spend months, make that years, telling the gullible working-class Poms exactly how they should vote, and the bloody whingeing bastards go and do the opposite.

Jeez, that's not democracy!

That's sheer bloody mindedness. I mean we make it so bloody simple for them – we don't even bother with words, we just use pictures. Corbyn with an ISIS flag up his bum.

Strewth – what don't they get?! The white van brigade just aren't paying attention anymore. Maybe it's time to put the knockers back on Page 3!

I feel better already! Rupe, you're a genius – give yourself a tax-free pay rise!

FRIDAY, JUNE 16, 2017

ENEMIES OF THE PEOPLE

THESE unelected members of the public have betrayed Britain.

Defying the will of the people as told to them by Paul Dacre, these unpatriotic, disloyal, traitorous voters have proved themselves to be completely out-of-touch with ordinary people like Paul Dacre, and have come up with an indefensible decision to express their own point of view, which threatens all that Paul Dacre holds dear.

They're trapped in a bubble of normal life and no longer understand what is really going on in Paul Dacre's head. Surely it's time for them all to stand down in shame and give power

back to the people who matter, ie Paul Dacre.

These saboteurs must be crushed before they inflict any further damage on Paul Dacre and his strongly held belief that nine pages of bonkers bile about Jeremy Corbyn's desire to establish a Caliphate in Islington does anything but increase the Labour vote. *(You're fired, I've finally read this paper – Lord Rothermere)*

London Evening Standard

HA HA HA HA HA HA

On other pages Ha ha ha ha ha ha ha ha ha ha ha ha ha ha ha ha
Tomorrow Ha ha ha ha ha ha ha ha ha ha ha ha ha ha ha ha ha again

TO CLARIFY, I HAVE ALWAYS THOUGHT JEREMY IS WONDERFUL

by All Labour MPs

A LOT of Labour members have been asking me exactly what my opinions on Jeremy Corbyn are, in light of the fact that Labour has gained seats in this election. I wish to make a few things clear.

I would like to clarify that when, in August 2015, I said that "Jeremy Corbyn is a spineless, IRA-loving, Hamas-appeasing, peacenik who would hand the keys to Trident over to Putin in a heartbeat", what I really meant was that I have an immense and deep respect for his credentials as a muscular pacifist, and there's no question the UK's nuclear arsenal would be safe in his hands, if indeed we think we need one. *(Jeremy, if you're reading this, please do answer my calls.)*

Furthermore, when I stated in July 2016 that "this nasty, toxic clot is dragging a once-proud party along a one-way road to electoral oblivion", what I was trying to say was that only Jeremy's unique mixture of vision and style could help Labour make substantial gains at the ballot box, and that he is an electoral genius to rival Disraeli, Churchill and Tony Blair, although obviously his views are much more sound than all the above. *(I've left three voicemails, but in case you didn't get them, I'll ring again now.)*

Finally, when I described him last week as a "Pathetic Commie hangover just desperate to nationalise everything he can, so thickos like him don't feel left out", what I meant to say is that he is a master tactician, the Che Guevara of Islington North, and I can only humbly say that I would be honoured to serve in his shadow cabinet in any capacity whatsoever. *(Still waiting. Please do ring, JC.)*

HAMMOND SURVIVES CAR CRASH

by Our Disaster Correspondent **Ian Ferno**

THERE was a lucky escape for one of Britain's least popular TV personalities, when he emerged unscathed from one of the most spectacular car crashes ever seen on television.

Spectators gasped as Philip Hammond walked away from the flames that only seconds before had threatened to engulf him.

Said one, "One minute he was in the driving seat, with everything apparently under control, the next moment the wheels had come off, he was on the skids, and heading downhill fast."

Said another, "To be honest, we all thought Jezza would be the one to go down in flames, he was steering so wildly to the left, but instead he went on to finish second in the race, or as he put it, 'win a famous victory'."

Mr Hammond was in no doubt as to what had caused the crash, "It was a disaster waiting to happen – I blame May."

(That's enough political motoring metaphor wrangling. Ed.)

FEMINISTS OUTRAGED AT BANK OF ENGLAND'S NEW AIRBRUSHED JANE AUSTEN £10 NOTE

PRESIDENT MACRON IN VERSAILLES

From The Message Boards

Members of the online community respond to the major issues of the day...

Manspreading banned

In The Year Of Our Lord Two Thousand And Seventeen, Madrid's transport leaders did no more than ban 'Manspreading', whereby men do no more than sit with their legs apart, invading the personal space of others. Inasmuch and insofar as they did so do, then they did no more than The Lord, who did no more than berate the wicked powerful man 'spreading himself like a green bay tree'. (Psalm 37:35) – *Mr Salmon*

I am a MAN. I take the tube to the City. My long muscular legs are at 90 degrees, allowing my 14-inch dick to rest comfortably after servicing my beautiful wife. On my left a woman sighs loudly as my thigh presses hers. She shifts away from me and frowns, trying to suppress the passions I arouse. On my right a cringing cuck cowers and leans on his wife. She stares at me, angry with envy, knowing her four-eyed faggot husband can't satisfy her financially or sexually. The cuck's micropenis has the erection of its wretched life as I crush his feeble leg. The woman opposite stares at her phone – anything to distract her eyes away from my crotch. Or is she secretly filming? – *Jay*

poof's with small bollock's sit with leg's together im no poof and my bollock's r fucking massive 😎 anyway wat about fat bird's with big arse's and shoping bag's? – *bonksy*

Without condoning your sexist language, it's true that the 'manspreading' narrative is insufficiently socio-sexuo-gender-nuanced. As a Reader in Sexual Cultures, I am mindful of the full spectrum of genital behaviours, be they 'male', 'female', or trans. While it is possible that extremely large penises or scrotums (or labia) could make it difficult to sit with legs closed, this is highly unusual. There are, however, more common socio-sexual factors which could physically impinge, be they mainstream (penazzling, enhancement underwear, penis weights) or sexuality-specific (genital cages, etc). To answer your second point with an everyday example that I used recently on Woman's Hour – a 350lb woman identifying as, say, exhibitionist and femdom (straight or lesbian) may find it physically impossible to rest bags on her lap while wearing a strap-on dildo. – *Dr Sarah Reeves*

My husband and I are in our sixties and have many hobbies, including real ale, non-league football, swinging and dogging. I am a sprightly "womanspreader" and can still open my legs 180 degrees! The last time I did this was on a night bus in Birmingham. I took up five seats at the back, and the only people who complained were the ones who didn't get a go on me before we reached our stop. 😄 I plan to go for the world record to raise money for Help For Heroes, but I haven't had a reply from the bus company yet. – *Gilfy Gracie*

THAT DAVIS/ BARNIER SUMMIT IN FULL

by Our Brexit Staff **Quentin Lettscelebratethismarvellousday**

AT LAST, the great day has arrived when Britain begins to throw off her shackles of the European tyranny which has enslaved us for 44 years.

Yesterday's Britain's Mr Brexit, David Davis, squared up across the table to the EU's top negotiator, Michael Barnier.

It was a clash of the Titans. Mr Davis opened the proceedings with a no-nonsense speech that made Britain's position crystal clear.

"The British people," he said, "are fed up with being told what to do by foreigners, and have voted unequivocally that they wish from now on to decide their future for themselves.

"That is why," he continued, "we would be grateful if you could tell us how we are going to leave the EU and exactly what sort of a 'relationship' you are prepared to allow us when we've left."

Monsieur Barnier, visibly shaken by Davis's trenchant broadside, could only stammer in reply, "Mr Davis, I think we'd better begin with this agenda I've drawn up here."

So saying, he pushed across the table a 550-page document headed *"What the UK must do since it is obvious that they don't have a plan".*

"If you look at the first page," said Barnier politely, "you will notice that the first item which has to be agreed before we can discuss anything else, is the little matter of the bill.

"As you will see, it amounts to a modest 2,000 billion euros, payable in instalments over the next two years."

At this point, Mr Davis exploded. He leaned across the table with a lantern jaw and declared in Churchillian tones, "Yes, Monsieur Barnier, that all seems fine. I'm sure we can scrape it together somehow, or the next government will."

And then Mr Davis launched his devastating bombshell.

"So now can we start discussing our new trade deal?" he demanded.

"Non," replied the intransigent Frenchman *(to be continued for the next two years)*

"Look at the Joneses pretending to get all the jokes in a Stoppard play"

H. D. HERNEMAN

QUEEN'S 'EU' HAT GIVES CODED MESSAGE

I'm a remainer

Tell me about it

CONCERN ABOUT CAPACITY OF ANTI-TERRORISM HOTLINE

Hello? Hello? Is anybody there?

May's shock new answer to suicide bombers

by Our Terror Staff
Phil Space

THE prime minister last night reacted to the latest terrorist outrage by unveiling her surprise new plan to deal with the threat of suicide bombers.

"There is only one way to stop these people who are prepared to die for their cause, and that is to put in place a real deterrent.

"What I am proposing is to introduce much longer custodial sentences for anyone found guilty of suicide bombing.

"Any would-be suicide bomber is really going to think twice if he is facing the prospect of as much as nine years in prison, possibly reduced to five for good behaviour – such as promising not to be a suicide bomber again when they are let out."

THAT SOCIAL MEDIA TERROR ATTACK CYCLE IN FULL

■ Reports of fresh terrorist atrocity

■ Hashtag 'Pray for *(insert city name attacked here)* immediately trends

■ Calls by police for gruesome images from the scene not to be posted

■ Numerous gruesome images from scene posted

■ Right-wing newspaper columnist tweets something offensive

■ The President of the United States tweets something more offensive

■ Tweets insisting *(insert city name here)* will never be cowed by terrorism RT'd thousands of times

■ Pictures of Eiffel Tower going dark/lit up YET AGAIN in colours of country targeted RT'd tens of thousands of times

■ Piers Morgan tweets

■ Everyone says just ignore the attention-seeking twit

■ No one ignores the attention-seeking twit

■ New terrorist atrocity happens

■ Hashtag Pray for *(insert city name)*

CONT. FOREVER...

THIS ISN'T GOOD ENOUGH. I DEMAND TO SPEAK TO A FRIEND OF YOURS PRETENDING TO BE YOUR SUPERVISOR.

Realistic complaint

Grenfell Tower Tragedy Why It Happened

Our team of experts (since yesterday) provide the definitive answers to the questions everyone is asking

Q. *Is the cladding to blame?*

A. Yes. According to Wikipedia, this type of cladding has caused previous fires in tower blocks above 94 storeys all over the world.

A good example was shown in the film *The Towering Inferno*, where fortunately all the main characters escaped in a helicopter.

Q. *Why wasn't a helicopter supplied by Kensington and Chelsea Borough Council to the residents of Grenfell Tower?*

A. According to this blog I've just read, it's all down to savage Tory cuts. Helicopters are, of course, very expensive and the residents of Grenfell Tower would not have been high on the priority list for one of the richest Tory boroughs in the country.

Q. *If we can just get back to the cladding, is it true that the panels used in Grenfell were banned, as we were told by the Chancellor of the Exchequer Philip Hammond?*

A. No. I've just read this piece by some technical expert which explains that the panels were perfectly legal.

Q. *So who is to blame?*

A. Well, there is going to be a full public inquiry, but this will probably not report before 2025. So, in the meantime, the consensus seems to be that it's all the fault of the heartless Tories, which is why Mrs May refused to hug any victims when she went there, leaving it to Jeremy Corbyn to show us what true compassion looks like by giving his backing to the "day of rage".

Q. *What should now be done for the dispossessed residents of the tower?*

A. The council should immediately requisition all the nearby properties owned by rich foreigners and fill them with the poor foreigners who used to live in Grenfell Tower until it was burned down by the Tories.

Q. *Where did you say you get your information? I've been following this story round the clock and I've never seen any of this stuff before.*

A. We rely on highly-placed experts, who cannot be named but who are permanently online, reading each other's blogs and claiming that there has been a massive anti-establishment cover-up of everything, the details of which cannot be revealed under the Official Secrets Act for at least 100 years.

Things That Won't Happen, No.94

THE OLD TIMES
1666
GREAT FIRE OF LONDON
'LESSONS WILL BE LEARNED' SAYS CAVALIER GOVERNMENT

BY DIARIST AND BLOGGER SAMUEL PEPYS

It started in Pudding Lane and quickly spread to the rest of London, causing destruction on an unprecedented scale.

The people of London reacted to the Great Fire with remarkable bravery and an impressive sense of community, but questions have been asked about the Cavaliers in charge. The Government failed to heed the warnings about the combustibility of the substance known in the building trade as "wood".

Said one expert, "This was a disaster waiting to happen, building all these houses on top of each other out of inflammable material with no fire exits."

The poor suffered the worst, crammed into their crowded dwellings, with little regard for their safety.

The Monarch put the

politicians to shame, and was swiftly on the scene, bringing comfort to survivors with a common touch, but the First Minister was nowhere to be seen, leading to cries of, "Resign! Or at least show you care."

A Government spokesman said, "We must immediately have a public enquiry, which should report within the next 100 years or so, making it impossible for there to be fires in this great City ever again, and certainly not in 451 years' time."

McDonnell Fails Safety Test

THE Shadow Chancellor of the Exchequer was under threat of removal last night following tests which prove that his language is "highly inflammatory".

Said a senior fire officer, "McDonnell is an accident waiting to happen. It only takes a little spart *(surely "spark"? Ed)* and he becomes incendiary, accusing politicians,

other than himself, of mass murder."

Concerns over McDonnell's dangerously explosive rhetoric have been ignored for years, but finally the alarm was raised in Glastonbury when toxic phrases were seen belching out of his mouth.

People ran for the exits saying, "He should be fired."

(Reuters)

Dave Spart (Co-Chairperson of the Neasden Proto-Revolutionary Yurts for All Gender-Neutral Foxes for Momentum Alliance)

Once again it is absolutely sickening to see the mainstream capitalist media attempt to belittle the totally successful non-political Day of Total Rage Against The Tories by suggesting that a million ordinary people did not turn up to express their solidarity and that the figure was closer to er... a couple of hundred, which is a total and sickening lie put about by the fascist police and firefighters to cover up the real scandal over numbers, ie how many died in the Grenfell Fire or rather the Grenfell Tory War Crime as it is referred to on our placards er... a total which is actually in the thousands and nowhere near the supposed official figure of 79 which is nothing more than a laughable example of fake news to support the racist, fascist and frankly Brexist government of Mrs Murderer May which needs to be democratically removed by force if necessary from its totally illegal occupation of Downing Street er... which was obviously the whole point of the massively successful mass protest viz to channel the justifiable anger of the families of the fire victims into direct nationwide political action of the type that led to the regrettable if understandable beating up of a man in a suit in the lobby of Kensington and Chelsea Council HQ in the belief that he was a Tory councillor rather than as it transpired a volunteer helping the victims... er... er... however the attempt to hijack this tragedy, or rather Tory Government Genocide as it is rightly called on our blog, by the reactionary forces of the right-wing-centre-left neo-Blairite establishment is a total and utter disgrace and one which should lead to the immediate placing of all media under a responsible nationalised body by the legitimate government, ie Jeremy and *(cont. p94)*

Death toll change

■ It was confirmed today by the Home Office that in future the official death toll from all disasters, such as the Grenfell Tower fire, will be decided by Lily Allen on Channel 4 News.

"Having seen Lily Allen disputing the official death toll of 79 we realise that the red tape, regulations and procedure surrounding official death tolls needs to be swept away and transformed," said a Home Office spokesman.

"In its place we will simply send Lily Allen to the disaster scene to talk to obviously distraught and grieving locals and then she can just decide on a figure for herself."

Lily Allen later confirmed that 678 people had died in the Grenfell fire, a figure she reached after speaking to two local residents who said they'd heard that figure from someone else who had seen the refrigerated area where those hundreds of bodies are being secretly stored by the Government to quell public anger.

Twitter on fire safety

■ There was no surprise at all that every Twitter user instantly became a fire safety expert following the devastating fire at Grenfell Tower.

"From the moment I logged on I was able to surmise the exact reasons as to why the fire spread so rapidly, without having to wait for accident investigation experts to comb the scenes for clues," said all Twitter users.

"We instantly became experts on building cladding materials and why certain materials were used in preference to other materials.

"It's incredible how simply having an account on Twitter totally outweighs the 20 years' experience of accident investigators on the scene, meaning they may as well not bother to scour the building for the precise reasons for the tragedy, as we've already reported exactly why it happened in under 30 seconds."

Fury as tower block failures escalate

■ As the number of dangerous tower blocks rose to over 60 in 25 local authorities, there was widespread anger that they weren't all Tory.

Said one furious protestor, "This is appalling. It doesn't fit at all with our agenda that the Conservatives are to blame for everything. How dare Labour councils ruin things by being equally culpable?"

The Mayfly

It's a mystery

WHATEVER could have led Darren Osborne to despise Muslims so much that he would drive his van into a group who were leaving prayers at the Finsbury Park Mosque?

How could his brain have become so warped and twisted and filled with hateful far-right propaganda?

We may never know.

ON OTHER PAGES

● The Sun ordered to admit that front-page story which claimed "one in five British Muslims had sympathy for ISIS" was significantly misleading

● The European Commission against Racism and Intolerance (ECRI) attacks The Sun for use of "offensive, discriminatory and provocative terminology" which fuels racist attitudes

● The Sun newspaper deletes heavily-criticised article by Katie Hopkins that calls refugees escaping Syria "cockroaches".

Cartoonist In Hiding After Blasphemous Drawing

by Our Media Staff **Polly Tickle**

A CARTOONIST responsible for producing a forbidden image which was deliberately calculated to be offensive to believers was last night said to be "in fear for his life" after a Fatwah was decreed.

The image of a white van bearing the label "The Daily Mail" outraged fanatical supporters of the religious leader Paul Dacre, who issued a full-page article denouncing the cartoonist for blasphemy, hate crime, and disagreeing with him.

The cartoonist who cannot be named (Martin Rowson) is said to be "hiding" where no one will ever find him, ie in the middle pages of the Guardian.

Fury As Musicians Interrupt Political Rally

by Our Corbyn Correspondent **Ray Bid**

THERE was widespread fury amongst Corbyn supporters as the Tory BBC allowed a three-day political rally celebrating Jeremy Corbyn to be hijacked by popular musicians.

Said one, "You could almost see the glee in Tory stooge Laura Kuenssberg's eyes as the BBC sought to lessen the impact of Jeremy Corbyn's historic centrepiece speech by sandwiching him between people playing guitars, drums and saxophones."

He continued, "They even sought to downplay the size of the crowd who flocked to hear Jeremy deliver his commandments by suggesting that some of them were 'music fans'."

Another supporter claimed, "Only the Tory-loving BBC could have cut away from Corbyn after his speech ended to show hour after hour of musicians like Stormzy, Katy Perry, The Foo Fighters and Ed Sheeran playing songs, thus giving the wholly misleading impression that the entire Glastonbury audience hadn't attended solely for the purpose of chanting 'Oh Jeremy Corbyn' for hours on end."

Viewers who witnessed this spectacle were urged to take to Twitter to share their hatred for the British Tory Broadcasting Corporation with all the other Twitter users who agree with them.

Corbyn speech in full

■ JEREMY Corbyn used a speech on the Pyramid Stage at Glastonbury to send out a message to President Trump to "build bridges not walls".

He told the audience, "You'll find the message on that massive wall over there which was built to keep out the poor people who haven't got a spare $250 for a ticket."

"Apparently, they're some of the young people who voted in the General Election"

The Eye's Controversial New Columnist

This week I am very angry about criticism of the Conservative Party. There have been many unkind comments saying there isn't the talent within the party to lead it out of the chaos that Theresa May and David Cameron have wrought upon it. What rubbish! Of course there is talent within the party! And the Tories know exactly where to find it. Looking at the current mediocre crop of contenders (Johnson, Davis, Gove, Hammond), it is perfectly sensible for the 1922 committee to decide to skip a generation. And looking at the next generation of mediocre contenders, (Priti Patel, Amber Rudd) it is perfectly correct for them to skip that generation too. And the next. And the next. And the one after that. And so, to cut a long story short, I am honoured to be selected by them to be the next leader of the Conservative Party! I promise to be at least as bald as William Hague and Iain Duncan Smith, to dribble as much as Michael Howard, and to continue the sensible policy of napping in the afternoons begun by David Cameron. Can I just say, in the words of Francis of Assisi, "Where there is discord, may I bring Harry Potter, where there is error, may I bring Tweenies, where there is doubt, may I bring Fireman Sam"... *(cont. p94)*

SPORTS DIRECT
COMPANY MEETING
THOSE MINUTES IN FULL

CALL TO ORDER
The Chairman ordered 12 pints for himself and called on everyone else to do the same.

MINUTES
The Minutes of the last meeting were read. It took 27 minutes for everyone to get pissed.

ATTENDING
Mr Ashley, Mr Toady, Mr Yesman, Mr Time-Server, Mr Free-Lunch.

FINANCIAL REPORT
The budget for the evening was set at £270,000 (not including food).

ANNOUNCEMENTS
Mr Ashley told Mr Toady: "I really love you."

Mr Toady told Mr Ashley: "I really love you too. Can I have fifteen million poundsh?"

Mr Ashley told Mr Toady: "Of coursh you can. You're my besht mate!"

PROPOSALS
Over a round of vodka chasers it was proposed the company name be changed to Shorts-Direct or possibly Shots-Direct.

The proposal was carried, as was Mr Yesman, who had passed out.

MOTIONS
Everyone did the Locomotion, then the Conga and then sang "Ole! Ole! Ole! Ole!"

APOLOGIES
Mr Ashley apologised for vomiting in the fire-place.

ANY OTHER BUSINESS
Mr Ashley then did his business in the toilet.

FURTHER ACTION REQUIRED
The meeting was interrupted by a stag party asking them to keep the noise down.

Mr Ashley told the stag party: "I'll take you all on. Outshide NOW!"

ADJOURNMENT
The meeting adjourned to Mr Iqbal's Kebab Direct.

MEMORANDUM
Mr Ashley could remember nothing at all.

Exclusive

That New Daniel Craig Bond Film

Working title: **'The Man With the Golden Handcuffs'**, starring 00alrightthen

(Bond enters M's office)

M: Ah, Bond, I wasn't expecting you. I thought you'd handed back your licence to make a killing.

Bond: I'm very reluctant to work for this outdated, sexist, misogynist organisation. To be honest, the way MI6 works is gratuitously violent.

M: For God's sake, Bond, we pay you enough, don't we? Just get on and do the job!

(Cut to Q's laboratory. Q hands Bond a cheque)

Q: This is an amazing gadget. It looks like an ordinary piece of paper, but it turns into a Lamborghini or a yacht, or a villa in Tuscany, or seed money for an avant-garde Indie film no one wants to see.

Bond: Ok, it's a deal.

(Cut to Bond in villain's lair. Bond is tied to chair with golden handcuffs)

Bond: Do you expect me to talk?

Villain (Barbara Broccoli): No, I expect you to glumly mumble your way through the next 90 minutes and then spend the next three years saying you'll never do another mission again.

(Cut to Bond in bed with Miss Moneyforoldrope)

Bond: I'm worried that I'm just a sex object and no one respects me for my mind.

Moneyforoldrope: Shut up and get your trunks off.

COMING SOON: *'Sourpussy'*.

OwenJones @OwenJones Queue ten deep for a simple ice cream. What an insult.

Owen Jones @OwenJones Ice cream isn't the problem: the problem is the Tories.

Owen Jones @OwenJones Opportunistic Tories united in slashing ice cream provisions for working people.

Owen Jones @OwenJones Hear me discuss loathsome Tory ice cream austerity cuts on @BBCRadioScot at 6.15am.

Owen Jones @OwenJones My wait in ice cream queue has been vindicated. OK, so I am now at the front. But I am well aware there are others at the back, worse off.

Owen Jones @OwenJones Hear me discuss the disgraceful plight of those at the back of the queue this Thursday on @Worldatone.

Owen Jones @OwenJones Kids as young as five forced to build beach-based **castles** using only bucket and spade. Tory housing policy in shreds.

Owen Jones @OwenJones I stand by helpless, watching kids' castles washed away by sea in one of the richest societies that ever existed.

Owen Jones @OwenJones Let's be absolutely clear about this. Sandcastles are a con, a lie. Kids' lives ruined.

Owen Jones @OwenJones The look of disillusion on the faces of those kids will never leave me. Not now. Not ever.

Owen Jones @OwenJones Watch me debate appalling sandcastle crisis with Julia Hartley-Brewer and Daniel Hannan on @skynews.

Owen Jones @OwenJones You drive a dodgem for three minutes and end up battered and bruised having gone precisely nowhere. Britain is in a total mess. End of.

Owen Jones @OwenJones The dodgems are nothing more than a racket for their wealthy backers, a crude Tory instrument to inculcate shameless bad driving.

Owen Jones @OwenJones The helter-skelter offers no viable accommodation. No one in this day and age should be asked to sleep outside, on an incline.

Owen Jones @OwenJones Lugged a rotten doormat up 120 steps. Sat on it. In six seconds, I'd been whirled back to where I'd began. Call that progress?

Owen Jones @OwenJones Goldfish has spacious bowl all to itself, 360 degree views, fresh water, food on demand. Tory bastard.

Owen Jones @OwenJones Hear me debate housing crisis with two leading goldfish in five minutes on @LBC

Owen Jones @OwenJones Totally brill photos of me and two leading goldfish sharing a post-debate pint now available on Instagram.

Owen Jones @OwenJones Fact. Candy floss has ZERO nutritional value but continues to be sold in vast quantities to underage kids, nurses, firefighters. Where's the sense?

Owen Jones @OwenJones I paid 35p into a **Penny Falls** slot machine and got a paltry and iniquitous 12p back. Calamitous failure of the system.

Owen Jones @OwenJones Join me on BanPennyFalls protest this Sunday.

Owen Jones @OwenJones Hear me talking about BanPennyFalls with @VanessaFeltz on @RadioLondon Friday 9.23am

Owen Jones @OwenJones Proud to support our BanPennyFalls protestors! Return all tragically wasted PennyFalls investments now!

Owen Jones @OwenJones Penny Falls cover-up spinning out of control. Tories running scared.

Owen Jones @OwenJones Heartless Tory government continues to ignore widespread calls for official inquiry into Penny Falls scandal.

Owen Jones @OwenJones It's impossible to countenance a government that continues to permit such a grossly unfair and ruthless institution as the coconut shy.

Owen Jones @OwenJones 3 balls for £1.50. Hurling them at a coconut takes 10 seconds. That's £6.00 a minute, £360 an hour. So this is how the rich get their kicks. Do you laugh or cry?

Owen Jones @OwenJones No Tory government will ever force me into throwing balls at coconuts. No way. You must be joking.

Owen Jones @OwenJones Throwing hard balls at coconuts for **fun** plays into the ongoing media narrative of persecuting the defenceless.

Owen Jones @OwenJones Nearly 13m people didn't vote Labour to see cocophobic thugs destroy our compassionate country.

Owen Jones @OwenJones Proud to support coconuts.

Owen Jones @OwenJones Why are they called **funfairs**? Unfairs, more like.

Owen Jones @OwenJones Just went swimming in sea. Can you believe it? Stung by Tory jellyfish.

Owen Jones @OwenJones Total cost of Trident? £167 billion. Money to be spent on ridding our coastlines of jellyfish? Zero. What an insult.

Owen Jones @OwenJones Watch me discussing growing jellyfish peril with @davidaaronovitch and @andrealeadsom on @BBCNewsnight

Owen Jones @OwenJones Grave danger that fretting about jellyfish will redirect anger away from the powerful to those who have to spend their lives floating aimlessly in water.

Owen Jones @OwenJones Proud to ignore jellyfish and concentrate on more important things.

Owen Jones @OwenJones FACT: No jellyfish has ever stung anyone. Reports to the contrary are simply hate-filled propaganda and an insult to commonsense.

Owen Jones @OwenJones Watch me condemning merciless calls for persecution of jellyfish on @BBCRadioLondon.

Owen Jones @OwenJones At last, this hateful, pointless Tory govt have dropped all plans for eradication of jellyfish. Further proof that protest works.

Owen Jones @OwenJones Just spotted children as young as five or six with buckets and spades, set to work on the sand.

Owen Jones @OwenJones And this is the 21st Century! Intolerable conditions for anyone, let alone little kids. Profound lessons here.

Owen Jones @OwenJones Women, children, LGBTI people denied basic human dignity of a table, forced to eat food between two slices of bread. Shame on you, Tories!

Owen Jones @OwenJones Listen to me @BBCRadioSouthend debating the sandwich issue with @TimmyMallett and @LauriePenny.

Owen Jones @OwenJones Horrific Guardian report: 37% of Britons go out in the blistering sun with no type of sunscreen. You know what? This Govt just doesn't care.

As tweeted to
CRAIG BROWN

"Describe what you can bring to this company"

GARDEN BRIDGE SCRAPPED – A NATION MOURNS

WHY I, AS THE PARENT OF A STUDENT, AM SUDDENLY VERY KEEN ON THE ABOLITION OF TUITION FEES

by All Middle-aged Hacks

AS AN independent, objective observer of government, I can't help but notice that my son is about to go to university. Blimey, have you seen how much they're charging? It's a disgrace! I've no time for Corbyn, but come on now, you've got to admit he's got a point... £50k? How many holidays is that? *(Cont. p94)*

Shylock Defends Venetian Student Loan Scheme

by Our Financial Staff
Will Shakeup

THE government of Venice was last night unrepentant about outsourcing its student loan scheme to the SLC (the Shylock Loan Corporation) which was asking for "a pound of flesh" as interest on a "three-year educational debt package".

Said the Doge, "I can't see what the fuss is about. It seems only fair that we should get a reasonable return on our investment. It's not as though we're asking for an arm and a leg. Although we may do somewhere down the line."

Said one legal expert and critic of the scheme, Portia,

"The quality of mercy is not strained". She continued, "It droppeth as the gentle rain from heaven upon the place beneath."

Rialto Bridging Loan

Essentially, she argued that students are being "bled dry" by an unfair rate of interest, ie the pound of flesh, and that the Doge should step in and abolish student loans.

The head of the SLC said, "I absolutely resent the accusation that I am overcharging my younger clients, such as Antonio. What next? Are you going to compare me to Wonga?"

CORBYNOMICS EXPLAINED

Q *Why do all young people think Mr Corbyn is wonderful?*

A Mr Corbyn has invented a brilliantly imaginative new economic theory. He proposes that we should remove all caps on public spending and in particular abolish the hated tuition fees paid by all students (ie more than 50 percent of all 18-24s).

Q *Why hasn't anyone come up with such a brilliant idea before?*

A Critics do point out that there is one problem with Corbynomics. All the extra money he wishes to spend has to be borrowed and will one day have to be paid back.

Q *Who will pay it back?*

A The 18-24s of today will one day be the 35-50s and will find that it is they who will be paying huge amounts of tax to fund, firstly, the interest paid on the money the government has borrowed and, secondly, repayment of the money itself.

Q *Won't they be very cross with Mr Corbyn?*

A No, because by that time he will no longer be around to blame. This is the key to the Corbynomics theory. Anyone who puts forward such a theory must be very, very old and anyone who believes him must be very, very young...

HISTORIC DUP/TORY AGREEMENT

Oh no, there are two men holding hands

A Doctor Writes

Diabetes

AS A doctor, I'm often asked, "Is Boris Johnson suffering from Di-abbott-es?"

The simple answer is "yes". The foreign secretary, like the shadow home secretary, exhibits exactly the same symptoms in media interviews – confusion, inability to remember figures and details, and loss of the power of speech.

However, there is no need to worry about this because *Di-abbott-es* or *Arrogantus Non-Preparens Normalis* lasts a very short time and Mr Johnson will no doubt be as right as rain in a couple of days.

If you are worried about Boris Johnson becoming Prime Minister, you should be.

© *A Spin Doctor, 2017*

News in brief

Love Island

■ 2.6 million viewers all watching ironically, say ironic viewers, unconvincingly.

TV HIGHLIGHTS

Gove Island

ITV2

Tacky reality show in which all the contestants try to screw each other whilst pretending they are all friends.

Contains repetitive and tawdry scenes of flirtation and betrayal which are unsuitable for children or indeed adults.

This week, will Michael make up with Boris who is trying to get into bed with Theresa even though she is already in bed with Arlene, while Philip has been rejected and tells David that Andrea lied about Theresa?

EYE VERDICT: Depressing and DUPraved

"He believed Nick Clegg AND Jeremy Corbyn"

AUSTERITY
An Apology from the Conservative Party

IN RECENT years we may have given the impression that we placed the highest priority on bringing Britain's public spending back under control after the reckless spending spree of the Labour government, which was threatening to drive the country into bankruptcy.

We may have reinforced this impression by promising to slash the defict and "to restore some sense of fiscal discipline" to an economy where we were adding tens of billions of pounds a year to a national debt that competed with Greece for reckless management.

It was for this purpose that we may have encouraged the idea that Britain would need to go through a period of "austerity".

We now realise, in light of losing the election, that there is nothing this country needs more than an end to hugely damaging cuts in our spending on our NHS, our schools, our police and, of course, our wonderful emergency services, whose response to the Grenfell tragedy was an inspiration to us all.

This is what the people of Britain have made clear is their highest priority, by their rejection of so-called "austerity" and their overwhelming support for Mr Corbyn's policy that there should be no limit on the money that we will have to borrow to give the people of Britain what they so richly deserve, ie a national debt even larger than the one we have already managed to double since 2010 to an eye-watering £1.74 trillion.

We apologise for any confusion that we may have caused among voters by any seeming contradiction between our earlier position and the one we adopted this morning after we locked Philip Hammond in a cupboard.

SHOCK TERROR REPORT FINDS SAUDI ARABIA HAS BEEN FUNDING TERROR

Those other findings:
- Catholicism funding Pope
- Bear has been funding woodland toilet facilities

LATE NEWS
- Chilcot says Blair not straight with nation
- *Vogue* boss says "Glossy mags encourage women to buy things they don't need"
- That's enough. Ed.

IRAQ CELEBRATES AS RUBBLE LIBERATED

THERE were scenes of wild celebration today after Iraqi Government forces confirmed that after nine months of constant bombardment from the air, and a siege on the ground, it had retaken control of a large area of rubble from Isis.

"This large area of rubble is roughly the size of what was once Iraq's second largest city, Mosul," said delighted Iraqi President Fuad Masum.

"This rubble has been totally liberated from the oppressive Isis regime and is 100 percent back under government control," said an Iraqi tank commander, proudly driving through the rubble.

"It is a fitting testament to the ongoing success of the West's war on Isis. We're fully expecting that within a few weeks, the millions of displaced residents driven out by Isis will return and use the rubble to make a nice gravel driveway leading to where their homes used to be." *(Reuters)*

Tips for spotting false news

1. Be sceptical about headlines
...headlines such as 'Tips for spotting false news'

2. Check the source
Is it trustworthy and reliable? Or is it Facebook?

3. Look closely at the web address
Is it www.facebook. com?

4. Check the evidence
Has Facebook ever done the right thing in the past? cf terrorism, paedophilia, gathering information about everyone without their permission.

5. Is the story a joke?
Yes – it is. The idea of Facebook being remotely concerned about anything other than making money is risible.

NB For any American academic or member of the Trump administration, this is genuine fake news, courtesy of the *Private Eye* fake news factory in Macedonia *(Uri, age 19½).*

May says 'I am listening to the electorate'

by Our
Political Staff
Peter O'Bore

In a conciliatory speech to Tory backbenchers, Theresa May last night offered to drop almost everything listed in the manifesto which won the Conservatives the election.

She told them, "More people voted for us than for any other party, so we must respect that choice by dropping everything that they thought they were voting for, such as means-tested winter fuel allowances, a triple-lock on pensions, scrapping free lunches for children of the better-off and a strong and stable government."

She continued, "All these silly ideas must go. I can't think who came up with them in the first place.

"We will, of course, be keeping the really sensible policies that everyone is in favour of, such as HS2 and the Hinkley Point nuclear power station, whilst maintaining our wonderfully strong and stable alliance with our new friends from Ulster."

Sarah Vain

Exclusive Fashion Verdict

DID you see that the Duchess of Cambridge has had a new haircut for Wimbledon?

She's had six inches chopped off her ridiculously girly, flicky-flicky hair. And about time too!

There comes a time in any woman's life when she has to admit that she is no longer a girl but a mature mother of two, married to a very important person in public life!

And you can't carry off that role with hair that's

halfway down your back and gets blown about in the wind.

My advice to Kate is that this is a good start. She's obviously been looking at older female role models like the one you can see at the top of this column! But if she really wants to copy me, she needs to cut even more of it off, and I can assure her, from personal experience, that only then will she really be taken seriously.

(Sarah Vain's column has had to be cut by six inches. It is still too long and next time may be cut altogether. P.D.)

"Please look after this author..."

WORLD APPALLED AT TIME TRUMP SPENDS ON GOLF COURSE

by Our Sports Staff **Phil Cardin**

THERE was shock around the entire globe today when it was revealed that Donald Trump had spent one fifth of his presidency on the golf course.

Said one international leader, "This is terrible. If only he'd spent more time playing golf, the world would be a safer place."

Said another, "Only 20 percent? It's a disaster. That leaves the other 80 percent of his time spent watching television, tweeting about television, trolling critics on television and, worst of all, being president of the United States."

A spokesman for the White House, Mr Sean Spicegirl, was, however, quick to reassure the global community.

"This is typical fake news put out by the failing mainstream media. The president has not spent one fifth of his time playing golf. I do not accept that figure. The president has spent over half of his tenure in the Oval Office – that's a total of nearly 80 percent of his working hours – on the greens. Which is more time than any other president in living or future memory. Fact."

When asked for a comment, the president was unavailable, due to a prior commitment addressing a putt at the 14th hole of his own golf course in St Andrew Marr-a-go-go *(cont. p94)*

That Rees-Mogg baby name shortlist in full

THOSE names even his wife vetoed before settling on Sixtus Dominic Boniface...

- Floccinaucinihilipilification Rees-Mogg
- Antidisestablishmentarianism Rees-Mogg
- Supercalifragilisticexpialidocious Rees-Mogg
- Eton Trinity Oxford Parliament Rees-Mogg
- Griff Rees-Mogg
- Brooklyn Apple Zowie Blanket Lourdes Rees-Mogg
- Moggy McMoggface
- Poshy McPoshface
- The Sir David Attenborough Polar Exploration Ship Rees-Mogg
- Jacob Rees-Sprogg
- The next leader of the Conservative Party

Late News

■ "This is the worst name with which one could saddle a child," says leading child psychologist Verity Dimm. "This poor boy has to go to school and answer to the name 'Rees-Mogg'."

Even Later News

■ "Given that there are now five Rees-Mogg boys and they will all go to Eton, the school will be in a quandary as to their correct nomenclature," says leading Professor of Snobology, Sir Jolyon Good-Fellowes.

"Might I suggest that Sixtus, as the 'fifthtest' boy, will take the title of Rees-Mogg Miniminimissimus in the descending order familiar to anybody who's been to a good school, such that the boys will be known as follows: Rees-Mogg Maximus, Ress-Mogg Major, Rees-Mogg Minor, Rees-Mogg Minimus, and the aforementioned Rees-Mogg Magnum Classic White Chocolate. *(That's enough Rees-Mogg. Ed.)*

HRH the Duchess of Cornwall
AN APOLOGY

IN COMMON with all other newspapers we may in recent decades have given the impression that Camilla Parker-Bowles was in some way totally unsuitable to be considered as a future Queen of England and, in the meantime, should certainly never be known as the Princess of Wales, a title reserved in perpetuity for Diana, the People's Princess and Queen of All Our Hearts.

Headlines such as "Did Di Die So Chazza Could Wed Camilla?", "Now Lovecheat Cami-Knickers Wants To Be Queen" and "Charles Bids to Crown Mistress as Tampax Britannica" might have reinforced the view that we were in some sense dubious about the advantages to the monarchy of allowing the heir to the throne to marry another man's wife.

We now realise, in the light of Camilla's 70th birthday, that all this was a long time ago and, frankly, she hasn't done too bad a job and anyway Charles is going to be king soon, so we'd better start ingratiating ourselves with the inevitable.

Our headlines this week, such as "The Queen is Nearly Dead – Long Live Our New Queen Camilla!", "All Hail Mrs Parker-Bowles, Our New Gloriana!" and "Yes, She's More Popular Than Diana, It's Official" will, we hope, go some way to correcting any misunderstanding to which our thousands of previous news stories, features and editorials may possibly have given rise.

New time traveller revealed

IT WAS the news that the whole world had been waiting for! The voyager who travels back in time is now a woman. Camilla, formerly 70, is regenerated via a picture by the Master, Mario Photoshoppi, and becomes a radiant, gorgeous 50-year-old who *(That's enough. Ed)*

MURDER ON THE HIGH SPEED EXPRESS
Chapter 94

Poirot stroked his chin thoughtfully, and twiddled with his moustache. "Zis is indeed a mystery, everyone seems to be making a killing." He gazed round at the assembled suspects in the First Class carriage – a group of lawyers, bankers and party donors, all of whom looked immensely guilty.

"Perhaps you will explain, ladies and gentlemen – zis train is ahead of schedule, you 'ave, 'ow you say, already received £2.3 million, yet nothing haz happened! Eet iz deeply suspicious."

Poirot was searching for a motive – was it greed, or was it incompetence, or more likely, both? Either way the victim, the tax payer, who had been bled dry, was crying out for justice.

"Now, tell me again about ze routes. How does the money get to your bank accounts at such high speed?"

There was silence in the room as the assembled professionals sweated and looked anxiously at each other. Said one accountant, "But Monsieur Poirot, we have made sure the public are not offended by seeing what we've been up to."

"You have been covering your tracks," retorted the Belgian sleuth, "not that there are any yet." Poirot decided to stop playing his elaborate game of cat and mouse.

"I know who's guilty! It is... George Osborne!!"

A gasp went up – they had all got away with murder. Poirot looked out at the news vendor giving away free copies of the Evening Standard on the platform: "Read all about it – George Osborne totally innocent. Theresa May should go to jail!"

Poirot sighed "Plus ça change", as the gravy train continued into the night... ∎

"*And the new Dr Who is to be a woman...*"

DOCTOR WHO *ROUND-UP*

DALEK 'OVERLOOKED AGAIN'

■ There was fury amongst the Dalek community after the role of the thirteenth Doctor Who went to a human rather than a Dalek.

"This is so typically Dalekist – a number of extremely competent Dalek actors have been overlooked in favour of a female human," tweeted one furious Dalek.

"Why do you think young Daleks grow up to be the most evil creatures in the galaxy when they have no positive role models on the telly to aspire to?"

The head of BBC Drama, Mr Placeholder, refused to comment on the casting, on the grounds that he had been exterminated.

BBC ABANDON NEW SERIES

■ The BBC confirmed today that it was abandoning the new series of Doctor Who after a recently divorced 48-year-old postal worker from Kidderminster, tweeting as TardisGuy4 ,said he'd no longer be watching the children's Sci-Fi show now it had a female Doctor.

"We had been looking forward to another series of the hit Sci-Fi show watched by hundreds of millions of people in 75 countries around the world," said a BBC spokesman, "but after TardisGuy4 said he'd given up on the show we have no choice but to abandon it.

"Thank God the BBC has come to its senses," said TardisGuy4. "Having a 2,000-year-old woman rather than a man travelling through time and space in a police box, fighting space aliens, totally destroys the realism of the show.

"I was confident that by tweeting to my 83 followers that I would no longer be watching Doctor Who, it would bring the show crashing down.

"Seriously, what other choice did the producers have?"

THERESA MAY 'WELCOMES FEMALE DOCTOR WHO'

■ Theresa May has welcomed the news that the thirteenth Doctor Who will be a woman.

"I'm certain that initially she'll be very popular, seen as a strong and stable new Time Lord, but after disastrously choosing to go into battle too soon against the Daleks, she'll be left humiliated and largely powerless inside the Tardis, as the infighting and backbiting about her replacement on Gallifrey rages on.

"So yes, enjoy."

SEXUAL OFFENCES ON TRAINS DOUBLE IN FIVE YEARS

Thank goodness they are going to scrap the guards and make them driver only!

Those John Humphrys Interviews In Full

LAST WEEK
John interviews the tennis player Johanna Konta

Humphrys: Konta... that's a foreign name. So what are you? You were born in Hungary, you're really an Australian, and then you come over here and pretend to be British.

Konta: Good morning, Mr Humphrys, thank you for inviting me on your show. I was actually born in Australia...

Humphrys: But let's face it, you were never any good at tennis, were you? You were only ranked 994th in Australia, so you thought you'd try your luck in Britain. That's about the size of it, isn't it?

Konta: Well, no, actually, Mr Humphrys. I won the Australian Under-12s and then my parents moved to Britain, so it really wasn't anything to do with...

Humphrys: Yes, well, that's your story. And now I suppose you expect us all to be cheering you on as a Brit?

Konta: Well, I would like to thank the Centre Court crowd for being so...

Humphrys: Well, I'm afraid that's all we've got time for.

NEXT WEEK
John interviews the Olympic athlete Mo Farah

Humphrys: So, Mo Farah, that's a foreign name, isn't it? You were born in Somalia, and then you came over here as a kid, and ever since you've been pretending to be British.

Farah: Good morning, Mr Humphrys. Thank you for inviting me on your programme.

Humphrys: So what are you? That's what everyone wants to know. Are you an African, just another economic migrant? You're not really trying to tell us you're a Brit, are you?

Farah: Well, I have lived here most of my life and I'm very proud that the Queen gave me a knighthood for my services to the British...

Humphrys: Well, that's your story, but you never made any mark as a runner before you came to Britain, did you?

Farah: I was only eight, Mr Humphrys.

Humphrys: Well, that's all we've got time for.

THE WEEK AFTER
John interviews himself

Humphrys: That's a silly name. Is it Welsh?

Humphrys: Good morning, John.

Humphrys: So you were born in Cardiff and you came over here looking for a job. You're just another economic migrant, aren't you?

Humphrys: I have lived here most of my life, and I've been very proud to work for the British Broadcasting Corporation.

Humphrys: Well, that's your story. But the truth is that you came over here for the money, didn't you? And quite a lot of it, I read in the newspapers.

Humphrys: Isn't it time for *Thought For The Day*?

Nick Robinson, Justin Webb, Mishal Husain, Sarah Montague (*all together*): Yes, we were all thinking that we wished we had John's agent.

COULD YOUR JOB BE DONE BY A MACHINE?

by Our Flesh and Blood Correspondent **A. Person**

THE growing tide of automation is the biggest crisis facing industries across the world today. There is no doubt that the world of work as we know it is dying, and that millions and millions of now totally useless people will lose their livelihoods as a result.

Almost every industry is going to suffer massive job losses. Obviously, all the estate agents and lawyers and doctors and train drivers and car manufacturers will be sacked, and there will be huge gains in efficiency across those sectors of society, even though it's sad that they won't be working. But it is important to remember that there are lots of jobs which cannot be done by machines. Jobs which require great skill, and care, and the sort of nuance that no machine could ever be capable of.

To pick a random example,

take the position of a newspaper journalist.

This is a precision role, requiring a human's delicate touch, which definitely COULD NEVER be done by some robot. It would have to check all the facts – alright, admittedly using Google, which is sort of a machine – but it would also have to think of new stories – alright, admittedly much of it is copied wholesale from press releases and news agencies – but it would also have to compare bits of information, perhaps using some sort of automated system – but... look, it's obvious, there's definitely no way a machine could ever – I mean, it's completely ridiculous – get away from me, you bastards – no, you can't sack me like this – please, I have a family to support *(We apologise for the interruption to this article. The article will now continue as normal.)*

TOP BREXITEER THREATENED WITH TRIPLE LIBEL SUITS

by Our Court Staff **Sue Everyone**

MR DOMINIC Cummings, the former head of the Leave campaign, faces multiple libel actions after describing the Minister for Brexit, David Davis, as "thick as mince, lazy as a toad and vain as Narcissus".

Writs have been issued on behalf of a bowl of mince, a toad and the late Mr Narcissus, all of whom have claimed irreparable damage to their reputations in being likened to Mr Davis.

Said the mince, "How dare anyone compare my mental agility to that of the leader of the Brexit negotiations?" Said Mr Toad, "To suggest I am the sort of amphibian who would turn up to an important meeting without any notes is a gross defamation of character."

The late Mr Narcissus said, "Before accusing me of vanity, Mr Cummings should take a long, hard look at himself in the mirror, which is what Mr Davis does *all* the time."

Mr Davis, however, has decided not to take legal action against Mr Cummings for suggestions that he is thick, lazy and vain.

He said, "To be honest, I don't understand his point, I can't be bothered to sue him and, anyway, it would make me look bad."

Downward-facing Dog vs Upward-looking Cat

PRINCES REMEMBER THEIR MOTHER

Let's make a TV programme that really embarrasses our father

It's what she would have wanted

Prison 'Staffing Levels' Adequate

by Our Prisons Correspondent **Harry Grout**

THE Home Office has hit back at claims by the president of the Prison Governors Association that the recent spate of riots prove staffing levels in jails are at dangerous levels.

"This is absolute nonsense and a baseless scare story," insisted a Home Office spokesman.

"We have spoken to the prisoners currently running a number of prisons across England, most recently they have taken over the running of The Mount in Herefordshire, and they say they have more than enough inmates to seize control of the jail and run it on a day-to-day basis."

Speaking from The Mount prison, where guards are currently being kept in their cells 24 hours a day, the prisoner running the jail from B-Wing, who wanted to be known as Rude Boy, insisted that the prison was operating normally with more than adequate numbers of inmates roaming the cell blocks dishing out punishment beatings.

TORY MP SACKED FOR 'N-WORD'

by Our Westminster Staff **Rod Black**

A CONSERVATIVE backbench MP was today summarily dismissed after evidence emerged that she had used the "N-word" in a discussion about Brexit.

A Tory spokesman confirmed, "The word she chose has become synonymous with old-fashioned racism and has no place in the modern Conservative party."

The offensive word is "Nigel", which has become unacceptable in polite society in the last five years.

Nigel in the Woodpile

The MP concerned was shocked and horrified at her slip of the tongue and immediately apologised to anyone who might have been offended.

"It was careless, crass and inappropriate to talk about 'Nigel', even in an innocent phrase about him hiding in the saloon bar of the Woodpile Arms. I accept that the word 'Nigel' has a long and unpleasant history of creating division and intolerance in our society."

One of her defenders, Mr N. Farage, said, "Oh, for Heaven's sake, this is political correctness gone Paul Nuttall."

Mr Farage later apologised for his use of the N-word "Nuttall", which he agreed was offensive and inappropriate in a modern *(cont. p94)*

Exclusive to all newspapers

Mother loved children

A TV documentary yesterday revealed that a mother loved her children. The children said, "She was like a mother to us". *(Reuters)*

On other pages

■ Children of divorced parents didn't see enough of either parent **2**

■ Children sad when mother died **3**

■ Plus hundreds of pages of pictures, analysis, comment, more pix, more analysis,more comment, even more pix **94**

Another exclusive to all newspapers

Boy is four

A boy was four years old today. His parents said, "Happy Birthday, George". *(PA)*

DUP LEADER IN LONDON

What's the time?

1956

"It's not a sex robot, you've been had..."

THIS WEEK

JEREMY PAXMAN
(in conversation with top spoon journalist Rod Ladle)

Do you have a favourite spoon?

Mind your own bloody business.

You are not on the BBC now, so you don't have to be impartial or objective any more. What is your favourite spoon?

I'm not telling. You can ask me as often as you like, but you won't get an answer.

Come on, you're a national treasure, people have an interest in your spoon preferences...

I don't care. They can bugger off. It's none of their business.

Would you say then that you hate all spoons?

Don't be ridiculous. Next question.

OK, could you name a single spoon that you admire?

Er... er... not off the top of my head, no. I've got no interest in looking at spoons. End of.

So what do you do in your spare time?

I quite like looking at spoons. Often in box-sets. There's a lot of good cutlery being made nowadays.

So spoons aren't all rubbish?

I didn't say that. And you won't catch me out that easily. Next!

OK, last question... Do you have a favourite spoon?

Harrumph. For the last time. I WON'T TELL YOU.

All right then, will you tell me about you and the much younger fruity blonde researcher?

Did you say favourite spoon? Yes, well, there are a lot of interesting spoons around and, as a One Spoon Tory, my favourite spoon is of course *(continues to try and flog autobiography "A Life of Spoons" for 94 pages)*

NEXT WEEK: *James Stunt, "Me and My Stunt".*

PM ON HOLIDAY

When's check-out time?

Probably when you get back to London

Daily Telegraph Friday 11 August 2017

Letters to the Editor

The National Trust Row

SIR – My good lady wife and I have been supporters of the National Trust for over 100 years, and indeed for the last 30 years have been volunteer guides at the charming Jacobean country House Wolfenden Hall where we happily welcomed guests of every description to the property.

You can imagine our dismay then when we were suddenly instructed last week, on pain of being demoted to serving in the gift shop, that we had henceforth to wear a garish "Rainbow Badge", bearing the logo "I'm LBCBTQI!"

This was, we were told, part of the National Trust's ill-advised "House and Gay-Den" initiative in which it attempted to woo the so-called "pink pound" by rewriting the history of some of its most treasured properties in a more "inclusive" manner.

As someone who knew the late owner of Wolfenden Hall, Cedric Wimpole St John Screamer, I was appalled by the attempt of the "politically correct" brigade to try and claim Cedric as "a gay hero". Cedric was a quiet, unassuming bachelor who wrote poetry and had a number of close friends in the creative and artistic community. There was never any suggestion during his life that he might be homosexual and indeed the matter was never referred to by him and certainly not by those of us amongst his acquaintance who used to drop into the Hall of an evening to drink sherry and listen to his collection of Judy Garland records.

For the ubiquitous Mr Stephen Fry to try and turn Cedric into some sort of martyr figure is deeply regrettable and is a grotesque retrospective invasion of privacy. I am delighted, however, that after we made our views plain to Dame Helen Gush, the retiring NT leader, the badge edict has been rescinded and we have received an apology in which Dame Gauche says that she was wrong to assume Lady Gusset and I were the type of "blinkered homophobes who would refuse to wear a rainbow badge".

I do hope that we can now put this matter behind us and once again concentrate on educating our visitors about the delights of Wolfenden Hall, including Cedric's historic collection of Arab tea pots amassed on his visits to Tunisia and Morocco.

Yours welcomingly,

Sir Herbert Gusset,
Rainbows End,
Oscar St Wilde,
Dorset

Corbyn and Venezuela – why the silence?

by Our Political Correspondent
Anne R. Key

As riots continue in Venezuela, following President Maduro's fraudulent victory at the polls, and Jeremy Corbyn enjoys a cycling holiday in Croatia, calls are intensifying for him to go on the record with a public denunciation of the out-of-control socialist leader.

"The way in which he is repressing internal dissent is totally unacceptable and risks the country descending into chaos," said one political commentator.

"For Maduro to have any credibility he must publicly reject Corbyn's tyrannical U-turn on student tuition fees, not to mention his suppression of any realistic conversation about Brexit."

Asked by a Croatian news reporter where he and the rest of the Labour Party were heading, Mr Corbyn said there was only one option: Split.

On other pages
Livingstone 'shock'

Ken Livingstone has broadly defended the brutal crackdown on democracy in Venezuela by President Maduro.

"I will of course be reserving judgement and not offering my full support for him until he burns down the parliament building and invades Poland."

School news

St Cakes

St Cakes is to become a gender-neutral, independent fee-paying school with a new motto *"Qui/Quae/Quod Paget Entrat"*. The academic year will consist of three terms: Michael/Michaelamas, Hilary/Hillary and Trinity/Tristram. There are 72 boys (formerly girls) in the school and 73 girls (formerly boys). The Head Person is L.G.B.G.T.Q. Jenner (Caitlins), who was known in the Lower School as J.C.T. Jennings Minor (Buckeridges). Confused Parents Evening will take place on John (formerly June) 27th. Skirts will be worn by boys and trousers by girls. The school production is Shakespeare's *Two Gender-Neutral Men of Verona* and will take place in the Janet (formerly the Gym). *(That's enough of this. Ed.)*

MERKEL GOES WALKING

Oh no, it's Theresa May

And she's seen us

CHRIS EVANS REVEALED AS BBC'S HIGHEST PAID STAR

Everyone agrees that abuse in politics is the fault of 'those c***s on the other side'

by Our Political Staff **Peter O'Bollocks**

FOLLOWING reports of endemic abuse spreading itself through political discussions in Britain, both the Conservative and Labour parties have held a joint summit and issued a statement clarifying who is responsible.

They also vow to remove vicious personal abuse and trolling from modern political dialogue. The statement reads as follows:

"For too long, British political discourse has been poisoned by a filthy streak of abuse a mile wide which runs – regrettably – directly through our opposite numbers.

"We are fortunate indeed that our own party has been completely unsullied by abuse, despite the unedifying sight of our opponents falling on each other like starving, mutinous dogs desperate to gnaw one

another's feeble bones. Indeed, the most severe incident in our history was many years ago when one member muttered that another member was being 'a bit of a prat, though he has only the best intentions'.

"Sadly, not every party can be as blissful and united as ours. Indeed, we need only cast our eyes to our opposition to see a party where vicious slanging of the most outrageous, hurtful, personal kind has become de rigeur, and where you may be killed simply for offering to make someone a cup of tea.

"Now, when we look across the aisle, we see dreadful disarray, and a mob of ugly scumbags shouting abuse at each other. Why don't they just hang themselves?

"We hope this clarifies our position on the matter."

BBC PAY SHOCK

Have you heard how much the Daleks are getting paid?

WHITE HOUSE – NEW COMMUNICATIONS DIRECTOR APPOINTED

by Our Political Staff **Michael Whitehouse**

AFTER another chaotic week in the Trump administration, Washington was reassured at the announcement of a new Communications Director.

A mayfly has been given the job, to the delight of insiders.

Said one, "At last an element of stability has been restored. What any administration needs is

continuity and now we know that the mayfly will be in the job for at least 24 hours, possibly even 24½, depending on his natural life-cycle."

He added, "There's a massive buzz about the mayfly, not just because of his longevity. But because of his experience in operating in close proximity to a massive turd."

"We're heading for another crash"

81

Exclusive to the
DI-LY MAIL

DAY ONE

HOW DIANA INVENTED RED CARPET GLAMOUR

Never before had anyone graced a red carpet like she did, except the women who did.

DAY TWO

HOW DIANA MADE SWIMWEAR SEXY

Never before had anyone ever worn a bikini and looked good, except the women who did.

DAY THREE

HOW DIANA MADE BREATHING FASHIONABLE

Never before had anyone thought it was a good idea to breathe until Diana bravely showed us the way.

DAY NINETY FOUR

HOW THE DAILY MAIL INVENTED RUBBISH ABOUT DIANA

Never before had anyone printed such drivel until the Daily Mail showed us how to do it.

Diana Tapes:
Grubby
Blood Money

CHANNEL 4 should be ashamed of itself, giving 30 pieces of silver to the Judas, Peter Settelen, who betrayed the trust of Diana, the late Princess of Hearts.

How dare they try and exploit the memory of the tragic princess for their own squalid financial ends?

How dare they inflict further suffering on the Royal Family at this terrible time, purely for commercial gain?

How dare they deprive Sky of the exclusive footage purely to boost their own ratings and cause poor Mr Murdoch the anguish of watching those bastards get what is rightfully his.

On other pages

That disgraceful, grubby, hurtful, squalid transcript in full.

DAILY EXPRESS

FRIDAY AUGUST 11, 2017

WHY DIANA WOULD HAVE VOTED FOR BREXIT

by Our Royal Staff **Lee Vuralone**

THE *Express* can exclusively reveal today that the late Princess Diana would definitely have voted to leave the European Union in any referendum and would currently favour a hard Brexit.

This extraordinary finding is the result of in-depth research of her political and economic opinions by top Dianaologist, Professor Charlotte Tan. "Let there be no doubt," said the professor, "all the facts point to only one possible conclusion: Diana would have been a committed Brexiteer and would strongly have resisted membership of both the Customs Union and the Single Market. Her objections on an imposed tariff wall were well known."

The professor's research document backed up these points with the following irrefutable proof:

■ Diana hated Germans, particularly the Queen, who wasn't very helpful when she complained about Charles

■ Diana hated Greeks, particularly Prince Philip, who told Charles it would be acceptable to take Camilla as a mistress

■ Diana hated Italians, particularly the paparazzi

■ Diana hated Brussels, particularly at Christmas

"How much more evidence does anyone need?" asked the professor, "Can I have my cheque now? In Euros, please."

BBC Defends Entirely Different Cooking Show

by Our Plagiarism Staff **Kat Koppy**

BBC executives leapt to the defence of their new programme "Strictly Come Baking" yesterday, insisting it was in no way similar to their previous show "The Great British Bake Off" for which Channel 4 paid millions for exclusive rights last year.

"For a start, it's got a completely different presenter," said one executive. "Her name is Mary Berry and she's a whole year older than the one who presented the original show that this one is nothing like."

He added, "This new show is a cooking show, which has nothing to do with baking cakes, except when the cooking task involves the baking of cakes. Oh, and by the way, the contestants in 'Strictly Come Baking' are members of the public who

are totally different from the members of the public who were in the original show. The presenter is Claudia Winkleman, a witty female Cambridge graduate who is entirely different from Mel and Sue, who are two witty female Cambridge graduates."

The BBC has just announced a spin-off show called "An Extra Spice", which will analyse the highlights of the cooking show in a totally amusing and different way with a comedic cooking enthusiast, possibly Katy Brand, or maybe Jo Caulfield, or some combination of the two.

Channel 4 is outraged by the attempts to copy the "Bake Off" format. Said a furious executive, "Why can't the BBC come up with an original idea for a programme instead of just copying the one we bought off them?"

Stoical Aussie terror threat levels explained

Not expected — *Bonzer*

Attack likely — *No worries*

Could occur — *Fair dinkum*

Imminent — *Another prawn on the barbie*

"I'll leave that with you then"

PETER ACKROYD: QUEER CITY

Before the Romans came, most male Londoners favoured eye-liner. Those in the military preferred to sashay rather than to march or stride. Or so the historians tell us. Indeed, some suggest that the name "London" is itself an amalgam of "don", meaning to wear or vest oneself in, and "Lon", an abbreviation of "loon pants", the close-fitting casual trousers, flared from the knees downwards, which have remained popular with the queer community throughout the ages. Others have argued that "Lon" is derived from "Loin", while "don" is a well-known abbreviation of "dong", ancient slang for the penis or male appendage. So we may safely conclude that same-sex relations were irresistible to ancient Londoners. Indeed, news of their popularity may have offered Julius Caesar the impetus for his invasion. Caesar was himself notoriously effeminate, telling his cohorts to refer to him as "Julia", and letting it be known within their ranks that massed winking and pursing of lips was his preferred form of salute.

The earliest collections of Anglo-Saxon laws make no mention of same-sex activity, which indicates that the great Anglo-Saxon warriors, with their distinctive moustaches and tank-tops, could not keep their hands off one another. Christianity did not arrive formally in England until 597, when Augustine arrived at Thanet, having heard of the all-night "dogging" sessions taking place every second Thursday at gay clubs situated on the site of what is now St Paul's.

By the twelfth century, same-sex love came to be considered as the prevailing vice of Norman nobles, princes and kings. How could it not be so in a military caste that relied upon masculine loyalty and friendship? Many etymologists believe that William the Conqueror was so-called because his male organ had the smooth, slightly shiny, brown surface of a conker, and he loved nothing so much as standing beneath a tree and knock it against others of a similar hue.

Most areas of London were originally named to celebrate queer activity. The "dilly" in Piccadilly is believed, by me, if by no one else, to have been the Norman name for a male whore; it was customary for elderly judges, bishops and civil servants to go to that area to "pick a" dilly, before retiring with them to their clubs, where special cupboards would be set aside for their mutual gratification.

Other stations on the Piccadilly line stand as testament to the popularity of the act of sodomy. "Oakwood" is self-explanatory, as are "Cockfosters" and "Arsenal". Turnham Green – literally "Turn 'em green" suggests that some Tudor novices to the act may have felt a little queasy before getting the hang of it. This is, at least, one explanation. Knightsbridge was where the knights would pull out their "bridges" to show how they could go up and down, while Hammersmith was, in all likelihood, the area where a well-known male concubine called Smith would parade up and down, waiting for a "Ham-erd", or hand-job. Even today, if you ask a stranger to direct you to Hammersmith, you are more than likely to end the day enjoying a same-sex session in a basement flat in Earls Court, which was, it has been suggested, named in the late 16th century after the oft-heard exclamation,

"I say! Look what Earl's caught!" when the notorious Earl of Monmouth would parade his new young catch, clad, most likely, in Tudor "loon-pants" along the streets of one of London's most licentious boroughs.

Many of London's best-loved snacks have their origins in same-sex activities. Dr Samuel Fish, the infamous 18th century apothecary, was discovered wrapped in newspaper with his naked young assistant Tommy Chips; between the two of them they gave rise to the city's most popular takeaway food. That is, at least, one explanation. The Mars Bar is believed to echo the exact proportions of the "bar" of Jeremy Mars, the licentious 16th century poet; when its manufacturers reduced the bar's overall size in 2009, some experts imagined this to be the direct result of a re-examination of his withered corpse. Londoners still love Mushy Peas, yet few of them realise that their favoured dish is named after the "Pea-nis" of Mr Archibald Mushy, a notorious Victorian kerb-crawler who liked to smear the young men he picked up on his travels in a gooey green substance before having his way with them. As the bawdy old nursery rhyme, still sung in many parts of the East End to this day, has it:

> Mushy peas, oh, mushy peas
> Mr Mushy doth touch my peas,
> And now sup we all your Mars Bar
> And prod our dongs in Fish, and Chips.

In his day, King Henry VIII was as notorious a homosexual as Giacomo Casanova. Like most Londoners, Henry employed six wives as an elaborate smokescreen. When suspicions had been aroused, he began to behead them in order to show how heterosexual he was. At least two of his wives – Anne of Cleves and Catherine Howard – are believed to have been young men, while a third – Jane Seymour – was a lesbian, or, as she made clear by her silence, would almost certainly have been a lesbian if she had felt so inclined. That history holds no firm proof that she ever engaged in a lesbian act is evidence of the lengths to which she went to keep her sexual drives hidden.

Generations of queer Londoners continue to throng to the city's most prominent buildings for same-sex pursuits. Three times a year, they put on their campest costumes – tail-coats, floral dresses and baroque feathered hats – and make their way to the celebrated "garden" party at Buckingham Palace. "Garden", is, of course, old English slang for sodomy. The present British Royal Family is predominantly queer, with the possible exception of HM the Queen, who is famously transsexual. Other public buildings used primarily for purposes of cottaging include both Houses of Parliament, St Paul's Cathedral, the Royal Opera House and Chelsea Barracks. In the year 2000, the "London Eye" was erected to cope with the overflow.

Each morning, millions of men flock to London from the suburbs, finding the combination of alleyways, elevators, public toilets, open plan offices and Royal palaces irresistible. Special trains are laid on for them. These eager and enterprising queers are known to each other as "commuters", and can be identified by their propensity to wear "trousers" and "shirts", with many lesbians preferring the easier access afforded by a "skirt" or "dress". Their continued presence represents the ultimate triumph of the Queer City.

As told to
CRAIG BROWN

Fallen angels

"This is what we call a 'patient' or, more accurately, a 'potential profit centre'..."

"You got it wrong... a 'seven-day NHS' is how long you have to wait to see someone!"

"Well, we did tell him we couldn't operate until he lost weight!"

"We might not be the 'envy of the western world', but I hear there are still some districts in Kazakhstan that are a little bit jealous of us!"

"We've conducted a thorough investigation into the death of your father and, in the interest of full disclosure, we've determined 'shit happens'!"

"I'm going to look for a bed... I may be some time!"

DUNKIRK SPIRIT 2017

It's harder to leave Europe than we thought

A Doctor Writes

AS A doctor, patients often appear in my surgery, saying, "Doctor, I'm suffering from acute anxiety."

What I usually say is, "Me too. Have you seen the news? Bloody hell. If it's not North Korea, it's Spain and the next time you look, it's Finland... and it never stops."

The patient then tends to ask, "Is that why you are hiding under the desk, Doctor?"

The simple answer is "Yes". We are all suffering from

Smartphone Syndrome or what is technically known as *Nervosa Mobilis Novellum Alertus Normalis.*

What happens is that the patient attempts to live a normal life, but is constantly reminded via his or her device that atrocities are happening around the world practically 24/7 and it is fantastically depressing.

If you are worried about being anxious, then we are in a bit of a logical conundrum, but I would recommend a quick visit to the lavatory to relieve the problem – by throwing the phone down the toilet and flushing it away.

© A doctor, 2017.

"Do you think she ever gets bored?"

ROYAL POETRY CORNER

In Memoriam HRH The Duke of Edinburgh

So. Farewell
Then Prince Philip.

You have died
At the age of XX
(FILL IN DETAILS)
Or so said
The Telegraph
Online.

But actually
You are still
Alive.

Sorry
About that.
The mistake,
Not the fact that
You're still alive.

So. Farewell
Then the Intern
Working in the
Obituary department
Of the Telegraph
Online.

E.J. Thribb
(17½ Deceased)

Lines on the Retirement from public duties of His Royal Highness, Prince Philip, Duke of Edinburgh

So. Farewell
Then
Prince Philip.

After unveiling
216,412 plaques,
Attending
1,437,602 events,
Shaking an estimated
2 billion hands and
Making 474,816
Off-colour remarks,
You have decided
That you are now
Too old.

And you are
Handing
over your
Duke duties to a
Younger man, ie
Prince George.

E.J Thribb (97½)

Film highlights

Zombie Apocalypse

Horrific dystopian fantasy set in the present day in which the living dead stalk the streets in search of a way out of their nightmare.

Who unleashed the toxic Brexit virus and is there a cure? No. Viewers may find the scenes of zombies eating each other rather unpleasant, but alternatively they might find them quite amusing.

Starring Theresa May as Dead Woman Walking (see still).

EYE RATING: *It'll have you on the edge of your cliff!*

News in brief

Western tourists – 'We will support Spain in its hour of need'

■ The West has voiced its unconditional support for Spain following the recent terror attacks.

Tributes and vows to continue visiting the beleaguered country – and not let the terrorists win – have poured in. Said western tourists, "We will carry on visiting and will stand by Spain in their hour of need, just like we stood by er, Egypt... and er... Tunisia." *(Rotters)*

I DON'T NORMALLY GO THIS FAR ON A FIRST DATE

LEST WE FORGET
A Short Story Special

by Dame Sylvie Krin, author of *Duchess of Hearts* & *You're Never Too Old*

THE STORY SO FAR: Charles has been attending the Memorial Service for the 100th Anniversary of the Battle of Passchendaele in Belgium.

CHARLES lay back in the cast iron Victorian Flanders and Swann baignoire in his suite at the Chateau Watteur La Voliwarre, contemplating the events of the day. His aide-de-very-camp, Sir Alan Fitztightly, poured into the steaming water a soothing balm of Duchy Original Organic Dung and Dandelion Bath Essence and complimented the heir to the throne on his earlier performance.

"A very moving reading, Sire. It bought a tear to the eye. It really reminded us all that we must never forget."

Charles, however, seemed distracted, his mind clearly elsewhere.

"Really, you think so?"

"Oh yes, Sire," repeated Sir Alan, "we must make an effort to remember those who have passed on forever."

"Don't you think that sometimes it's better to forget some of them? Just one or two. Or one?"

Sir Alan looked confused, while Charles continued, "I mean it's very sad when people die and all that but you know it was all a long time ago and one should really move on."

Sir Alan then noticed a newspaper lying underneath the discarded beige Hacket and Brooks safari suit that Charles had controversially chosen for the memorial service. The headline shouted "Dynamite Diana Tapes Speak From Beyond Grave". Now everything was becoming clear.

"Remembrance is all very well but there does come a time when one has to start afresh, let bygones be bygones, end the chapter and close the book."

"Very good, Sire," Sir Alan deftly removed the offending newspaper from beneath the pile of clothes and soothed, "I understand completely, Your Highness. Let's hear no more about this whole unpleasant business, as Backstairs Billy used to say to the under-valets when they were caught without breeches in the overbutler's pantry in the days of your dear departed Nan."

For once, a grateful Charles did not cut short the louche reminiscences of his loyal Equerry-as-a-Corkscrew and he let Sir Alan twitter on.

"Let's put it all behind us, whoops, there I go again…"

Charles gloomily prodded the plastic miniature British Grand Fleet at Jutland, a gift from the King of Walloonia, which bobbed unsteadily on the frothy, soapy main.

"I mean, all these anniversaries, like say the 20th… it is of no significance really, is it? It's just a date, surely? No, I mean this endless obsession with the past, it really is…it really is…"

Sir Alan, as ever, completed his master's sentence. "It really is an essential part of our nation's story."

Charles looked unhappily at his confidant and counsel, his eminence rosé, his keeper of the Royal Ear.

In the silence that followed all that could be heard was the gurgle of the water heading down the plughole like so many memories, circling and circling until they disappeared for ever. If only…

(To be continued…)

Your new-look Independent, complete with 20% Saudi ownership

by Our Riyadh Correspondent **Alan Akbar**

THE Independent website has announced that its new minority shareholder, a Saudi Arabian millionaire, will have no influence whatsoever on the future direction of the newspaper's editorial department.

A spokesman for the site said, "We have agreed that the Independent will remain completely editorially independent. This will not be like the last time, when Evgeny Lebedev bought the Evening Standard and it was suddenly full of profiles of oligarchs' daughters, or the time after that, when George Osborne became editor and it was suddenly full of features about how marvellous David Cameron was and don't we all miss him now. No way.

"To calm everyone's nerves, here is an exclusive look at the new-look Independent we're putting together."

● 12 Great Things Women Can Do With The Time They Used To Spend Driving

● This Thief Lost His Hand, Which Is Justifiable Under The Laws Of Allah

● Someone Tried To Vote For The Opposition. What Happens Next Will Not Astound You, Because They Were Beaten Soundly, As Is Appropriate

● New Amusing Cartoons Of Literally Anything But Mohammed

● Isn't Qatar Shit?

The Independent. It is[1]. Are you?[2]

1 In hock to one of the wealthiest members of an appalling, human-rights abusing Middle Eastern theocracy with no press freedom.

2 See above.

Tragic Anniversary Remembered

by Our Entire Staff

It's unbelievable to think that it was exactly 10 years ago that Britain was plunged into a state of shock by the heart-rending news that came suddenly out of the blue.

Everyone remembers exactly where they were on that fateful day when we learned that the Northern Rock building society had gone bust.

As a tearful prime minister Gordon Brown told the nation, "This was truly the People's Bank", millions of ordinary people queued up outside branches of the bank to buy flowers *(surely to take out whatever was left of their money?)*.

Many left handwritten notes and cards with emotional messages such as "You bastards sold my life savings" and "That Matt Ridley should be strung up".

No one will ever forget whatever it was that we've already forgotten *(cont. p94)*

Battles of the American — Civil War —

No 94. Charlottesville, 14 August 2017

ONE of the most significant confrontations in American history came in the late summer of 2017, when an armed militia from all over the southern states descended on the Virginia town of Charlottesville to defend their legendary leader Robert E. Trump *(surely General Donald J. Lee? Ed)*

In the middle of the town they were met by a hastily assembled company of militant anti-Confederates, including many black volunteers to whom Trump's racial record was one of the gravest blots on the moral standing of the United States in the dock of world opinion.

No sooner had the two groups come together than scenes of extraordinary violence ensued. On one side, the elite Nazi KKK Division swung into action with clubs, shields, sticks, hunting rifles and even an automobile, which they used to deadly effect by driving into the crowd.

On the other side, the opposing forces angrily hit back by shouting such slogans as "No to White Supremacy", "Down with Anti-Semitism" and "Didn't we Defeat the Nazis Once Before in 1945, or Perhaps you Haven't Seen the Movie?"

As the battle made headlines across the world, the President of the United States delivered one of his most memorable orations, which would become known to future generations as the "Gettysburger With Fries" address, containing the immortal lines "Government of the people, by myself, for myself, shall not perish for at least another four years. Fact."

EXCLUSIVE TO ALL TABLOIDS

MONTH OF AUGUST TO BE RENAMED

by Our Entire Staff **Phil Space**

Yes, it's official! Due to immense public pressure, Britain has decided to rename its eighth month, as a tribute to the greatest woman who ever appeared in a newspaper.

From next year, July will officially be followed by the month of Diana. Starting on Diana the 1st and continuing all the way through Diana to the 31st of Diana, with 30 days of Diana inbetween, the nation will be reminded that this is the month that newspapers finally lose the plot and run thousands of pieces about her, until the anniversary of her death is over.

ON ALL OTHER PAGES

How Princess August re-invented the handbag, wore hats in a way that was different from everybody else in history, and was a better dancer than Elvis (Presley).

The Mogg Dictionary

Moggmentum Made-up phenomenon where people think Jacob Rees-Mogg could be Tory leader

Moggazine Any publication which desperately writes about Mogg because it's August

Moggnetism State of raw attraction of right-wing newspaper editors to Mogg

Moggnum Opus An extremely long and boring article about Mogg in the Spectator

Moggnifying Glass Device used to spot Mogg's chances of becoming PM

Moggna Carta Interview with Mogg where he clarifies that he definitely has the right to be PM if that is what he wants, which he doesn't

Moggalomania Deluded state of mind where Mogg thinks he could do it

Moggshots Pictures of Mogg and his amusingly named children

Moggadon Intense state of sleepiness brought about by reading endless articles about Mogg

TORY LEADERSHIP

Jacob Rees-Mogg gets his valet to throw his hat into the ring

---

POETRY CORNER

**In Memoriam
Sir Bruce Forsyth, showbiz legend, song and dance man, TV's Mr Light Entertainment, Strictly's evergreen star, etc, etc**

So. Farewell
Then Brucie.
Brucie, then
Farewell. So.

Yes, that was
Your sort of
Catchphrase.
Though, over 50
Years on telly,
You had too many
To list in a
Short poem.

My favourite
Is particularly
Apt now.
Did you play
Your cards right?
Where are you going?

Higher? Lower?

That is the
Question for us
All in the game
Of life.

E.J. Thribb
(17½ plus Brucie bonus)

Lines on the silencing of Big Ben

So. Farewell
Then Big Ben.

Bong, bong
Bong.
Bong, bong, bong, bong,
Bong, bong,
Bong, bong, bong.

That was
Your catchphrase.

E.J. Thribb (17½ years' temporary maintenance)

TRUMP'S VIEW OF THE GREAT CONFLICTS OF HISTORY

Second World War

Good and bad on both sides. Sure, there were lots of Nazis, but then some very violent people tried to stop them holding a legitimate march though Eastern Europe. You want to pull down all the statues of Hitler next? Outlaw salutes? Get real. I blame the Alt-Allies!

Lord of the Rings

Good and bad on both sides. Was that evil eye really all evil? No, it was not! Should you trust men with very hairy feet who steal other people's rings? And just 'cos a guy dresses up with a pointy hat and says he's a wizard doesn't mean he's a fascist. And even if he is, so what? It's a free Middle Earth. I've met some of those Orcs, and they're fine human beings, even if they're not human beings.

Star Wars

Good and bad on both sides. Those Storm Troopers certainly know how to maintain law and order. Sometimes the guys dressed all in white are the good guys. It's something I've spotted 'cos I watch it more carefully than you. And just 'cos he covers his face, and blows up entire planets doesn't make Darth Vader a bad guy! I've met some of those Ewoks – everyone says they're so cute, but they're not. I hate them. And they didn't have a permit. I know things you don't know!

Tom and Jerry

Good and bad on both sides. I mean, did you see the mouse use that frying pan?! Right in his face! Okay, so Tom was trying to eat him, but he's a cat. Jerry's a mouse. That's how it is! Doesn't mean Tom should have pianos dropped on his head. Think about it!

God and Satan

Good and bad on both sides. *(At this point, many Americans finally realise there may be problems with a democratic system that allows Trump to become President.)*

TRUMP DENIES WHITE SUPREMACIST SYMPATHIES

It's Fake Noose!

The Eye's Controversial New Columnist

This week I am very angry about the namby-pamby hand-wringing health and safety brigade. Stopping the chimes of Big Ben for four years while the tower is being refurbished? Outrageous! You couldn't make it up! It always comes down to taking account of the snowflake sensibilities of those who raise objections, and never those who want the chimes to sound out come hell or high water. In light of this, I have made a principled stand. The mobile hanging on my cot now plays 'The Wheels on the Bus Go Round and Round' twelve times an hour. I know this because I have pulled the cord myself every five minutes for the past week. Does the fact that it is causing my parents deep emotional and psychological distress give me any pause? No! Did the fact that my mother wept behind the sofa this morning, and yesterday my father tried to hold a bus driver hostage, ordering him to stop the wheels of his bus from going round and round? No! The important point is that this majestic bus-shaped piece of plastic needs to be heard by the nation, and not silenced over the objections of one or two weak-minded *(cont. p94)*

Jeremy Corbyn WRITES

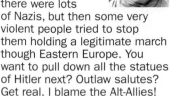

HELLO! It's me again. Again. Well, you could imagine the spring in my wellies when it was announced that Big Ben was to be finally silenced for the next four years!

And you could also imagine my manure-soaked disappointment when I heard that they were actually shutting off a CLOCK and not the hated centrist warmongering Blairite stooge Hilary Benn!

Oh well! I should have realised that's what they meant, but I'm not really a details person. I leave my underlings to note trivial things like the difference in spelling between "Ben" and "Benn"!

But in more cheery news, my rusty old heart was gladdened this week, when I heard about Stephen Hawking blasting Jeremy Hunt, complaining about Hunt cherry-picking research to justify what he's doing to the NHS. Good old Hawking, I say!

Cherry-picking is a terrible thing to do, and we should all listen very carefully to what Dr Hawking has to say. Not the things he says about me having to resign for the good of the Labour party of course! Or those things he says about Brexit being rubbish. Not those things! We should all focus on his criticisms of cherry-picking, because cherry-picking is the worst thing of all.

Anyway, I think we can all safely agree that his comments about the NHS are the words of a world-class genius and towering intellect, and that his comments about me are the words of a very sick disabled man edging ever closer to senility.

Truth to tell, I didn't really read his whole interview. Like *A Brief History of Time*, I read the first couple of sentences, gave up, and left it on the coffee table to impress people. I was told the universe dies at the end. I hate books with sad endings. Try *Das Kapital* instead. At least it's got jokes on every page! Cheerio!

Gnomemart

IT'S THE BIG BEN DOORBELL! BONG

Deafen yourself and your loved ones with the full-volume Big Ben chime!

Don't miss your favourite iconic national noise, with this incredible Westminster-style *Bong!*, as your house shakes to the sound of Big Ben every time someone comes to your door with your neighbour's Amazon delivery.

PRICE: £6 billion

THE BIG BEN BONG!

REALLY annoyed by the silencing of Big Ben's bell? Then relax and unwind with this replica **Big Ben Bong!**

Time will stand still – literally! – as you enjoy the magic chilling properties of the scale-model Elizabeth Tower Bong.

Get off your face next to the world's most famous clock face!

PRICE: £29 Plus police caution

The Delhi Telegraph

Friday, August 25, 2017

'Partition is the only solution' says India

by Our London Staff
Salmon Rushjob

IT HAS taken a top Indian civil servant, Sanjit Penpusha, to come up with the answer to what is to happen to Britain after it becomes independent.

Sent out from Delhi to assist the new UK government with how to solve the problems posed by a population bitterly divided by their religious views, Mr Penpusha has decided that there is no prospect of the two main mutually hostile groups involved ever living together peacefully again.

Penpusha has therefore drawn a line down the middle of the country and ruled that, post-independence, all the Leavers should live on one side in the north, and all the Remainers should live in the south.

This partition plan is controversial because, on each side of the line, there are substantial minorities who do not fit into this sweeping division of the country.

It is feared that the moment independence comes, at the stroke of midnight on March 19 2019, huge numbers of devout Brexiteers and Remoaners will be forced to flee from their homes to seek refuge the other side of the line.

Said one elderly British observer, Mahatma Gandalf, "It's going to be total chaos. I foresee millions of refugees desperate to board trains in each direction, hoping to join fellow believers as the country is irrevocably split into two.

"The only hope," he concluded, "is that the train service has now become so bad that no one will be able to go anywhere. So they'll just have to stay where they are and learn how to put up with each other."

DAVE SPART (Co-Chair of Neasden Anti-Sexist Pro-Chavez Freedom for Grouse Solidarity League)

It is totally and utterly sickening for the likes of Jess Phillips to claim that sexism is actually far more rife on the left of the political divide than the right and that it is actually male socialist activists who are the most misogynistic of all those men operating in the current repressive and intolerant climate er... er... this lying, cynical, offensive and deliberately damaging accusation from a neo-Blairite proto-globalist-capitalist-imperalist-centrist is absolutely typical of a treacherous tier of middle-aged so-called Labour women who should leave the important business of overthrowing the state to those of us who know what we are talking about, stop making silly remarks to try and get noticed and stick to what they are good at, ie childcare, healthcare, social care... er... care generally... and of course supporting Jeremy, whose attitude to women is totally and utterly well-known to be 100 percent... er... *(cont. p94)*

"You're not saving enough for your retirement"

A-LEVEL MATHEMATICS 2017

Question 1

If student X takes out a loan of £9,000 a year for 3 years, at an interest rate of 6.1%, and goes on to earn less than £25,000 a year for the next 20 years, and if student X is representative of the 2.3 million students studying at University...

A) How enormous will the Government's bill be for covering the debt?

B) How on earth are they going to pay that bill?

C) How ironic will it be if the Government has to take out a loan of its own at a punitive rate of interest linked to the retail price index in order to finance their own scheme?

D) Should the letter D be on the cone-shaped hat of the Education Minister?

(Answer to all questions: Get in thousands of under-qualified foreign students who pay up front)

An Uber Taxi Driver writes

Blimey! You're not going to report me, are you, lady? I wouldn't waste your time, love, Uber never pass it on to the police. Do you want to get out here? That'll be £27. What do you mean, it's a disgrace? *(Continued for 94 more offences...)*

Oxford Dictionary 2017

Celebrity *n.*, person who is not famous, and of whose identity the public have no idea.

Example: *"Who is that celebrity on Strictly Come Dancing? Weren't they previously on Celebrity Masterchef? Or was it Celebrity First Dates?"*

Non-celebrity *(see above)*

Who will play Nigel Farage in the forthcoming blockbuster Hollywood Brexit movie that is certainly going to happen? You decide...

Himself

Johnny Depp

Johnny Sessions

Meryl Streep

Michael Caine

Dr Who

Idris Elba

Could The Next Queen Be A Man?

by Our Royal TV Correspondent
Jenny Flect

THERE was outrage yesterday, when it was rumoured that the role of Queen in the long-running royal soap opera could be given to a man named "Charles".

"This is a disgrace," said one fan of the hit Royal TV drama. "The Queen has always been a woman. To change her into a man now is tokenism of the worst kind.

"This would be the end of it for me if they try and screw with such a successful format. I will refuse to watch the Queen's Christmas Message ever again if they do this."

The palace has denied the role change will ever happen, but refused to rule it out, with this statement:

"The part of the Queen being a man is always a possibility. It might be very timely to change the character, as the media is awfully short of role models for jaded, bitter, grey-haired men with nothing to do."

It's goodbye to Bolt

by Our Man at the World Championships
Lunchtime O'Lympics

WE shall never see his like again. Usain Bolt was a sprinter like no other, ie clean. *(Is this right? Ed.)*

It is, of course, a tragedy that in his last race he pulled a hamstring, but, to the delight of journalists everywhere, he went out clubbing and pulled again. *(Get back to the athletics. Ed.)*

09:58 – that is the time that will be forever etched in our memories because that was the time he left the nightclub, the morning before *(You're fired. Ed.)*

NEW BAKE-OFF —THE JUDGE'S VERDICT

This feels terribly stale

TV NEWS

Channel 4 'delighted by new Bake Off format'

■ CHANNEL 4 says it's delighted with the new Bake Off format after it was revealed that 6.5m had tuned into the first episode.

"Sandi, Noel and Prue were great additions, but the tweak to the format we loved the most, compared to the BBC version, was the endless advert breaks," said one Channel 4 exec. "They really delivered huge amounts of dough which rose beautifully during the 75 minutes.

"Obviously, there was a lull as the ad breaks were interrupted every now and again by people baking cakes, but this was kept to the absolute minimum to ensure maximum enjoyment for our executives desperate to recoup the £75m we paid for the show."

Twitter users 'deceived by Russian agent'

IT WAS revealed today that millions of Twitter users have been deceived into following an account that is just a mouthpiece for Russian propaganda which goes under the name of "Donald J. Trump".

The Trump account has built up a following of 37 million people, including prominent British right-wingers, and has been retweeted by senior Ukip officials.

A statistical analysis of recent tweets suggests that they were all posted between 3am and 5am and emanated from a notorious "troll factory" in Washington DC called "The White House".

"The Donald J Trump account is typical of Putin's propaganda war, pumping out an endless stream of fake news and pro-Russia stories to millions of social media users," said an MI5 source.

Daily Tudorgraph

1545 AD

Crowds Cheer Massive Warship In Portsmouth

by Our Naval Correspondent I. I. CAPTAIN

The entire population of Portsmouth (350) turned out to welcome the largest vessel in the British fleet as she sailed into the harbour.

At a price of 3 billion groats, the Mary Rose represents the very latest in maritime wood technology, and is the proud flagship of the monarch's Royal Navy. The ship is a symbol of British sovereignty at a tricky political time, as Henry VIII looks to leave the European Catholic Union.

Named after a member of the Royal family, the Mary Rose has been criticised for having an unusual design which means that it is unable to fly any aircraft, even though an order has been placed for a squadron of Signor da Vinci's prototype flying machines, which looked excellent on paper, but has proved difficult to deliver on time and budget.

The Mary Rose is also said to have problems with stability, and critics suggest it could be easily toppled by a freak gust of wind, or a Russian interfering with the ship's highly advanced technological communications system (pigeon), but Britain's First Minister, Lady Jane May (famous for her short reign), said, "This warship is a symbol of resurgent British power around the globe – the last thing it's going to do is sink without a trace."

LATE NEWS

Mary Rose sinks without a trace.

H.M.S. QUEEN ELIZABETH

Cluff

JOY AT ROYAL BABY NEWS

by Our Royal Correspondent **Peter Patteroftinyfeet**

THERE were celebrations last night all over Fleet Street at the news that a new Royal Baby supplement was on the way.

Said one tabloid editor, "We're overjoyed. We've been hoping for some happy news for so long. We really don't care what kind of baby supplement it is, so long as the sales are healthy."

Another editor said, "You can expect all the usual symptoms of a royal pregnancy, like morning sickness – when you look at all the royal baby coverage in the papers each morning, you'll feel nauseous."

He continued, "My brain's already gone to mush, which makes me ideal for editing a tabloid. I'm taking the pregnancy very seriously and already I'm drinking for two."

It is thought to be only six months before we can expect to hear all newspaper editors shouting: "Push! Push! Push it out, you bastards or you're all fired!" And in no time an eight-pound Royal Baby souvenir edition will be delivered.

Already people are speculating about what the name of the Royal Baby supplement will be. Front runners include: "Royal Baby Supplement", and "Your 94-Page Guide to the New Royal Baby", but the smart money is on "Supplementy McSupplementFace".

BREXIT ROUND-UP

'Stumbling block identified' claims Davis

As talks stall once again in Brussels over Britain's divorce bill from the EU, Britain's chief negotiator, David Davis, has identified what he sees as the major stumbling block to a smooth Brexit… namely, the EU.

"If it wasn't for the EU, these negotiations would have finished long ago, with everyone agreeing that Britain can leave the EU, not pay any money towards it, and continue to enjoy full tariff-free access," David Davis told reporters.

"But instead of that, the EU insists on taking the opposing view that, as we're leaving the EU, we can no longer enjoy all the benefits of being in the club.

"To make matters even more annoying, the EU negotiators arrive each day fully prepared and carefully briefed, whereas I arrive each day with something that I read on Michael Gove's Twitter feed scribbled on the back of a fag packet."

Said Davis, "I'm just asking them to show a little more imagination and imagine I know what I'm doing," Davis said, staring out the window and whistling the Colonel Bogey theme.

The EU's chief negotiator, Michel Barnier, has criticised Britain's Brexit papers, calling them shoddy and poorly thought out.

"The Express is the worst, but the Mail, The Telegraph and The Sun are not far behind."

Fury Over Exam Cheating

by Our Education Staff
Ivor Cribsheet

PARENTS of pupils at St Cakes, the £30,000 a minute Midlands public school (Motto 'Quis Paget Entrat'), have demanded refunds following the revelation that several public schools have been engaged in systematic cheating in A-Levels.

Said one irate Cakeian parent, himself an Old Cakeian (Battenberg's 1948-72, due to numerous retakes), "There is no evidence whatsoever that St Cakes has been cheating. This is not why I sent my sons to this boarding school from the age of three!

"What one expects from a public school is an unfair advantage wherever possible. How can Cakeians compete with boys from Eton, Winchester and Charterhouse if their teachers refuse to tell them the answers to every question in their forthcoming exam?"

Cakes' headmaster, Mr Kipling, defended the school's reputation, "We may have slipped up in our academic duties, but if it's any consolation, I can assure parents that school sports day will be a veritable drugs fest!"

When asked how much cheating was going on in economics classes, the headmaster of Eton said, "That's a very difficult question – I knew you were going to ask me that."

WHERE'S WALL-Y?

Can you spot Wall-y on the Mexican border?

Answer: *That's right, Wall-y's in the White House.*

A Doctor Writes

AS A doctor, I'm often asked, 'Doctor, should nitrous oxide inhaled from a balloon be classified as a legal high or should hippy crack be illegal?

The simple answer is… "ppphhhhttt …Ha ha ha ha ha ha ha ha ha ha ha ha ha ha ha ha ha ha ha ha ha ha ha ha ha ha ha ha ha ha ha ha ha…hold on a second, where was I? …ppphhhhttt …Ha ha ha ha ha ha ha ha ha ha ha ha ha ha ha ha ha ha ha ha ha ha ha ha ha ha ha ha ha ha ha ha ha ha ha ha ha ha ha ha ha ha… actually, excuse me, I'm feeling a bit dizzy, got a bit of a headache, get me a doctor… ppphhhhttt…that's better, ha ha ha ha ha ha ha ha ha ha ha ha." (*That's enough nitrous oxide, ha ha ha ha, Ed. Ha ha ha…*)
© A doctor

"Blimey Sharon… how much prosecco did you drink during pregnancy?"

Driverless trucks 'welcomed'

THERE was a major boost for driverless trucks today as Isis said they would in future be carrying out all their terrorist outrages in Central Europe using driverless trucks to plough into densely-packed tourist spots.

"We believe driverless truck technology will revolutionise how we terrify the Western infidels," said a senior Isis spokesman.

ROONEY SCANDAL LATEST

I'm making Wayne available on free transfer

PROBLEMS AT WATERLOO

The New Brussels Dictionary

Barney A noisy argument, involving two parties in disagreement.

Barnier An even noisier argument, involving two parties in extreme disagreement, that shows no sign of ever ending.

Barniest The inevitable result of a 'Barney', which has got 'Barnier' and ends up completely out of control as the argument reaches its 'Barniest' stage. At this point, the two parties resort to pointless name calling followed by punch throwing, spitting and hair pulling. The result of a 'Barniest' argument is always one big loser, namely everyone.

Daily Mail, Friday, September 08, 2017

WHAT SHOULD THE WEST DO ABOUT NORTH KOREA?

AS THE world holds its breath and teeters on the brink of Armageddon, we spell out the only options available to prevent the end of the world:

1 SANCTIONS These have been tried but don't work.

2 DIPLOMACY Utterly pointless as Kim Jong-un is totally mad.

3 INVASION Far too dangerous, as this could trigger counter-attack, risking the death of millions of South Koreans.

4 ASSASSINATION This is out of the question because it would be in breach of international law and might risk turning Kim Jong-un into a martyr and lead to

President Trump facing trial for war crimes.

5 THE NUCLEAR OPTION Launching nuclear weapons may not be the best way to stop a nuclear war, diplomats warn.

6 THE UNTHINKABLE This is unthinkable because nobody's thought of it yet.

7 Er…

8 …that's it, folks.

I've made a model of Mount Everest

To scale?

No, just to look at

Moose

Brexit – New Hope For Remainers

by Our Brexit Correspondent
Cliff Edge

As the third round of negotiations start, there is an increasing chance of Brexit never happening, according to leading figures in the Remain camp.

Said one, "We have serious grounds for optimism now. It is looking increasingly likely that the UK will not leave the EU at the end of March 2019, as Kim Jong-un and Donald Trump will almost certainly have blown up the entire planet well before the leave date."

Said another, "I was fearing a hard Brexit with the horrific economic and social consequences, but this is going to be far less painful."

He continued, "I feared I was going to have to pay a lot more for my prosecco and foreign holidays, but happily I'm just going to have my eyeballs explode and the flesh ripped from my melting bones instead. What a relief!"

In the City too, banks are no longer planning to relocate to Frankfurt, but are now favouring a move to an underground bunker in New Zealand.

However, one minister for Brexit dismissed this as typical Remoaner nonsense and scare-mongering. "Even if the world does end," said Liam Fox, "We will still be able to do fantastic deals with other planets".

Boris Johnson weighed in, adding, "Don't be bamboozled by those wimp-hearted harbingers of doom! Johnny Martian and Ginny Venusian will be queuing up to buy our good old British cheddar, Union Jack boxer shorts, and Beefeater teddy bears!"

A spokesman for Mars said, "Zzzzzzgglllxxx xrrrruuuullllgu luuxxrrrrgle Boris Johnson glllurrrzzzzzglllxxxrrr twat."

Police pay rise 'essential'

by Our Industrial Relations Staff
Cormoran Strike

THE Home Secretary, Amber Light, yesterday defended the decision to abandon the pay cap in the public sector for police and prison staff.

She explained to TV's Andrew Marrvellous, "It is vital that we give the police more money, as they are going to have to work hard over the next few months dealing with industrial action from the nurses and teachers."

She continued, "There will be marches, demonstrations and walk-outs, all of which will have to be policed – that doesn't come cheap."

She concluded, "Given that union bosses have admitted that some of this action will be illegal, it is likely that militant members of the teaching and nursing unions will end up in jail.

"And we will need well-paid and well-motivated prison staff to keep them safely locked up and off the streets."

MAY FURY OVER BORIS BREXIT PLAN

I'm driving from the front...

...last thing we need is a back-seat driver

Cabinet Agree on Future Action

KEY

THE TELEGRAPH

MODERN NURSERY RHYMES

We send the EU £350 million a week let's fund our NHS instead Vote Leave

#TakeControl

Let's take back control

"The lies on the bus come round and round, round and round, round and round"

This childhood favourite is based on the old saying "You wait ages for a bogus statistic on a bus and then 350 million come along at once"

Scotland reels at resignation by woman no one has heard of

by Our Political Staff
Robert Haggis

The world of Scottish politics was rocked to its foundations last night by the shock resignation of a woman no one had previously heard of.

In an exclusive interview with the BBC, the woman no one had heard of explained that now was the right time to step down as leader of the Scottish Labour Party and retire from the limelight which she had never experienced.

"Many people may be surprised to learn that I am resigning," she said, "because they were never aware that I had been leader in the first place."

She went on, "I am very proud of what I managed to achieve as the woman no one has ever heard of, including our hugely impressive performance at the last general election, which we lost by much less than we had done previously."

The Labour Party leader, Jeremy Corbyn, was quick to tweet his response to the news.

"Very sad to hear of resignation of the woman whose name escapes me."

Pundits were last night unanimously agreed that the now former leader of the Scottish Labour Party will be remembered as the most famous woman no one has ever heard of in history.

Terror As Stalker Found At Prince George's New School

by Our Royal Correspondent
Rick Spittle

An obsessive has been seen wandering around trying to get into the new school of Prince George in Battersea, London.

The intruder was believed to be a figure known to the authorities who for months has been prowling around the area hoping desperately that something will happen so he can photograph His Little Highness

and get his story into the newspaper the next day…

Where are you, George I know you must be here somewhere… Wait, take your hands off me, officer, I can explain, I'm the Prince George correspondent for the Mail… It's perfectly innocent, I assure you… Please, I just need to phone my editor and tell them that little George seemed a bit nervous on his first day but that his colly-wobbles will doubtless subside…

TRUMP CHOOSES NEW COMMUNICATIONS CHIEF

Next comes the swimwear round...

NORTH KOREA THREAT
WEST ANNOUNCES TEN-POINT PLAN

1. Right, that's it, mister!
2. We're going to count to three!
3. And then there's going to be trouble!
4. Right, One!
5. Two!
6. Two and a half!
7. Two and three quarters!
8. Two and seven-eighths!
9. Two and nineteen-twentieths!
10. Right, that's it, we're going to count to FIVE. One. Two…

Rest of the world

Japan

Boris Johnson, the Secretary of State for Foreign and Commonwealth Affairs, writes exclusively for Private Eye

Wednesday

CRIPES! Guess where old Bozza has been? Only the British Virgin Islands! And no jokes about virgins, thank you very much! Bojo's a serious international statesman now. And not just a world-famous ladies man who turned up hoping to meet this "Irma" everyone's talking about! Anyway, no more talk of dusky maidens or trousers at half-mast – this is proper relief, Bozza style! Stop it, matron!

First up, Mrs May called me in and said, "It's terribly dangerous over there and somebody might get lost in the whirlwind and never come back – I know just the chap to send on the first plane over. You!"

My retort? "Plane, Mrs M? A big chopper's more my style!" Mistake, as Mrs M's not known for her GSOH. And she sat there stony-faced and shouted "Get out!", clearly wanting yours truly to get out to the Caribbean before the storm petered out.

So I put on a natty, crumpled linen suit, looking suitably Raj – though the FO spoilsports told me to leave the pith helmet at home! And Shazam! I was off on a mission to reassure Johnny Native that he was just as British as the rest of us, and that Her Maj was doing everything she could to rebuild his hut, just as soon as we could get the navy to send over HMS *Inadequate* with enough mud and straw!

And it all went very well – I was greeted at what remained of the airport, armed with a jar of Marmite and a mug saying "Keep Calm and Carry On", by hundreds of grateful coconut munchers singing, dancing and holding up banners reading, "Haven't we suffered enough?". Good to see they've kept their sense of humour. They appreciate I'm flying the flag for Blighty, which is pretty easy when the wind blows this strongly.

Anyway, I've promised the downtrodden denizens of the Caicos and Eatos Islands a whole load of dosh, courtesy of the British taxpayer, so they can rebuild all their fine offices with shiny new brass plates on the doors, so that those clever chaps can show everyone how to avoid paying any tax. Whoops! Bozza's put his size tens in it! Still, think I got away with it. Nobody noticed. Now, where are all those British Virgins I keep hearing about?

Saturday

DOUBLE CRIPES! Bozza flies into another disaster zone! Can he rescue another island ravaged by Hurricane Brexit? Cue hot air and windy bluster from yours truly as I hastily put pen to paper to write a 350-million-word piece for the Daily Bozzagraph (motto: *We'll print anything!*).

In it I set out my glorious vision for a triumphant future in which Britannia rules the waves, the British lion roars once again and yours truly takes over as... whoops! Steady on, Bojo! Don't let the cat out of the bag...

I don't want to blow my own trumpet but Toot! Toot! only a blithering nincompoop would fail to accept the all-round brilliant logic of my 100-point plan, including the masterstroke point 94: "Brexit will be a success because it is so successful!"

That's what comes from a classical Oxford education – rigorous intellectual argument!! That and setting fire to Dave Cameron's trousers after trashing his rooms in Brasenose (obvs)!!

Sunday

TRIPLE CRIPES! Instead of an entire grateful nation recalling Winston Bozza to be prime minister and win the war against Europe, all the rotters in the party are putting the boot in and calling *me* a shameless opportunist! Me! The future PM!!

Only one thing for it. Eat toad, crawl up Mrs May's leather trousers and declare undying loyalty to Theresa No Mates.

With any luck, she'll be so desperate for chums she *won't* give me the heave-ho and we'll kiss and make up (Bozza's two favourite pastimes!) and trundle on as if nothing has happened – which, unfortunately, it hasn't! Whoops! Bozza telling the truth there – it won't happen again, I promise! Phew! Crisis averted! That's real disaster management for you!

Now off to Florence! I hear she's rather fruity!

Yours,

Blow-Jo!

FAILED PLOTTER CAUGHT

The whole thing completely backfired

Was it incompetence or just bad timing?

It's what everyone's wearing this year

BUCKET LIST
1. GET BUCKET
2. PUT BOMB IN IT

R♦J

"WELL I DID THINK IT WAS A BIT ODD SEEING A LIDL BAG AROUND PARSONS GREEN"

There once was a man from Isis

"Nobody got killed this time so the poem doesn't have to be so serious"

Let's Parlezment Franglais!

Numéro 94
L'address annual au Parlezment Européan

Président Druncker: J'ai un dream des Etats-Unis de l'Europe, d'une suele currency et d'un toujours closer union.

Tout le monde: Ce n'est pas un dream, c'est un cauchemar!

Président Druncker: Et un Président qui contrôle everything, ie moi-self!

Tout le monde: Avez-vous been drinking?

Druncker: Mais, of course, c'est breakfast time! Et maintenant je veux sharer avec vous mon vision...

Tout le monde: C'est double vision!

Drunckest: C'est un slur! Or rather, comme je dis, un schlurrrrr....

(Continues 2094)
© The late Kilometres Kington.

How the amazing new £1,000 iPhone X facial recognition technology works

High definition camera scans face

Camera recognises loyal Apple customer

Camera checks features for wide eyes and open mouth

Phone rates gullibility factor at X out of X

Apple checks bank balance of buyer

Apple Pay automatically opens wallet

Mugshot confirmed

Mug £1,000 poorer

Apple £1,000 richer

Taxman gets £0

James Murdoch's Argument for Allowing Fox to Take Over Sky, as Presented to the Competition and Markets Authority

"My father's a patient man, but he feels he's not getting the respect he deserves. Do you understand? Loyalty is very important to him and our family has been very loyal to this government and it would be a great shame if there was an accident and the whole of the CMA were, say, to fall under a bus. I'm not saying it will happen, but we live in dangerous times and if, for example, a piano fell on the head of everyone at Ofcom whilst they were walking under a window, it would be a shame. Do you follow me? I mean, all we want is for this little matter to be resolved amicably, as a mark of respect and loyalty to Rupert, without anyone falling under any buses or any pianos dropping out of the sky or without Karen Bradley, the Culture Secretary, waking up to find a horse's head next to her on the pillow. What I'm saying is that we're reasonable people and all we want is for everyone to be happy – particularly Rupert. Do you follow me? These are concrete proposals, as concrete as the boots that unfortunate people find themselves wearing when they accidentally fall off the end of piers and sleep with the fishes. And we don't want that to happen, do we?"

© "The Ozfather", now showing on Sky Classics.

McDonalds Introduces New Menu As Employees Strike

- Quarter-pound-an-hour
- Chicken McNuggetory-wage
- Filet-o-Fishing-for-a-PR-solution
- Sausage McNuffin-paid-to-employees
- McFlurry-of-panic-at-board-level

MONKEY SELFIE COPYRIGHT – TWO-YEAR BATTLE ENDS

You think *I'm* smiling, you should see the lawyers

Jacob Rees-Mogg's Reasons To Be Uplifted In Modern Britain

1 Food banks A marvellous example of philanthropic charity at work.

2 Rickets A splendid opportunity for the medical services to show their commitment and skill.

3 Chimney sweeps An inspiring opening for entrepreneurial cleaning start-ups to send 10-year-old boys up the flue.

4 Workhouses A heartwarming indication of Britain's desire to get the unemployed out of welfare and into work.

5 Top hats A headwarming symbol of Britain's return to a golden age of prosperity, order, paternalism, steam railways spats, typhoid, child prostitution, back-street abortions, Molly houses for sodomites, and old Etonians running the country as is only right and proper, *"vox snobuli, vox dei"*.

YOU DON'T HAVE TO BE SESQUIPEDALIAN TO WORK HERE, BUT IT HELPS

–PILBROW–

TV celebrity caught on camera in Nazi uniform

by Our Late Night Staff
Phil Space

THERE was outrage in our office last night when evidence emerged of a TV celebrity wearing a Nazi uniform.

This amazing still photograph taken only decades ago shows a well-known actor, the late Sam Kelly, deliberately dressing up as a Nazi.

His excuse that he was in the hugely popular TV comedy 'Allo 'Allo, playing the part of a Nazi, has been branded as "pathetic" by my editor, who went on to say, "Don't ruin the story by adding in any extra facts that make it look less important!"

He continued, "It's a thin news day and this story's got everything. Someone from the telly! Nazis! Bingo! Okay there's no bingo – that's on another page."

So there you have it – the worst example of dressing something up as a Nazi story. As a journalist, I'm somewhat ashamed, but I was only obeying orders!

Paul Hollywood is 94.

RYANAIR CANCELS FLIGHTS TO IMPROVE PUNCTUALITY

by Our Aviation Staff **Phil Departure-Lounge**

THE low-budget airline Ryanair yesterday announced a new policy to boost the reliability of their service.

Said Ryanair boss Michael O'Really, "We've gone from no-frills to no-flights. It's a brilliant strategy. With no planes taking off they can't possibly be late."

He continued, "We learnt how to do this by studying the operating practices of other leading transport practitioners like Southern Rail. It's marvellous really, no one goes anywhere, but they do it *on time!*"

Mr O'Really concluded, "OK. The passengers aren't very pleased but it means the staff can catch up with their holiday entitlement. Obviously they won't be able to fly anywhere, but they *can* go to Stansted airport and have a fortnight in the departure lounge."

A spokesman for Mr O'Really last night said, "There is an extra charge for this statement from Mr O'Really and if you don't print out the statement yourself there is another extra charge of £94!"

 Daily Tudorgraph

1534 AD

Protests Over Henry VIII's 'Power Grab'

by Our Political Staff SIR THOMAS 'CHARLES' MOORE

Parliament has this week been in a state of continuous uproar, as MPs from all sides expressed their ire at what they all called "an unprecedented power grab" by His Majesty.

The King has shocked the whole of Europe by his arbitrary decision to take back control from what he called "an unelected continental bureaucracy which for too long has imposed its foreign laws on the proud people of this island".

"It is time," he decreed, "that we reclaimed our English sovereignty, so that it can be exercised by myself."

In recent weeks, His Majesty has shown what is intended by his insistence that "Rexit means Rexit", by issuing executive orders that all the monasteries should be dissolved, all his wives should be divorced, beheaded or die, and even that the author of this article, Sir Charles Moore, should be sent to ye Tower for his head to be parted from his shoulders, thus ensuring that for centuries to come he will be remembered as a saint and martyr.

"I originally set up this coffee shop because I was sick of working in an office"

THE FOUR HORSEMEN OF THE APOCALYPSE ARE READY FOR THE OFF!